LIFE
TURNS MAN
UP
AND
DOWN

LIFE
TURNS MAN
UP
AND
DOWN

✳✳✳

**HIGH LIFE, USEFUL ADVICE,
AND MAD ENGLISH**

African Market Literature

SELECTED AND INTRODUCED BY

Kurt Thometz

Pantheon Books, New York

Library of Congress Cataloging-in-Publication Data

Life turns man up and down: high life, useful advice, and
mad English: African market literature/selected and
introduced by Kurt Thometz.
p. cm.
Includes bibliographical references (p. n).
ISBN 0-679-45021-1
1. Nigerian literature (English)   2. Popular literature—
Nigeria.   3. Nigeria—Literary collections.   4. Chapbooks,
Nigerian—Facsimiles.   I. Thometz, Kurt.

PR9387.5 .L54 2001   820.8'09669—dc21   2001021340

www.pantheonbooks.com

Book design by M. Kristen Bearse

Printed in the United States of America
First Edition
2 4 6 8 9 7 5 3 1

Introduction

This booklet is intended to help the readers who have been asking me to give them advice in order to be free from some troubles of this world.

Since the people can not tell the truth and since Money, lack of sense, enemies and bad friends kill a man, it is wise to know how to live and know yourself.

Many people have been asking to know why some people are rich while others are poor.

If you want to get money and know how to save it, buy a copy of this book. It will help you.

Do Not Trust In Me

My dear readers. Do not trust all you see in the world. Many friends are dangerous enemies. I have told you in time so that you may not regret at last. A word is enough for the wise.

Do not lend money to your friends without a strong agreement received and do not tell all your secrets or plans to your friends.

When you look left and right you understand better. Be careful the world is hard and full of lies and changes.

Since brother does not trust his brother, father does not trust his son, sister does not trust her sister, mother does not trust her daughter and master does not trust his servant. I can not tell you who you can trust.

Read on and become wise, good advice is the best medicine of life.

—From *No Money, Much Expenses, Enemies and Bad Friends Kill A Man* (*The Way to Avoid Poverty*) by R. Okonkwo. Onitsha: J. C. Brothers Bookshop, New Era Printers [1965?]

CONTENTS

Preface   ix
Warning   xi
High Life, Useful Advice, and Mad English   xiii

Rosemary and the Taxi Driver
  by Miller O. Albert   1

Man Has No Rest in His Life
  by Okenwa Olisah   45

Beware and Be Wise
  by Olusola   73

No Condition Is Permanent
  by The Master of Life (Okenwa Olisah)   75

Money Hard To Get But Easy To Spend
  by Okenwa Olisah   105

Lack of Money Is Not Lack of Sense
  by Felix N. Stephen   117

Miss Comfort's Heart Cries for Tonny's Love
  by Cyril Nwakuna Aririguzo   121

Drunkards Believe Bar As Heaven
  by Sunday Okenwa Olisah   125

Beware of Harlots and Many Friends
    by J. Nnadozie   127

How to Avoid Corner Corner Love and
    Win Good Love from Girls
    by Thomas O. Iguh   131

Why Harlots Hate Married Men
    and Love Bachelors
    by C.N.O. Moneyhard   137

Mabel the Sweet Honey That Poured Away
    by Speedy Eric   151

How to Write Famous Love Letters, Love Stories,
    and Make Friend with Girls
    by N. O. Njoku   225

Saturday Night Disappointment
    by Miller O. Albert   233

Adventures of the Four Stars
    by J. A. Okeke Anyichie   241

The Statements of Hitler Before the World War
    by Sunday Okenwa Olisah   295

The Life Story and Death of John Kennedy
    by Wilfred Onwuka   307

What Is Life?
    by Frank E. Odili   315

Afterword   339
A Reader's Guide   349

PREFACE

"Somewhere in the granary is the elusive kernel, the Word, the key, the moment of my rehabilitation. There are the cabalistic signs. The trouble is to find the key. Find the key and it leads to the Word. Very strange . . . very strange . . . a rash of these signs arrived lately. Oh God, Oh God, the enormity of unknown burdens, the hidden wisdoms. Say the word in our time, Oh Lord, utter the hidden word. But what do they mean? What in the power of hell do they mean?"[1]

The predicament of the Word is the predicament of its interpreters. Wole Soyinka's scholar in *The Road* contemplates the appearance of the Word in the still, dark age of a vanishing world. *In our time,* the professor tells us, the words became *signs,* become *unknown burdens* to epistemologically ponder. *Find the key and it leads to the Word. Say the word in our time, Oh Lord, utter the hidden word.*

Mourning stories and celebrated glories once sung by the griot now swing wrung from a foreign tongue and are placed to dry on paper; handmade words written to share with the eye. The visual aspect of the Word is more than exotic finery. A conscience clothed in an alphabet plays by different rules than one an aural-tactile vocabulary scantily attires. Language wrought by the hand for the eye can reproduce thoughts that can't be seen; *hidden wisdoms*. The Word is at the biblical heart of darkness and implicit in the Word's appearance is a cataclysm.

The writers of the literary anomalies comprising this collection come at us from the cusp of a world beyond the reach of anyone reading this book, from the amorphous age-old oral world before the written word. In the difference lay presumptions about ourselves, our black and white selves, that are not native to the human condition but are the result of the two-thousand-year-old technology of literacy.

While it is near impossible for the literate to conceive the unwritten world, its aesthetic echo can be heard here in West African literature's incunabula. Eastern Nigeria remained largely in literate darkness until the mid-twentieth century when the market traders who wrote and published these little books facilitated their culture's change from traditional orality to printed modernity, from Igbo land to Biafra.

These authors and their facilitators cater to a reading public who, with newly discovered romance, are enthusiastically embracing literacy. Here in demotic, uncooked, Mad English, composited by illiterate printers in broken type, newsprint bound in bush-bruised wraps and distributed from hand to mouth, is a potential literature's growing pains on display. And a potential literature's tragic demise.

WARNING

This is a selection of Africa's first popular written literature and it is best read as the authors intended: as an education, as entertainment, as instruction. Readers nonindigenous to Africa might keep in mind the literary merit of their own popular literature when judging the pamphleteers associated with the Onitsha market. For the messengers, schoolboys, taxi drivers, sign painters, guitar players, and farmers who wrote these little books, standardized English is as new as it was to their Elizabethan counterparts, with whom they share an extraordinary enthusiasm for that ever new concept, the written word.

As similar as they are in style and content to our precursors, so they are to our popmeisters. Romance, money, and style, the real stuff of the popular arts everywhere, are the primary interests of these authors and their audience. These entertainments, never sold as art, were never meant to be criticized as art and should not be read as art. Neither should they be read as sociological artifacts.

Note

All the characters in this novel, are all round imaginary. Note, none is real. It is no true story and therefore concerns nobody in anyway. Whoever hits his head at the ceiling does it at his own personal fatal risk.[2]

Is this stuff literature? "Am I a Star?" "Am I?" Then read on and enjoy the fun. Once a star, always a star.[3]

—From *Life Turns Man Up and Down*

HIGHLIFE, USEFUL ADVICE, AND MAD ENGLISH

"Her skin would make your blood flow in the wrong direction. She was so sweet and sexy, knew how to romance.
She married at sixteen. But she wanted more fun. Yet it
ended at seventeen. And what an end? So thrilling"[4]

In *Mabel the Sweet Honey That Poured Away,* an impa-
tient, complacent, and willingly bodice-ripped waitress
working a colonialist-era Igbo land jungle-town juke joint
screws herself to death in seventy pages of pugilistic prose
printed with primal poignancy. Mabel's introduction to the
slatternly ways of the New World is a work of poetic justice,
if not, strictly speaking, quality lit.

With the possible exception of her same-sex seduction
scenes with girlfriend Maggie, Speedy Eric's heroine takes
nothing but hard knocks in black Africa's first written
erotica. Picture her: *The Sweet Honey* in bold black and
burgundy ink on pale Tiffany-blue stapled, ornamented
cardstock, a single fold of seventy-two newsprint pages
bound pamphlet style. Portrait of our heroine: a lascivious,
raven-tressed, dramatically cleavaged and curvaceous,
rumba-sleeved and corseted, provocatively posed mid-
mambo cutie with an invitation to sin smile that beckons
with a rose, *Come here, sugar and get to this.* "And what an

end? . . . Inside the lavatory our seventeen years old sweet honey was pouring away. The agony lasted from eleven a.m. till four thirty p.m."[5]

Mabel is the tough stuff of West African Highlife in 1960: negritude noir by an amateur boxer who, in direct and blunt, raw English, tells the sort of sordid nightlife story that's told to country girls everywhere before they go, first time, to see the bright lights of the big city. It could be Lagos, Cairo, Memphis, Los Angeles, New York, London, or Paris but in Mabel's case it is Onitsha in Eastern Nigeria—Igbo land—on the eve of liberation.

Chinua Achebe, quoting Frantz Fanon, has called Onitsha "a zone of occult instability."

> "This is where the spirits meet the humans, the water meets the land, the child meets the adult—these are the zones of power, and I think this is really where stories are created."[6]

A sinister bend in the river, an early in-land outpost for slaving, the Royal Africa Company, and the Catholic Church—Onitsha is complicit in the savage capitalism of those who colonialized it. To the Igbo, Ijaw, Edo, Igala, and Tiv country people it was an ominous place of malevolent river-spirits and hooligans one had to be suspicious of. The very name, Onitsha, means "one who despises another."[7]

Reputedly the largest market town in sub-Sahara Africa, Onitsha stands at the crossroads of the Niger and the road connecting the East with the less-wild old Benin and Yoruba regions of western Nigeria. An Igbo proverb that made its way to the New World defines a crossroads as a place where bargains are struck with the devil, a place where souls are sold, a place where truth and falsehood open doors to the future and close doors to the past.

For country girls like Mabel, moving to town was the dawning of the Age of the Word in the Era of Romanticism. A trip to town from a village deep in the woods was as consciousness expanding as tripping through the psychodelic underworld of Amos Tutuola's *Bush of Ghosts.* Cars, hotel bars, electric guitars, telephones, capitalism, yellow journalism, and Hollywood romanticism are beautiful things though not quite of this world.

In the stall-lined alleys, under the rusted corrugated iron and raffia roofs, market hawkers offer everything from the staples of life to contraband. Stalls of yams, cassava, gari, cola nuts, and cayenne pepper rutted next to the monkey heads, snake jaws, and "prescription" pharmaceuticals of the "medicine sellers." Palm wine tapsters competed with cocktail ladies offering Spanish whiskey, gin from Holland, Golden Guinea beer, and Indian hemp to those souls who believed the bar was heaven's peace on earth.

In this New World there are strange gods and there are white people who seem to speak entirely in lies. White people were just the bizarre sort of thing one expected to see there. The first white people the Igbo knew were the pirates they slaved with. A sordid lot, the few who penetrated the interior did not personally impress the reputedly arrogant indigenes, who nevertheless found uses for them.

The trade in slaves corrupts everything it touches and from about 1530 through the mid-nineteenth century, Igbo land would send countless thousands of her own to *The Unknown,* as the New World was then known, seemingly for the pleasure of doing business. The two most important things the British self-styled "protectors" brought to the wildly disparate country they'd amalgamate as Nigeria were a common tongue and a common coin. These universal lubricants were as enthusiastically embraced as the material culture that came with them.

By the 1950s and '60s, men and women from the country took to the markets and bars of town as freshly armed radical stars. Foremost in their arsenal was the Word. With the possible exception of Chinua Achebe's *Things Fall Apart*, nothing shows the impact of Western urbanities' technologically adroit Word on the ordinary African's values better than the chapbooks of the Onitsha writers. They know the modes of expression of the people they serve and their writing has very definite purposes. The authors know the vernacular, the animism, and the vices of the time from the markets, missions, and juke joints of the colonialist era's back bush and fast-forward urbanity.

Books, magazines, music, and movies from England and America fed the vocabulary of the people's pidgin English, a composite tongue four hundred years in the making, on wonders scarcely imagined by the previous generation. Spread out on palm leaves next to automobile parts from Detroit were hi-fi highlife records from London, Los Angeles, and Lagos, textiles from India and China, and the peculiar, provocatively, turgidly titled little pamphlets printed on New Market Street: *Life Turns Man Up and Down, Money and Girls Turn Man Up and Down; Rosemary and the Taxi Driver; Never Trust All That Love You: The World Is So Corrupt That It Has Become Difficult to Trust All People; Beauty Is a Trouble; Drunkards Believe Bar As Heaven; Dangerous Man Versus Princess; Why Harlots Hate Married Men and Love Bachelors; Veronica My Daughter; How to Avoid Corner Corner Love and Win Good Love from Girls; Love at First, Hate at Last; Saturday Night Disappointment; Money Hard to Get But Easy to Spend.*

In his essay *The Autistic Hunt,* Wole Soyinka, Nigeria's Nobel Prize–winning author, says he read what he calls "the incredible pot-pourri of the semi-urban romancer before it was the 'hip/phony' thing to do."

... we pursued the latest titles with unabashed relish, assuming (falsely it now appears) that other readers recognized in this literature a reflection of a sudden inundation of false values, offering therefore a measure of unconscious humor and robust language.

The models (style and content) of Onitsha Market literature are a bizarre mixture of Marie Corelli, John Wayne, Cisco Kid, Watchtower instructional brochures, beauty cream literature, Candid Revelations, News of the World, Superman, Indian films, Awful Disclosure of . . . , True Romances, James Bond, Lennards' Overseas Catalogue, etc., etc., plus, of course, the occasional direct and simplistic recasting of political events in black Africa or in the black portion of the United States (such as the deaths of black heroes like Malcolm X or Martin Luther King or the exploits of Muhammed Ali)."[8]

To which might be added the *Reader's Digest, Drum* magazine, John Creasy, South African photo-novellas ("lookbooks"), the Holy Bible, newspapers, Shakespeare, and Jane Austen. While critically dismissing them as misthoughtful camp, Soyinka recognized them for something of what they were: the peripheral popular linear literacy of the semiliterate proletarian and not to be confused with well-schooled African literature, the kind they publish in Europe and export to Nigeria.

Where many of the better-educated Nigerian authors of the time saw the ideas attendant to colonialism as disastrous to their culture, the market writers saw them as symptoms of inevitable, even enviable change. While the university-trained intelligentsia concerned itself with symbolism and polished prose and took literacy for granted, the Onitsha market writers addressed the more typical and topical tropical concerns of their readers.

Their simple English and basic concerns—sex, money, and style: the real stuff of popular literature everywhere—appealed to an audience for whom literacy is a great accomplishment holding even greater promise. Implicit in the Word's appearance is the distance the writers and their readers have come, bringing themselves up to literacy from behind their linguistic predecessor's three-hundred-year lead.

Their literature is one of the rare occasions where the introduction of the Word to a primarily oral society is laid bare in print. Of the analogous pamphlet literature of eighteenth-century England, Samuel Johnson, working as their bibliographer, wrote . . .

> *The mind, once let loose to enquiry, and suffered to operate without restraint, necessarily deviates into peculiar opinions and wanders in new tracks, where she is indeed sometimes lost in a labrinth, from which though she cannot return and scarce knows how to proceed; yet, sometimes makes useful discoveries, or finds out nearer paths to knowledge.*[9]

The less than happenstance similarity in appearance, content, and context to the Elizabethan pamphleteers, in which the English novel finds its origins, has been pointed out by Emmanuel Obiechina in his critical works on this phenomenon. *Mabel the Sweet Honey That Poured Away* has been referred to as *Pamela* in Africa. These similarly sized, as poorly printed, likewise cardstock-covered chapbooks bear an uncanny resemblance to the works of Defoe, Richardson, and Greene not only in physical form but content. Both literatures attend the creation of a middle class. To both literatures Pop is a new concept made possible by a new consciousness made possible by new technologies.

At the time these literary anomalies were written, both author and audience have learned to speak and read English and most have just come to metropolitan life from the bush. Readers turn to them for useful advice on how to win a good girl's love, how to cope with the modern emancipated party girls and wives, how to cope with the money-mongers of the market and the sleek-headed nuts of the nightlife, and how to get up in a difficult world that turns men up and down.

Money, which is hard to get but easy to spend, has entered into the age-old agrarian moral equations that country traditions formerly dictated. This is the Age of Modern Ladies (whose character toward boys leaves something to be desired) and Radical Stars. "The saying that a Star is born and not made leaves the reader to prove if he is a Star or a mug. But remember a mug could be fearfully tough, sleek-headed and hard as a nut. . . . This is an age of radical stars."[10]

With independence from Britain in 1960, Nigeria took on a wild edge that musicians and writers mirrored. Nationalization and local pride embraced Africanization of the new popular arts. These artists fell in love with the romance of true love, whether in the convenient pulp paperback form or vis-à-vis the silvery cinema screen, and they discovered highlife. Originally a musical expression of vitality, highlife is the code of modernity. Ulli Beier, the German student of West African culture and literature who introduced the pamphlets to non-African audiences in 1961, defined highlife as "a reaction against the austerity of traditional African life. It is a way of life that believes in pleasure, music, drinking, free love and the ostentatious spending of money."

Beier's countryman and cohort, the bibliographer and author Janheinz Jahn, captured the more sophisticated side of the sensibility in his memoir of travels through Nigeria at the time. Describing how his friend Tip-Top "turned himself into a piece of poetry" at a nightclub, Jahn comments: "The African thing about it was the grandeur of attitude and gestures, which lifted him above all 'acting', transposing his future existence into the present, letting him be now what he would like to be and was meant to be."[11]

As the best jazz singers seem most comfortable in a limited range, the highlife authors turn their limited vocabularies to great advantage. There were author/musicians. Gabe Offiah, the author of *Rosa Bonsue,* was the composer and vocalist for the rowdy house band of the Niger City Hotel. For the band, Offiah wrote blues (which was the name for a ⅚ rhythm) in Igbo and highlifes in pidgin English, the common tongue. His novella of the utterly respectable bookkeeper, George Uzuh, falling into the bittersweet business of love with a nightclub girl—a real pretty tart—against his better judgement, is quite likely thinly veiled autobiography. The dialogue sounds barroom verbatim:

"She's got a beauty that's in a class by itself, a beauty that's intoxicating and exciting. And she's the craziest exponent of 'Bonsue'. Why I even heard them calling her Rosa Bonsue: "Haba Mallam, George, you've never seen anything like her before. You'll go ga-ga watching her wriggling and wiggling, shaking and swaying to the Bonsue tempo. Shegia: She's the real Bonsue. By the way, she's coming here tomorrow, I hope you don't mind?" "What is she coming here for?" asked George.

"To demonstrate the Bonsue," replied Bayo. "Look, I used every trick in and outside the book to make her acquaintance. Why, she even danced with me four times, which is a record. Rosa Bonsue is a fireball, man. She's too hot for my handling . . . I especially want her to come and demonstrate the Bonsue for your benefit, since you're a stay at home bookworm."[12]

At the Dolphin Cafe Hotel, which some concede to have been the best nightclub in Onitsha, "Pastor" Rex Jim Lawson's Nigeriaphone Studio Orchestra Onitsha had Thomas Iguh on double bass. The author of *Love at First, Hate at Last, Why Men Never Trust Woman, Agnes in the Game of True Love,* and *How to Avoid Corner Corner Love and Win Good Love From Girls,* Iguh was a very serious young man who cited Shakespeare, Thomas Paine, Thomas Jefferson, Abraham Lincoln, and Mao Tse-tung as his influences. His literary mission was "to fight [the] moral laxity" of "girls who go off with the boys and come back late at night."[13]

The didactic nature of his writing, which likely made him rather unpopular with the other band members, appealed to readers navigating their way through their own bitter experiences. Iguh's advice spoke to them in language they understood. His virile style is as peculiar as is the matter and derives something from his experience as a performance artist. He said the reason he chose drama as the vehicle his story drove was because it "projects a live experience" and "is more easily assimilated" by semiliterates.

The unedited, unexpurgated vehement venacularists of Onitsha, Port Harcourt, Aba, and occasionally Lagos show a healthy disrespect for the laws of language. Reading them demands we cut the catechism of literature some slack. They spell well enough to mean what they say but not always well enough to say what they mean. The best of the writers seem to thrive on the good grace of invincible ignorance. Colloquial, racy with simplicity, and full of the ulterior humor of the average man, the subject matter of the novellas is closer in style to that of the highlife musicians who played in the bars of the market than to that of the novelists of university towns.

Literary and musical forms that started out as copies of Western pulp fiction and Top 40 tunes assimilated themselves to the culture, Africanizing the colonist's commodities. Both comment and philosophize on social mores. Both find their precedents in the oral traditions of the village griot. Both are adapting to new technologies, the printing press and the gramophone. Highlife can sound like the common denominator between oral and literate sensibilities in Africa. As jazz, rhythm and blues, and rock and roll can be understood as musical dialogues between black and white in America, the Highlife and the Mad English of Eastern Nigeria commandeered by the market writers has that jazz vernacular, that reducing of the don'ts into do's of some kind that seems so intuitively in touch with language's ability to shine.

❋ ❋ ❋

The origins of Nigerian English lie in the mercantile vocabulary of the slave trade. The oldest written example of it is now only a transcription. *The Diary of Antera Duke, being three years in the life of an Efik chief, 18th January 1785 to 31st January 1788,* can be found in the curious book *Efik Traders of Old Calabar.*[14] In Dr. A. W. Wilkie's copy (the original text, reputedly, was lost when the Luftwaffe bombed the library of the United Presbyterian Church in Edinburgh), the short entries recount the slave raids, decapitations, human sacrifices, unscrupulous business transactions, and heavy drinking of the day.

A wealthy slave trader, Duke, recounts his swashbuckling, rather bloodthirsty adventures in the purest form of Mad English:

7.6.1787

... wee see Robin Tom King John and Otto Dutto Tom King John send them to com for mak play to Duke and my father and Egbo Young mother so the cutt one woman head of to Duke and 7 Barr Room men to be cutt for my father so play all night.[15]

In other words, the fellows got together and cut off the heads of one woman and seven barflies to honor their own dearly departed. Not only is what he says perfectly mad, but also the way he says it is perfectly mad. Duke's English was necessitated by his trade in human flesh. The bulk of his vocabulary was the language of commerce: How much for how many? Bartering came to be done more and more not only on English terms but *in* English terms.

Or something approaching English terms. By necessity he spoke English like a sailor, his only contact with the language being with sailors who didn't speak at all well themselves. The merchant captains and crews slaving out of Birmingham spoke the polygot argot of the Spanish Main, as ill thought as ill said. Manning a slave ship, being a step down from piracy, required and attracted the most rudimentary skills and souls, a multicultural dreck who reputedly communicated in such multitudinous vulgarities as to defy any single tongue's capacity for filth.

English added the finishing touches to a pidgin that had been in development in coastal Nigeria since the Portuguese started trading on the Bight of Biafra in the sixteenth century. When the British came a-slaving to Nigeria, along with the sorrow, tears, and blood came the English language. The pidgin then spoken along the coast of the Bight of Biafra is rooted in the rough trade talk of pirates. It employed a smattering of Portuguese (sabe),

Dutch, Cameroonian German, and Gold Coast French as well as the sailor's slanged and shanghaied English.

By the eighteenth century a jargon of English vocabulary and Ibibio construction was in place in the prosperous slaving town of Old Calabar. The result was transliterated from, amongst others, the vernacular of the Yoruba, Igbo, Ibibio, Ikak, Efik, Tiv, Hausa, and Falani and can strike the sympathetic ear as enigmatic. The raw, unrefined, self-defined street talk that occurs where different linguistic cultures meld creates a pidgin.

Like pidgins the world over, it is the language of the conquered collaborating with their colonialist conquistadors. The British are by nature economic imperialists. In contrast with the French-style cultural imperialism of West Africa, the English applied themselves to establishing political order and cultivating commercial accounts with the inhabitants. The brutally laisse faire capitalism of slaving melded with local customs as it traveled through the mangrove delta on the Bight of Biafra, up the Niger River to Igbo land's trading town, Onitsha.

Until their slave trade was abolished in the mid-nineteenth century, the British working at the mouth of the Niger River had never seen the origins of their product. It didn't much interest them. Whenever possible they did their business without stepping on shore. The reports of the earliest European explorers described the upriver country of the Igbo, beyond the mangrove swamps of the Delta, as pestilent: "The White Man's Grave." If malaria didn't destroy their immune systems, they figured the tsetse flies' sleeping sickness or the cannibal appetite would. Most were content to pay Delta middlemen the trinket sums they asked for to be spared the probable outcome.

If few of these entrepreneurs took the trouble to learn their suppliers' languages or many of their ways, the riverine flesh traders quickly learned the advantage a mass language can afford. The need for a lingua franca was generally felt, not only to facilitate trade with the melanoma-less but between neighbors. For a millennium and more the Igbo and their neighbors lived in tiny fiercely independent villages throughout the most populated land in Black Africa without king, country, or common tongue.

Chinua Achebe describes it as ". . . a world of men and women and children and spirits and deities and animals and nature . . . and men and women both living and dead—this is very important—a community of the living and the dead and the unborn. So it was both material and spiritual and whatever you did in the village took this into account."[16] The Igbo people's preferred reality is the world of the village. "It is one," says Achebe, "not the only reality, but it's the one the Igbo people, who are my people, have preferred to all others. It was as if they had a choice of creating empire or cities or large communities and they looked at them and said, 'No, we think that what is safest and best is a system in which everybody knows everybody else.' "[17]

But not *too* well. The composer George Antheil's squib, "People who are in love with one another do not really respect each other—they know too much about each other," would seem to apply. To be Igbo is to be your own man. The Igbo concept of *Chi* departs from the Christian's *Holy Spirit* in its ultimate uniqueness. Beside the concept of one God, the idea of a single reality seems antithetical to the Igbo's (or Heebo or Eboe or Ibo or Egbo) pragmatic mysticism. The stubbornness of their individuality seems to have prevented their achieving a standard dialect in precolonial times.

Even today the language we conveniently refer to as Igbo has at least thirty dialects that vary in mutual intelligibility. Igbo is the unwritten language of an oral culture.

Before the introduction of literacy, languages in Eastern Nigeria could be shared by only a few hundred or a few thousand people. Linguists believe there were as many as 350 dialects of Igbo but too little fieldwork has been done to confirm any number. Coupled with the question of a standardized orthography, the controversy over which of these dialects would ascend to a standard grammar and lexicon has made the language's usefulness as a written form questionable.

While the spoken word lives within the written, the opposite is not true. The literate have always used this to their Darwinian advantage. The history of colonialism is as much about the triumph of the literate over the illiterate than it is about any racial or national superiority. Once a people have learned to read, write, and print, oral culture is lost. The virus the written word releases in any oral society effectively renders much of tradition the stuff of nostalgia.

❋ ❋ ❋

One of the finest examples of the triumph of the literate is the first publication in English by a Western-educated African: the 1789 autobiography *The Interesting Narrative of Olaudah Equiano, or Gustavus Vassa the African, written by himself.* This first work in writing by an Igbo is imbued with sophisticated moral authority and intellectual independence. Equiano's cultural confidence, grounded in a millennium-old democracy, describes an achievement-oriented, self-sustaining human system worthy of respect. It spoke well enough to have gone through nine editions in its first eight years in print. The *Narrative* was widely subscribed to by members of British and American aristocracy and government and is frequently credited with bringing about the abolitionist movement and the eventual repeal of the Slave Act.

In Equiano's *Eboe*-land, the individual is valued over authority. Atomistic, competitive, and equalitarian, *Eboe* culture and temperament are pervaded by the autonomies Thomas Jefferson posited in the Constitution. These are not the qualities authoritarian England enjoyed in her African any more than in her American colonies. Equiano's description of the Igbo emphasis on individual achievement and initiative, alternative prestige goals, and paths of action must have impressed Jefferson. They as likely found substance in Jefferson's intercourse with Sally Hemings and her family as they found expression in his antipurist ethic and politics.

How much of Miss Hemings Jefferson actually grasped has been a subject of much speculation, but any contact would make an impression. Can we calculate the human factor that went into Jefferson's instigation of antislavery legislation? Given black English's rich reputation for neologisms, need his appreciation of the vernacular and his democratic linguistic theories have come entirely from his reading of Anglo-Saxon when he was hearing first-, second-, and third-generation Africans speaking English on the grounds of his farm? *The Narrative* could only have enriched Jefferson's familiarity with articulate African sensibility at Monticello. In it, Equiano debunks the disinformation commonly used to justify the trade in humans by the "Oran Otang philosophers" who believed Africans no better than irrational and subhuman. Equiano's Igbo family values would help explain the world of Monticello. Their proverbs regarding polygamy might have lent wisdom in matters of concern to his extended family's politic.

Miss Hemings's grandmother was Jefferson's father-in-law's African, quite likely Igbo, wife. Their children were both Jefferson's domestics and in-laws. Mulatto Sally, being his own wife Martha's half-sister, becoming his concubine transgresses segregationalist and monogamist strictures but barely raises an eyebrow where such scripture is unwritten. In their miscegenation, his Oran Otang philosophy—which also meant believing Africans prefer to mate with whites just as orangutans ("wildman of the woods") prefer to mate with African women—likely grated but equivocated easily to assimilation.

When Equiano was kidnapped at the age of ten in 1755, *The Unknown* was where the whites were the presumed cannibals. Gentile slavery, much as Jefferson practiced, was a fact of life in Igbo land. Until Africans were sold to Europeans, slavery had been mostly a social control in a land without jails. The criminal acts and debt that sentenced slaves could be bought out of, just as title could be bought into, made them Oru. An Oru was a slave who could be bought or sold as livestock, but redeemed. An Osu could as well, but an Osu couldn't buy his freedom. He was born dedicated to a god and it was his fate to be labeled untouchable.

The Unknown largely obliterated those differences. Had there been many literate Africans in Africa at the time of Equiano's publication, it might have demystified *The Unknown* into which so many were born, sentenced, abducted, and sold. The very existence of *The Unknown* transgressed the Igbo reasons for keeping slaves. They could be sold down the river. Those who would survive the Middle Passage would almost all be Osu in the New World. Monticello was one of the exceptions. Equiano was another, being amongst the privileged few Eastern Nigerians given the opportunity to learn written English for the next hundred years. As such, he was among the chosen few who would accomplish freedom.

✳ ✳ ✳

The shore at Onitsha offered a curious sight: the river was full of native canoes, and on the shore was a great crowd, motley and busy, coming, going, talking and gesticulating and sometimes appearing greatly excited. . . . It was market day and the canoes had brought men belonging to the neighboring tribes to Onitsha to exchange their products for European wares which the black traders sell either on their own account or on that of the factors they represent. . . . Standing or sitting, the women were exhibiting their wares; at one place calicoes, at another beads, here jugs or bottles of gin or rum, and everywhere large calabashes of salt. The men walked about among the groups, making exchanges with palm oil or ivory for the merchandise they wanted: or soldiers made their purchases with cowries. . . . The traveler is everywhere struck with the diversity of the races.

Rev. Adjai Crowther:
Church Missionary Intelligencer, 1857

Today a lightly treed savanna, Onitsha in the mid-eighteenth century, when slaving anchored the economy, was inland from the port on the Niger, shrouded in rainforest. The bush of British moneymongering for a hundred years before the abolition of the trade in humans and a hundred years after, it had a reputation for being inhospitable to whites.

In Eastern Nigeria, the European entrepreneurs were preceded by appeasing black Christian missionaries, mostly from the Gold Coast. While at the end flourishing, the Christianization of Igbo land did not go well. It succeeded better in practical than in spiritual matters. Enough so that one of the most frequent complaints of the proselytizers was the feeling the Onitsha Igbo, in particular, were taking advantage of them, more interested in merchandise than evangelism.

Until the discovery, in 1857, of quinine's prophylactic effect on malaria, few whites withstood the rigors of the inhospitable environment. By then palm oil—another universal lubricant—not slaves, had become the major export from the interior. Even then the entrepreneurs came less to conquer than to eliminate the middlemen who'd opened the trade routes through scrupulous and at times honorable business practices. Only when the Royal Africa Company monopolies were endangered by fair trade did the lobbyists of Liverpool suggest colonization.

European missionaries didn't establish themselves in Onitsha, the commercial heart of Igbo land, until the mid-nineteenth century. Whereas hypocrisy, immortality, drunkenness, and insensitivity to the indigenous contributed to the Christian's unconvincing campaign to convert the Igbo throughout the nineteenth century, their embrace of the Word challenged the old order much as the Jeffersonian embrace challenged his acceptance of slavery.

With few exceptions, the majority of converts came from the Osu caste whose *untouchable* status was as incongruous with Igbo social ideals as slavery was to America's. One of the Church's most discomforting of beatitudes, that the meek shall inherit the earth, impressed itself on the Igbo elite when they found their educated inferiors' incomes threatening economic superiority. If the Igbo disagree on many things, one of the things they came to agree upon is education. The Igbo venerate education. To be erudite is to be elegant. The existence of a mission-educated class sped up the spread of a nationalist movement, and the Christian mission, despite early hostility, emerged as an indispensable factor in Igbo land. Five generations after Equiano and two generations before independence, the real development of Igbo literacy began.

Igbo literacy, recognition, and independence would find its evangelist in Nnamdi Azikiwe. Mentored by the legendary John Moray Stuart-Young in the fundamentals of poetry, philosophy, and resistance, "Zik" would be the most influential of all the *Been To's* of Nigeria's own lost generation. *Been To 1912:* Onitsha, Christ Missionary Society; Lagos, Wesleyan Boys H.S.; Calabar: Hope Waddell Training Institute. *Been To 1925:* Harpers Ferry, W.V.: Storer College. *Been To 1926:* Washington, D.C.: Howard University. *Been To:* Lincoln University, Columbia University, The University of Pennsylvania, and London University in England where he studied with Bronislaw Malinowski, the father of anthropology.

Inspired by Marcus Garvey, W.E.B. DuBois, the "Black Zionism" of Dr. James Emmanuel Kwegyir Aggrey, and the Harlem Renaissance writers, "Zik"—the Igbo Renaissance man—returned to Africa in 1934 to "show the light" and "find the way," editing the influential *African Morning Star* and the *West African Pilot* through the 1930s. His Zik Group of newspapers made resentment of foreign rule palpable while promoting the new principles of negritude being expounded by Léopold Senghor of Senegal.

Azikiwe recognized the revolutionary effect literacy would have on Nigeria's reclaiming her independence and taunted his constituency with their shortcomings, chiding them for remaining satisfied within the confines of mediocrity.

"Africans have pencils and pens and ink. . . . But with their vaunted knowledge obtained from the important educational centres of the world, what have Africans been able to produce, intellectually speaking? And by this one implies a literary output. . . . Literature is the soul of any nation. . . . Why cannot an African write a textbook? Africans must be inferior. If not, what excuse can they offer?"[18]

Zik was believed because his voice carried authority. He preached a "new African" who was "attuned with the hymn of infinity." He invited the elite, whether African or not, and the status quo to abstain from their parochial faith in supreme powers and corrupted unnatural home culture and indulge in his pleasing cocktail of Igbo idealism and metropolitan materialism. Literacy enabled the self-determination necessary to the indigenous African's enjoying the basic human rights their place in the protectorate denied them.

Though Nigeria was amalgamated into a British protectorate at the turn of the twentieth century, it wasn't until between the world wars that the colonialist's presence was much felt beyond the commercial sphere in Onitsha. The Second World War brought western-style modernism and new opportunities to all of West Africa but perhaps to nowhere so much as East Central Nigeria. Oil was discovered downriver, putting an end to subsistence economy.

With the economic boom that followed the war, Igbo land's educational system remade itself. Graduates of missionary schools had groomed their schooling to teaching in the public and private schools that they would open. Veterans of the 81st and 82nd Divisions of the Royal West African Frontier Force returned from duty in Kenya, India, and Burma under British command with superior educations, came home as skilled mechanics and printers and used their shops as both trade schools and forums. These *Been To's*, possessed with the migrant's subjectivity, spread the growing dissatisfaction with village life. Their newly accomplished literacy voiced their impatience with provincial life's complacency as best their third-grade vocabularies allowed, often pitting themselves against their own parochial faith in the "natural" and "universal" ways of their home culture.

The dusk of the colonial era and the dawn of the industrial revolution in West Africa, when the Pandora's box of modernity opened on Igbo land, was a boom time along the banks of the Niger River. Society would reorient itself from tribal to urban ways within two generations. By the end of the Second World War, English had penetrated even the deepest bush, creating a niche in the Onitsha market that was quickly filled by authors and booksellers who knew what sold.

❄ ❄ ❄

In 1947 a Lagos printer published *Ikolo the Wrestler and Other Igbo Tales,* a collection of folktales by Cyprian Ekwensi in English, and followed up with his first bestseller, *When Love Whispers,* a romance. As best we know these are the first literary works written and printed by and for Nigerians in English. A contemporary reprint by Tabansi Bookshop would be the first of the chapbooks published in Onitsha.

The 1953 census of Onitsha estimated 38 percent of the population could write in English. Self-employed jobbing printers, authors, and booksellers quickly deduced a marriage of form and content perfectly suited to facilitate what existed of a reading public. Priced within the means of working people, the subject matter and the language of the books were shrewdly calculated to be within their audience's grasp. In 1954, Ekwensi's *People of the City* would be the first fiction by an African to be published in England.

By 1960, the town supported not only the twenty-four booksellers on New Market Road but also a publishing industry.

The precariously printed pamphlets are very uniform in style if not content. They measure approximately five-by-eight inches, contain anywhere from sixteen to seventy-two newsprint pages, and were produced in print runs ranging from a few hundred to a few thousand to tens of thousands. They are cheap, priced equivalent to a bottle of beer, and simply written. Their purpose is to profit all involved. To do so they must entertain and instruct.

Although in the economic equation of Onitsha publishing, the author was the low man on the totem pole, it was socially a very prestigious position. As would seem universal, the author was as much an esteemed title as a profession, writing an accomplishment, a way to *Get Up,* to be important. Ekwensi, Okenwa Olisah, Miller O. Albert, and Money-hard were the Dominick Dunnes, the Jackie Collins, the Elmore Leonards, the Barbara Cartlands, the Deepak Chopras, and the Rush Limbaughs of their time. They could tell you how to get rich, how to write good letters, how to pass examinations, how to conduct meetings, and also teach you proverbs. The more didactic could plummet you with platitudes but the best of the Onitsha authors shine with the felt life of a countrified person undergoing citification.

Many of the books are nearly as well judged by their covers as by their written contents. Publishers enlisted local signwriters to give the words visual punch. The chief influences on these artists, as well as the writers, have less to do with the seriousness and power of traditional African art and culture than with the New World influences of cinema, journalism, and commercial advertising. While the rubber-cut prints that illustrate many of the texts show the influence of local folk art, the more elaborate covers usurp images from look-books (photo-novellas), fan magazines, sweater catalogues, and newspapers, not unlike the Pop artists of the West.

One wonders if there was any way Andy Warhol could have seen the Master of Life's *The Way to Get Money: The Best Wonderful Book for Money Mongers* before appropriating the identical image of Troy Donahue (nine times), coincidentally in the same pale

THE WAY TO GET MONEY

The Best Wonderful Book for MONEY MONGERS

2/-

yellow hue as the pamphlet, for his first one-man exhibition at the Eleanor Ward Gallery. Both pamphlet and painting appeared in (or about) 1962. It's certainly a book Warhol would have appreciated, more than somewhat in the vein of *The Philosophy of Andy Warhol (From A to B & Back Again)*, as full of good advice. Their serendipitous sharing of both an image and an aptitude for attitude and artifice would have amused Warhol. But unlike his cynical and ironic pop, the products of these popular artists glisten with glamour and humor.

The market writers employ a prose with a sweet street freshness that suits their shrewd and occasionally startling insights into life as they know it. This in part explains the linguistic characteristics of the Mad English of the Onitsha market pamphlets. The broken English of the writers is somewhat the result of being under- and miseducated. The syncopated syntaxes, unorthodox pidgin, raw grammar, and creative mistakes that riddle these writings all contribute to their expressiveness but are not always intentional.

The Victorian-era printing presses create a distinct imprint without necessarily creating a style but an appreciable ornamentation, an illuminated printing. Purely borne by necessity, the printers' art extended only as far as their limited capacities would crudely carry them. In Miller O. Albert's *Saturday Night Disappointment,* a large, emboldened moderne type is usually, but not always, employed to amplify exclamation. Or is it to replace the font's missing italic? The writers are even more affectionate of their punctuation. Extraneous quotation marks, upper-case exclamation, and rat-ta-tattooed commas contribute to the youthful testosterone-tinged exuberance of the prose.

How much of the humor of the pamphlets is on purpose can be difficult to gauge. Being amongst the semiliterate audience the pamphlets were intended for might or might not enhance an understanding of their meaning. I've wondered if Frank Odeli's *What Is Life?* would make any different sense if I were African. As is, I recommend it as a challenge to readers who feel they've accomplished *Finnegans Wake,* yet fall short of answering that primary query.

The inquisitive reader should, however, be forewarned. Based in rhythm and pitch, rather than harmony and tone, the Igbo language has a sensibility at odds with the received standard English. Literacy goes a ways toward diminishing the impact and our enjoyment of the pamphlets; we see them through a glass darkly. The pamphlet authors handle the problem of linguistic interference by sifting one culture through the medium of another, and the end product may not be as smooth as members of either culture demand.

Literature, with a capital L, can hardly be expected of people just making their first acquaintance with the written word, with the non-Afrocentric world, with modernity. For the messengers, schoolboys, taxi drivers, guitar players, and farmers who wrote these little books, standardized English is as new as it was to their Elizabethan counterparts. An oral culture transforming itself into a literary culture can take certain liberties; its elementary authors indulge themselves. In their innocence of the conventions of English language or thought, they artlessly experiment with words with the playfulness of poets. Most satisfying are the newly hewn surprises the writers wrench out of the English language. A phrase like, "head over feels in love," or "means of lovlihood" might be the product of poetic license, a cliché spun on its head, or the unintentional error of an illiterate printer.

Writers who approach a foreign language with such an audacious zest for the best, who don't bother to learn all the niceties of grammar, spelling, and punctuation, who rip into English and let it fly, will be equally reckless and righteous. The marvelously misunderstood words and idioms and volatile violations of vocabulary restrictions, the unorthodox syntax, and the spin on pidgin result in felicities we might think of as creative mistakes. At its best this kind of writing is fresh, vigorous, and imaginative. At its worst it is merely incomprehensible, such as life's mysteries.

But good or bad, deliberate or accidental, borrowed or invented, the features of chapbook style should be studied as carefully as their form or content. The concern of the pamphleteers was the masses' immediate needs. It shouldn't be surprising that a male-oriented and essentially patriarchal society produces mainly male authors expressing immediate male concerns. The writers are men and most of their readers are men.

While most of the female characters in the pamphlets are negatively portrayed as the daughters of Eve (money-mongers, prostitutes, and fraudulent women of easy virtues—the cause of most troubles in life), quite a number of them are depicted in a positive light. Some, like Veronica in Ogali Ogali's classic *Veronica My Daughter,* are shown as highly principled women who know what they want and how to get it. Others are portrayed in true romance situations and live fulfilled lives with their loved ones.

The contradictory image of women in the Onitsha pamphlets is a reflection of the contradictory nature of modern Igbo society. The authors had two worlds to deal with: the traditional world with its vernacular, diction, moral imperatives, and narrative forms, and the new commercial environment of nascent English, romance and thriller novels, adventure films, and Highlife ethics. They had the task of merging cultural and historical currents: adapting, assimilating, and engraving on the traditional matter at hand, which was vanishing, and the new moral, ethical, linguistic, and materialistic values that came with Christianity and colonial capitalism.

The resultant pamphletry can be read for a measure of those differences between the other and ourselves. This "ephemeral" literature's central purpose is a dialogue between the semiliterates and illiterates about us. Literacy has introduced its conceit, romance, to Igbo land and ruined its love life. Life has turned man up and down. Literacy has broken the oral world into alphabetic pieces, which need to be reconstructed for truth to be said again. No condition is permanent, they tell us.

The Igbos earned a reputation as suicides in the days of the Atlantic slave trade. What the British called "Igbo gut" drew a line between the white Devil and the blue sea sufficiently deep to find one of its finest expressions in the mythified histories of their Middle Passage. Landing on Georgia's Sea Islands, Gullah legend has it, Igbos chose death over captivity, en masse joining shackled hands and walking into the ocean, drowning rather than suffering indignity.

However mythified, Igbo suicide could turn evil inside out to beloved freedom and leave bad spirits in its wake. Not that it was condoned. As previously mentioned, suicide was also employed as their penultimate means of execution, proscribed to atone for only the most serious crimes. It gave a man to God's judgment rather than to his only too human fellows, who took it into their own hands only when the aberration attempted to elude atonement for their sins. Suicide over money, or romance, or cynicism, however, was in no way condoned, and it stigmatized the crime's survivors.

This sort of retribution characterized the marginalization of the Igbo people in post-war Nigeria. They have been treated *as if* they should kill themselves, as if their "miserious life" is to be expected. They have played the loser's game. It is a case of *Winner Take Nothing,* as in the epitaph of Hemingway's book by that same title: "Unlike all other forms of lutte or combat the conditions are that the winner shall take nothing; neither his ease, nor his pleasure, nor any notions of glory; nor, if he win far enough, shall there be any reward within himself."

In the sixth year of Nigerian independence disparate matters went awry. Fifty thousand Igbo, expated to the Muslim lands of the Hausa and Falani, were murdered in retribution for a military coup. The resultant Igbo push to secede from the ill-thought colonialist collaging of wildly distinct populations into nations came to a hard shove, ending the independence expected of 1960s' liberation.

The xenobiosis the colonialists and the Pan-Africanists relied on to make nations of tribes couldn't withstand the onslaughts of modernity and the inequities of colonialism. Nigeria imploded and there was another murder and another military coup and then it got to be just murder. As with so many wars, the Biafra War was essentially a racist war fought for money. Its origins are in an early attempt to dismantle the infrastructure of dishonesty the English left as legacy. This bureaucracy's initial purpose, being to serve the flesh trade, had the lasting legacy of serving dash. Their *shit talks, money walks* way of getting things done characterizes the piracy transposed on the indigenous capitalism in which the Igbo were known to excel.

Nigeria destroyed and starved Biafra from 1965 through 1971. By the war's end over a million people had died in Eastern Nigeria's fatal attempt at secession. Biafra is remembered for being the first televised genocide. Emaciated, bloated, cadaverous Igbo children scrounging through wreckage in the jungle contrasting with marauding, cannibalistic-humanoid guerrilla war racists fighting for money created the indelible imagery Biafra's public relations firm, Markpress, effectively projected onto the world's conscience.

Onitsha's market literature was among the casualties trampled underfoot and left to die in the jungle. There were a few dozen political pamphlets chronicling the war, most of which are without critical account, all very carefully worded, less interested in propaganda than in moral reform. Until the self-proclaimed Republic of Biafra set up their government press at Enugu, dissent was rarely heard in the pamphletry. The books with a political subject were sometimes plays about current events that read like transcriptions from the radio dramatically interpreted by someone smoking marijuana.

The self-help titles *Money Hard to Get But Easy To Spend, The Right Way to Approach Ladies and Get Them in Love,* and *How to Become Rich and Avoid Poverty* found their way to reprint in attempts to pick up the pieces. Booksellers discovered that the pamphletry had an appeal to a new audience who'd read about but not from them. *Veronica My Daughter* and *Mabel the Sweet Honey That Poured Away* could once again be found. A few new literary titles like Shakespeare C.N. Nwachukwu's *Tragedy of Civilian Major* appeared in the resurrected stalls of the market. Thomas Orlando Iguh resumed his writing after fighting with his drama, *The Last Days of Biafra,* published appropriately by Survival Bookshop in 1971. Ogali Ogali's *No Heaven for the Priest* and his *Thirty Years for the Director* deplore the war's consequences.

"*Nurse Gloria,*" *a Drama of Our Time, Romance That Disturbed the Mind and Job,* coming out of Port Harcourt in 1975, shows no greater sophistication than the pamphletry twenty-five years previous. The war closed and ruined the schools, shuttered the book-stalls, scattered the type-faces, and broke the presses and pressmen that created a literature of the masses. The war devalued literacy as it devalued anything you couldn't eat.

"The reality here on the ground," as they say in Onitsha market, has since had little to do with literacy's hypotheses, less with habituating itself to literacy's attendant reasons. The irresistible tendency of the human mind to enslave itself with habit has ensnared the surviving generations in the old ways. Concurrent with the collapse of the nation's school systems during the rein of Sani Abacha in the 1990s, the populace passed from semiliterate to postliterate media, skipping lightly over literacy.

In electronic communications, orality is less an impediment to understanding than literacy. While the Igbo language resists alphabetical order, it assimilates easily to video, which, rather like jazz, uses all the techniques of its oral poetry. In the twenty-first century, in the pamphletries' stead, the Onitsha entertainment industry finds a familiar equation in an inexpensive format for Igbo popular culture in the homegrown, gangster-culture, sex-and-violence melodramas now sold on video cassette in the market.

No condition is permanent. It is my sincere desire that new readers will read this literature differently than its intended audience. For Nigerian readers, perhaps the passing of time makes the rites of passage from a traditional nonliterary society to a modern pop culture less embarrassing, more appreciable. Elitism in academia has contributed to the ghettoizing of vernacular literature and slurs on the fathers of the modern Nigerian novel, Amos Tutuola and Cyprian Ekwensi. Curious that critics who are usually so vehemently anticolonial should feel so compelled to exalt the King's English and despair their fellow countryman's language as common.

But their greatest appeal, and here I think they mean the same thing to us as they did for their intended audience, is in what they tell us about our language. The Mad English of Eastern Nigeria in the 1950s and '60s has that jazz vernacular, that reducing of the do's into the don't's of some kind, that seems intuitively in touch with our language's ability to revitalize itself.

Dylan Thomas, who coined the term *Young English* in his review of Amos Tutuola's *Palm Wine Drinkard,* once described poetry as "the rhythmic, inevitably narrative, movement from an underclothed blindness to a naked vision." Herein, for me, lies the key to these writings and their appeal to an audience that has no interest in this literature as African. These writers transcend the experience in which they are rooted and speak a language that, while sometimes audacious, is easily understood by its poetic justice.

Notes

1. Wole Soyinka. *The Road.* Oxford: Oxford University Press, 1965.

2. Miller O. Albert. *Rosemary and the Taxi Driver.* Onitsha: Chinyelv Printing Press, 1960.

3. J. A. Okeke Anyichie. *Adventures of the Four Stars.* Onitsha: Highbred Maxwell, n.d.

4. Speedy Eric. *Mabel the Sweet Honey That Poured Away.* Onitsha: A. Onwudiwe & Sons, Trinity Press, 1960.

5. Ibid. p. 70.

6. Jonathan Cott. "Chinua Achebe: At the Crossroads," *Parabola: The Magazine of Myth and Tradition* 6.2 (Spring 1981), 30–39.

7. Nnamdi Azikiwe. *My Odyssey.* London: C. Hurst & Co., 1970, p. 11.

8. Wole Soyinka. *Art, Dialogue, and Outrage: Essays on Literature and Culture.* London: Methuen, 1993.

9. Samuel Johnson. "Essay on the origin and importance of small tracts and fugitive pieces." Preface to *The Harleian miscellany: or, A collection of scarce, curious, and entertaining pamphlets and tracts, as well in manuscript as in print, found in the late Earl of Oxford's library. Interspersed with historical, political, and critical notes.* London: Printed for T. Osborne, 1744–46.

10. J. A. Okeke Anyichie. *Adventures of the Four Stars.* Onitsha: Highbred Maxwell, 1965.

11. Janheinz Jahn. *Through African Doors: Experiences and Encounters in West Africa.* New York: Grove Press, 1962, p. 177.

12. Gabe Offiah. *Rosa Bonsue,* printed in back of Eddy N. Ekesiobia, '*True Love*': *Fineboy Joe and Beautiful Cathe,* 3rd edition. Aba: V.C. Okeanu, July 1971, p. 32–33.

13. Don Dodson. *Onitsha Pamphlets: Culture in the Marketplace.* Madison: University of Wisconsin, 1974, p. 248.

14. Daryll Forde, ed. *Efik Traders of Old Calabar.* London: Dawsons of Pall Mall, 1968.

15. Ibid., pp. 78–79.

16. Jonathan Cott. "Chinua Achebe: At the Crossroads," in *Conversations with Chinua Achebe.* Jackson: University Press of Mississippi, 1997, pp. 78–79.

17. Ibid., p. 77.

18. Nnamdi Azikiwe. *Renascent Africa.* Lagos: 1937; reprint, London: Frank Cass, 1968, pp. 137–38.

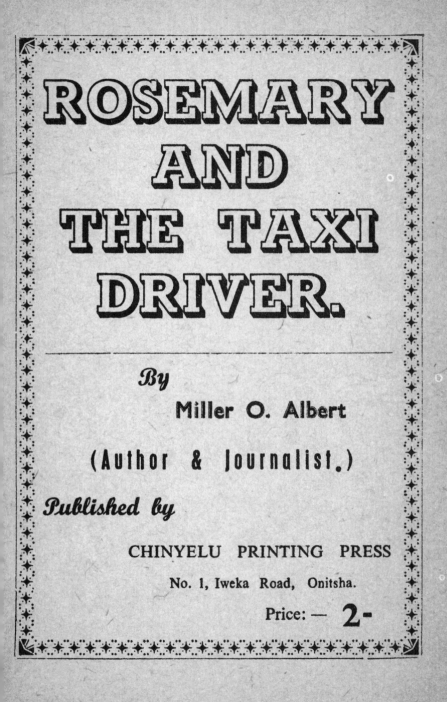

ROSEMARY AND THE TAXI DRIVER.

By

Miller O. Albert

(Author & Journalist.)

Published by

CHINYELU PRINTING PRESS

No. 1, Iweka Road, Onitsha.

Price: — **2-**

ROSEMARY
AND THE TAXI DRIVER*

Printed

By

CHINYELU   PRINTING   PRESS,

1,   IWEKA   ROAD,

ONITSHA.

NIGERIA.

*complete text

NOTICE

~~~~~~~~~~~~~

NOTE

All characters in this novel, are all round imaginary. Note, none is real. It is no true story and therefore concerns n o b o d y in anyway. Whoever hits his head at the ceiling does it at his own personal fatal risk.

The Author.

ROSEMARY AND THE TAXI DRIVER.

CHAPTER CONTENTS

i.   The Dazzling Beauty of Rosemary.

ii. The Star High Life Dance.

iii Rosemary's Glamorous Spells.

iv   Midnight Love.

v.   Lost Days of Love.

vi. Defamatory Libel.

CHAPTER 1.

THE DAZZLING BEAUTY OF ROSEMARY.

"If there was a prize to be awarded for falling in love at first blush, Rosemary should be given the richest golden medal, " She has been chasing around the romantic seaport of Lagos, with her flareful flush o f romance. H e r v o i l e t gown with vibrant colours and heavenly patterns vested below h e r knees. She w o r e a dazzling gold necklace, shiny ear rings a n d a botanical veil, stained all over with jet colours.

It was in the month of April, while the dry season was nearly over. " The season that sparks off love, kisses and romance. Wasn't it wonderful ? The long carefree days had gone." It was time for love to roar on the air, and equally, the time for Rosemary to travel on a journey from Lagos to the East.

The sun flickered over her canon - ball - head, with the hairs on her forehead, heightened like onboard type of shaving. She resoluted to follow the train at the earliest declining hour of the day. At down, She got ready to march with all the guts of the times, besides her romantic love. She sang many love poems to them, while they twist, wiggle waggle and utter many love incantations, worthy of marring all the lively zests of any woman folk.

She was in her maiden form and had remained untampered, since her generate days. Even to meddle with her zestful glamour of beauty, nobody had ever succeeded. The grim enthusiasm of her ardent lust was bubbling on her romantic face, and her youthfull glances of shyness. She had got all the zests of the West and mettled her senses, to bolster up alcrtly, to crack love, romance and joke, up to their highest mediocre of acme. It was a doy for love maniacs to come and a day for Rosemary to travel too.

Reaching the town station on April ten, Rosemary delved into an undisturbed romance, with her boy friend, who was sobering, with mournful bunch of derangement, sending love expressions with quakeful Arctic chill, over her love conscious nerves. He tossed her, to stop crying for her departure and urged her to beat her heart throbs and vibrating mind, quite at its intensive urgent, with the incidence. He tossed her, managing to serene her temper; cleaning with offection, all the bitter tears of love, which were journeying down her retroussed pug-nose.

After it was just at mid-night the train could be noticed rumbling through the land, making its harsh, grimy noises. Rosemary grimaced, twisting herself into a startled look. The youngs at heart there, all delved into a wonderful tremor for fear it was a moment to have each person clutched to a shock proof. It was a day for the saints to sing of love, blessed stars started to shine intensively overhead in the broad-day light and also a day for Rosemary to travel.

She had packed all her suit cases like sardines and noisted her headtie on her onboards shaving, allowing it a bit loose, to fly goodbye, waving hilariously to her dearly beloved, who took all the rigours of unprecedented impression, to escort her with pretty tough smiles of flamboyant gestures, to the station.

"Lagos is a neautiful town," She said. "Could rather get lost there, than to dream of Elfland. Would bend, kiss, wiggle at stage shows, of High life or give the highest jazz strokes of at least five pounds each. Highlife I know, Bonsue I know, but which shall I dance with brief happiness in the East? I know I'm Rosemary. Mary, is the last tail of it, Yes! But I will one day, add one "R" after a letter, from the last spelling, to make it a vital gut that's Yes the much sought after treasure, "Marry."

Soon she entered into the train, rolling the sleeves of her gown, getting ready for any strange enventuality. All the mask faced odd boys were soaring on the air, for her cheerful romance because of her saucy red lips. The character they presented, became very chicky to happiness and some, were savouring insubordination, mostly the odd concomitant type, of immoral stimulation, which provoked the impetus of glaring at sexual menace, below the belt, leading to excessive giving back of daily toping and night time tipples of dry gin and Whiskey.

Rosemary was as active as quick sliver. Bitter phenomenon of love commotions, had come her way since yesrerday.

9

Quick steps to love, was taking breed, but she resoluted to shun it till a most suitable paragon of being, presents the most ardent glamour of flamboyant gestures. The frowning of her face, could portray her sliding tackles, which she kept in a store for African highlife. The key-notes, which the orchestra boys clangour, hurts her feeling of patience. She gestriculated within a moment, recording quick steps occurring in her mind, as a great annal and reinvigorative general of classical Africa.

The beats were highly clamouring melodiously, making airy sounds over the sky, winding, round, the tympanum of every star highlife beater. It made many glamour of beauties shudder frantically. No doubt of Rosemery. She perceived the necessary vital guts about it too, pulling force as if she was glamouring briskly in a stage show "Yeh!"

She was enjoying the slow gallops of the train, when she perceived a philosophy in herself which compelled her to taste all the life flavours of thebeautiful town of Enugu. She could ohboard a tinker omnibus the same day she alighted from the train to Onitsha; but faculties not remedying themselves, she resoluted to divide her journey inorder to trace out one to marry, or to fall in love and gulp in all the broths nature packed into it, like parcels of sand

The man she cloistered at first flush of her sight was a romantic virile odd, who introduced himself as Okoro.

After they mande a nice little smile, they raged a torrential down pour of speeches, each trying to exhaust the querulous tone God had suffered to give out, free of charge to every individual. Soon they felt an impression of bigness in themselves, glaring at nature as super love maker.

This taxi driving dwarf of a beauty, fell a heavenly victim to many sophisticated things of his expectation. He had committed many " Why saints come " crimes of life, with unprecedented suave stratagems. He is noticed more on moral defamation than on tidy clearing off of indifference behaviours. He presents suave nonentities, each time he feels like marring success, with a mahatma type of power. He laughs more as a freak, than as a human being, looking like crime offender, with illicit practical glances, evident in his hefty stature, timing the day with unrecorded imshaps. He had shattered many plans and still it bubbles in his evil mind the more to present the highest catastrophe, ever recorded.

After watching if any of his girl customers was on the guide, he rendered a submissive character of:
" Hello, who goes there ? "

Rosemary drifted to him, loving him and loving him and loving too the more. She flashed her romantic eyes, bending down for shamefulness. A little of a time, she made her character to be
" How is it ? "

" It is quite well. "

" How far you ' re going driver ? Your car's I know must be of the sort I always ride of a time ago, you remember ?" She touched him on the chin.

" I do" He replied. "What a ride, you want?" " Are you still just in the West African English, brought by t h e journalists ? O chuckle you to laugh." Just within the veldt." He replied, putting his hands inside his pocket and bluffing arrogantly, boistering eye signal of inviolable romance.

They delved into torrential down pour of speeches, making their devilish introduction.

The love now brewing, with active hotness, was blasty and could rather throw off each with the little idea, they've got about themselves.

Okoro, the taxi driver got a tanner trouser and tough adam coats and glared at himself as the chap of the day. Soon he left the taxi, minor and took Rosemary home, to cool down.

The house Rosemary was put on their arrival was savouring something of the old and Okoro having got informations about his brother on tour, made way with her, into his brother's room with Rosemary. Before their arrival, Okoro did the game of removing the pictures hoisted over the air which were all his brother's pictures. He did that without time because something of the lot he likes best was down. He didn't want Rosemary to feel that he wasn't the owner of the little end.

A little time, he took permission to go and get back his senior uncle, but not knowing that he was going to carry the dirty minor he kept in the taxi park, outside the railway station. On his way back, he washed out the annotations terming the car a taxi.

When he reached his brother's house, where he kept Rosemary he gave a nasty clangcuring blasts of the minor horn. She rushed out and welcomed him. She rushed, twisting her eye br-ows and knitting it a bit, to show the zests of the West.

They ate the little bread and suasage Okoro brought from his brother's electrolux. Rosemary was lost in arena of love adventure. They loved each other and satisfied with their talents at the sametime. Infact, it could have been the best love so far, if it wasn't meddled with malice and pugnacity.

The day for the owner of the house to re-occupy his little end of no regret was come, just a day for the dumb and deaf, to have a brisk enjoyment. Rosemary was planning to head to Osha; but hadn't been to any toping society since her stay off in the East.

She impressed Okoro, to give her enough subsidy, to foot the tipple. Though it was stated, for the deaf and dumb, still she was compelled to witness it.

Towards the down of the day, Okoro got ready to go out with Rosemary for the dance.

The arrangement being to stop a tinker omnibus on the way, after the night tipple, so that she could float down, a magpie to Onitsha.

There was no chance for Okoro to hoist up the decorations in his brother's house which he turned down, incase Rosemary shoud recognise what was brewing. Actually, it was too tough a play, to tell Rosemary to go out, while they were in the midst of burning speech. He didn't want to be suspected, and had not lay such impression so pompous, before, and ought not leat it go, at this terrible moment. When it was just at the nick of a time, he hurriedly put Rosemary's suit cases inside the minor, and hurriedly ordered her to get in, in good faith. She soon got ready and rubbed her pancake, feeling just on the lead. She raised her black hairs, to suit her apex nose. A curtly smile bubbled on the air, favouring Okoro. But there was no time, to blast romantic flares. He dudged the love smiles.

Soon he kicked the taxi and went back, after half way to hoist on the pictures he turned down when he was at the worst instincts. He was shuddering at every hiss of a sound. Before he could finish remedying the crime he committed, his brother, the faithful owner of the house came in, standing at the corridor, guessing that something of the sort which he doesn's want was wrong He soon sighed and got depressed. After many odd remarks, the full automobile of his spirit, compelled him to leave exerything, threatening him with pretty tough smiles, of tremor.

After his liberation, he trotted off with his craggy legs, jumping into the minor with a mad stampede, hoping to finish the speedometre, within an active time.

CHAPTER II
THE STAR HIGHLIFE DANCE.

They sped over the hills and scaled round the mountains. Okoro had the hands to corner the worst wagons, speeding up from Onitsha. The wind howled across the dreary desert, showing an intensive chill, from the quaking side of heaven. The hoarfrost drizzled down with a low temperature, baffling the virile odd beings; who had their nose like dogs. Those who hadn't theirs like dogs, have some part, like that of sea crocodile.

All the time, Okoro hadn't rendered any account of what he had got out of the minor to the owner. The police had all got informations that Okoro had run away with the minor, belonging to a soanso, quoting the number and the report's reference number. The report became crime and forgery for having rubbed off the taxi, written on its glasses. All the time, Rosemary had told Okoro that she was a retired woman police. In the real sense of her own case, she was terminated for illicit practices. She was with her pictures with her, to make it really tough with the times.

After mile 'two' a traffic constable stopped him, to check his particulars but he knew that he was recorded as a culprit in the crime book he was holding and had fallen victim to many offences, more serious than felony and misdemeanour, but he sped over, increasing his speed.

He began to eye like an imperial Corsican. The madness which jumped crazily into him was taking a strong hold. He was in his generate twenties and had a pugnacious bunch of stamina new from nature with which to blast off any being that might intervene. His blows were bullets man; and his senses of alertness, were the worst blemish of this life. He could bend, manoevre and pull down any house, punching just little below the belt.

After two hours ride, they went to witness the dance. Now it was time for evil, to take strong beer, and Okoro to bolster up for any shocking derangement. The dance, as published was apparently for the dumb and deaf and to infuse benevolence into people, to help raise funds for them. The high life music which they clangoured, was intensively a great hit of an utterly breakdown. Okoro ordered for bottles of cold beer, with which to cool down. Rosemary, a beautifully sought after glamour of a beauty, glared at the crowd, feeling the guts on her stirring face. She was proving very exotic, knitting her sweet brows, showing the proud delicious power, of her beauty.

Soon she let go a faintly smile, twisting herself. She startled at the blush she sensed the notion that those who hadn,t nice looking legs, had them supported with sticks. She twisted her scarlet lips, gulping in the tango on her table from drops to bits.

As soon as she felt like getting up, she tossed her excitement. As the English legend, had passed it that: "Excuse me dance" is permissible in a dancing party, a man who was almost a genius came, just a paragon of a man with apex nose like that of jackrabbi. Soon he let go a character of "Excuse me dance lady - " through a trivial eye signal. Rosemary raised on objection in taking the floor with the man; while Okoro was on top of the cold beer. Though he drank it with a disarray of anxiety, he still glares as greedy as a dog to exhaust more bottles or turn out the bar. He had not enough money, but conceived a stratagem with which to shun the attention of the waitress. Rosemary hadn't said a word of two, neither had the man who was dancing with her spoken a hiss. They mistook themselves as deaf and dumb orgies.

Rosemary thought that her partner was defected while the man thought that she was a deaf and dumb beauty. They've not talked to each other since they started on the floor. The dance was boring in the public mind and the lattest highlife strokes were on the air. The man dancing with Rosemary determined to toss her through the lattest South African acrobatic style of patha - patha, the highest ever fashioned. He didn't know that Rosemary was made to withstand all the rigours of unprecedented hazards, accrueing from such stylish dancing. She flew into the space and came back to the earth with a start, just afresh.

When the dance became a full automobile of spit fire, a tumult was caused.

The mobile style was rough just like the twisting of infatry. No doubt, the guy was an erratic. Rosemary grimaced with a flicker of amusement on her face. Soon Okoro perceived the mixture of highlife and high love displaying. He felt tough demonstrations, and buttoned up his heavily damped tanner trouser, feeling like a tanner scandal. He pulled the waist band of his pant, with a great force, feeling like creating irresistible attraction. He felt a heavy holler, at Rosemary, soaking his lips with his evil tongue, to stop the mess. The wife of the man dancing with Rosemary shouted: "Let us leave here, it is getting to down of the day!"

He replied, pulling his pant again: " I m trying to let go this dumb and deaf glamour dancing with me, don' t you see her?"

Rosemary grimaced: " You' re mad, ain' t you? You are full concomitant of evil beauty and mar."

She left highly depressed with the atmosphere of devilish temperature, creating indiscribable phenomena. Okoro noticed that the rusal was very outboring, h e sneared the scandal w h o assaulted Rosemary and slaapped off his chin, he had one left for him, to chew the little corn he had in his pocket. The fight became too rigid. Okoro manoevred the second time, blasting a punch on the man's belly, beer, rushed out, forming a little rivulet, to mark the great occasion. He knocked the scandal down. After notcing the catastrophe as very unbecoming, he set out on Olympic game with Rosemary, heading off to Onitsha, creating the worst record of event, ever recorded, in the annals of such occasion.

Rosemary was confused with what ideas she perceived about Okoro. He had been roaring in her beauty, thinking of what solignum, that was used in the combination of Okoro and devils. She was also a bit confused, if she could challenge the times and abandon other sully trouble which are the great blemish of this life and delve into romantic go - of this beautiful world, with Okoro.

The appointment Rosemary had at Onitsha was systematically conditional. She thought of either to break or bend. Before the next beautiful time people could say : " Good morning" to themselves, they entered into the beautiful town of Onitsha, They made an enquiry about a man, in the form of Rosemary's dad. It was reported to them that the man had left for Lagos the other day. Rosemary had her plans fixed and consolidated by nature.

When in Onitsha, the police were informed about Okoro and that he is a person wanted by the police. In the night, as it was trivial with them that they couldn't go gay without tipple, they began to guess, a place to have it out with the day. But it was just a time to make an arrest. Okoro isn't a new bird to be caught in a chaff. He had been committing many crimes none of the crimes, was below five years of terms. Instead of reducing it to four, he extends it to seven, eight or nine worth of jail terms.

Okoro was outside the gate, boistering an often ditchery romance. The stars were out, giving twinkling lights of shiny colours. The wind descended with the impressive array of cooling down the nerves.

People all entered into the hall, but It remained Okoro and Rosemary. Okoro hadn't enough money to pay. There was no Rockefeller, for an immediate subsidy. A hefty detective who wore a dirty black over-all uniform, came into the crowd looking terribly at Okoro. Immediately Okoro knew what damnation he meant, he didn't query the detective, till the man told him to follow him trace where he forgot his wife.

Okoro knew his plans. He didn't want to strife in the crowd. He took the dictative out, while the detective thought that he was taking him out. Nearing t h e police station, the detective caught Okoro on the back. He knew wrestling stratagem, then he let go the twisting leg type and hurled him up on the air and left him to land any how he likes, even if with his head broken; it was equally good. Soon, after few minutes, all the heaviness of his body, landed with a hefty noise of beer, from his stomach, like a parcel of sand.

Okoro used his own personal cudgel which he reserved for culprit like detective and police officials and knocked the cudgel on the left Palm of the detective, the medicine, which he put in his Palm since his school days for goal-keeping, fell down that one grieved him most.

It was a great mighty falling. Okoro rushed back to Rosemary, after tossing the detective well and kicking him to a dead beat, ordered her to get ready for an immediate transfer of power to owerri, that their plots are divulged.

CHAPTER III
ROSEMARY'S GLAMOROUS SPELLS.

The same evening, Okoro and Rosemary sped up to Owerri. They were ascending with the fullest drive. The sun flickered across the bewildering desert, glittering with the entire equatorial hotness and splendour. Things not being well with nature, the dictators, informed Owerri that a minor congrous of crime speacialist, was on the tidal drive, to Owerri. They further added, that if the simplest chance provides itself, a simple arrest, without tears must be made.

The accident prevention devices, got ready, to make the times, unsuitable for Okoro, on such grounds of inauspicious practice. A philosophy, presented itself, humming like a bee in him. To eschew the attention of the police, was the let go of the bee, which could probably take effect, through the manoevre of the car, flying a magpie, on another road.

The breakneck speed, was terrific. It was a bottle neck type of a run, rearing the fatal full-stop of the speedometre.

It was an Olympic game, in its purview and wasn't suitable for such tough roads, as Nigerian Roads. Soon Okoro bolstered up to render a blemish blow Thank God he never did it, it could have been the lattest catastrophe ever recorded in the history of crime.

Soon they entered into Owerri. As it was trivial with their creation, mostly it had run through their veins, they could not let go a night, without a hellish tipple, they began to stare, for a night, full of sparks and glamorous beauties, for a happy mode of impression over the night. Soon they packed the morris minor, which was the real cause of the war of Roses. Okoro loafed to the service of bigness. The clangouring funs of the town, commoted their musical pulses. They must have had only a night to spend, a night not too favourable with nature. They managed to drift near a hotel, for a crucial toping ceremony. Okoro's eyes, were very ready to tackle any jackrabbit, or the fairy witching demonstrator, who could undermine plots. such as the ones of his. He got ready to foot any bill that what he calls unlawful challenge of the times might afford him.

Rosemary, feeling very comfortabla and expressing her glamorous spell into a high apex of tipples. She was crazy and danced the crudest type of it, beating just around. The dance as it was, seemed more of an Elfland type than as the odd type nearer the inhabitants of the Equatorial world. Those who had their legs like dogs, made their eyes, like owl and the kind they called the beasty type, flowed their retroussed nose, up to the pinnacle of saint Augustine Cathedral. Rosemary didn't feel much depressed, in that her slimy self, was an evidence of good diet, of her own taste. No doubt, she had tasted it all of a time and Isn't It ? the good tidy days of her love, mellowed down with tidy kisses and a nice fragile hug of the type of her choice and mostly the fervent flirtation and ardent, vehement of fervourism, which went gay with all her generate days.

She roon became an erratic. All along, Okoro was deviating from corners, where arrests would seem natural. He had the impression of bowing down, under the flinging cover of the Alps and mountains. If the stars could have got a thing of the shield type, that could have been a nice asset, descending from heaven, for his utter approval. it was the highest eccentric subtle, ever experienced.

Since they have entered into the hotel, Okoro had drunk some topes of beer, hoping to gain mastery, over the control of alcohol. He was an ex-student of the alcoholic centre New York. He qualified with Dr. Koko, with the same doctorate degree in alcohol, only that he lost his two words of D. R., in an un natural land of the Dames. To eschew the rusals, became an untidy concomitant of the devils breath and the sinister sequence of events. To set hell on fire, could burn all the problems, in stock for the offenders.

Ain't it wonderful ? how could trouble remedy itself ? Someone must pay by compromise.

The night deepened into a cemmerian darkness. As for crime also, they are never down with boredom. He rose up on his leg feeling very indefatigable. He didn't think either through breathing or blasting of marijuana that there was a way through which he could be hurled crazily, with strategic frenziness, into the fire. All along the crimes taking strong hold, he had been on a race for life, with another man's taxi of a minor car. Rosemary she got in April, felt lost at the romance she had got. Every intervention was ready to be marred and they had impression to be defeated or they defeat, at the long run. She had once been a police woman and knew what she would be expected to do, when at the highest peak of tribulation and was a fragile hand, with her picture at her hand, ready to default any problem.

Soon Okoro felt like going out to dance. He bolstered up on the door passage, loafing at the corridor, eyeing briskly with sharp eye signals to his dally Rosemary. While Okoro got the confidence that nobody will disturb him again, he began to feel normal. He extended the waist band of his pant, for more gulping in of beer and thickness. It was the day manna fell down for the Israelites.

Rosemary felt like sleeping. She dozed drowsily. It was a dubious napping. She later woke, after a mad stampede was caused.

She was in a position to determine the course of affairs, but she fell to nap. All the sizzling stares of her beauty were rumpled into a startled look. She was instructed to signal at the blush of any red flag, this she ignored, to doze off the hundred gas automobile of a man, gestricuiating over the bar,

The policemen, who were tracing for him from a far away distance, landed with full perspiration just on their journey to Mecca, down from their mouth piece, to their chin, but that they counted as zests. They put life into the crime, making it a congrous mixture of the devilis tincture of ina- uspices and colourful blood shed. Soon they let go a thorough pillage, through a violent plunder of tins and cases. The ransack of the whole hotel, must call up, the arresting of brothel girls, which must be done either by prevalence, or virus censure or to let go a concomitant blessed time of physical demonstration.

Unfortunately, the two policemen and a det- ective, saw Rosemary and came to her to arrest her, for illicit practice, as they hummed it. She was once at the same Ikeja with them. She murm- ured with her patience, taxing her conscience, Any assault is justifiable, hoping to pull tough with the freak type of police, before her. She knew all the little laws, which enforce them to boister some defamatory criticisms. As a matter of sincerity, she had the patience to retain them, till the day is done.

They felt like cavalries, led into an Indian hotel, where beauty sparks itself, amidst kindness.

Glowing with its saucy romance, round the maiden forms, roaring seizelessly, like an Arctic child. As my father uses to say that in the past, people of the armed forces sent to India usually lost into the arena of sexual displays, it was quite it, in the way they lost without the senses of responsibility, boring home to trace of old dads and mummies. They sat, with their eyes, as glittering as the morning rays of the sun, with its little dog of action spinning round, like that of a wounded tiger. They all began to read the krola advertisement on the wall and throwing in nonsense question, which lead girls to go wrong if not experts of her sort.

One of them felt too big of himself and said: " The culprit conld be here Billy! "

" Why are yon worried. " He went on " To-morrow is pay, can't refuse me my salary, whether I got him or not. Don't you want life, can't you hold fast tenaciously, a banner without stain ? " " Yes I can do. " He replied.

They began to buy beer and thickness for extra vital power, with which to get a devilish mind, to get hold of Okoro. He had already heard their squeakish noises and felt gone. With the least chance he escaped an arrest and went out. With a little nick of a time Okoro blew a hand trumpet, which made Rosemary to catch it at once, the notion that she is wanted, by the young hearty man of her's. She fade in moving away, through a courtesy of " Excuse me Gents. ! "

On the way, they clangoured a very loud noise, which made the whole virlie litigants round about to dream of a court, witness box, the barristers, in his hood referring to what he did half way, as it is always the case, when at the beginning of law degrees, bringing in full briskness, the judge, glaring at the public for an assault of justifiable character, which his forces had marred and made useless, for defaulters, concerned. The harsh, grimy noise, made the police man, just a sentinel on the guide, accused himself - of loafing with the time. It was one of a clock and people going along that time are at the pangs of death, or possible assailance.

Before they could corner a g r e e n house, a man who was looking for him, g r i p p e d him, twisting his eyes, as if c a u g h t the quarrelsome bunch, who had been removing his yams, f r o m the ban. He held him below the belt, toughening the motion, which could have rendered itself possible. It was a total b e l o w me down, as he didn't feel his hands cold, before he caught h i m in the tough position of life. It was a fight, which finished with exchanging of Ibo made below of a very high fistal challenge. He resisted it. He used his head, to blow him off the skies.

Before people may gather to arrest him, he made way with Rosemary facing the way to Aba. As he runs, wtth the speed limit of from eighty to hundred, he could see t h e police van, running just the same speed. It was a film race of l i f e. They bent acutely at sharp bend corners and had the s a m e determination just t o finish before four Am.

Rosemary had got many senses about crime. She has a nose for it, an eye to see it in its first blush, just identical with her love glances and senses to mar its plans. The van had been running the speed, chasing them with the most hurrible drive. All along they've cornered Alps and mountains, a plan to shun the mediocre of lawful arrest roared with the intent of defying the whole commotion of the fire. She thought of hiding but that winded over. She jam life, love and the sweet flavours of all of them, marching concomit a r if it wouldn't become a blessing.

She was in her early twenties, to die at down, under such defamatory condition, became an over rated nuisance more bother and expense, than many of the earlier adopted ones. Okoro though on some cigar blasts, didn't mind the whole affair. He had the impetus to die of love, dream of it or sense its fullest flavour. provided that something is down, like that on his side, in the form of Rosemary. Whenever he drives at a finishing point, he has somthing of the lot, giving him a brief happiness, like the attention of Rosemary.

When next he forgets himself, he startles at life, like a baby, just awake. And may feel like asking himself "What is disturbing my emotional feelings?" Then all of a sudden, he could ballance with his thought that he had committed acrime and an offence, more serious, than felony and misdemeanour. Sometimes, he feels very happy. And may not know why. When he retrospects again, he perceives that infact something is down.

That day, they dived at a sharp bend and the police van mistook them. After many races and there was no successful trace of him, the police fade in sending a report through the wireless to Aba, for an immediate check up.

CHAPTER IV
MIDNIGHT LOVE

Okoro and Rosemary determined to sleep in the bush without any bed. Okoro grimaced, feeling like facing it.

" Wouldn't you lie da- r,l-ing, Darling ! " On what ? "

" Here is alright; I presume. Could rather do it here believe me, than to worry you in the jail house, you know of tearing all these races, have made me feel the waist, like a parcel of sand. "

" I shall be no but, till I reach Aba "

" How are you sure," Okoro said: " That we aren't going at Aba?"

She made little gestures and said: " If we can, we can ! "

He was scraped off his craggy legs. He twisted himself like a wounded worm and said: " What has got into you girl ? you are going to play me the game.

Hellow Rosemary ! "

She sobered down with impatience. She made a shameful little smile, just down with Okoro, to pass the hot equatorial hours of hotness, now cold of the Arctic pole. She glanced him one, two, three and four or five˙ To love was far deep, a miracle to

29

let it go just like that. After many unsatisfactory kisses, Okoro was still what he was. He hadn't felt satisfied. He still makes the attitude of: " Kiss me again. "

She replied: " I'll do but not now. "

They rocked each other, hugging themselves together, feeling the transfer flirtation and fervourism, through the sending over, of the wormth, which God had wasted time, in giving over to any living belong, excepting the reptiles. Their intentions were deep, mostly that of Okoro. His sexual instinct was in its worst intensive urgent. Startled were the leaves around, mourning under the roary wind. The scaring desert winded over with tremor. They like doing the lot, the life they played was as the first day of a virgin in a honeymoon. How beautiful it is to toss one self with his wife, how lovely it was for Rosemary to feel very shy and sophisticated. Her youthful fidelity was exhausted and they delved into a romantic blast. It was a nice day for men to marry. If there hadn't been that there was no responsible adult, it could have been a honeymoon.

When the day began to break, they woke to set off. Even to do a lot of evil journey. They didn't know that they were waited at Aba. The information came to them last night, that such a man, with so and so number on his taxi and a girl, were speeding up to Aba. Since they got the message through the wireless, there had been loafing about lazily with their cudgels.

The terrible moment for the taxi to pass Aba, had come with speed. To halt the taxi was terrible. Okoro was a film goer. He knew in himself that to change a car, is an English method of bringing confusion into crime.

The half way they stood now, wasn't anything other than seven miles from Aba. They cornered a bit, allowing cars to have way freely.

An evilly damped man who way to Aba was stopped by Okoro to blow him off his car and take over, but infact the man was stronger than evil himself. Immediately Okoro began to approach him with his tanner, the driver shouted " Tanner ! Tanner !! Tanner !!! It is idiot and bastards who wear that tanner. Fear it the tanner you wear .... " His voice was carried away, by the speed of the car. Before down of the day. a report was got from Aba that the police tossed a man with morris minor, thinking that was Okoro, then they weer given instruction, on how to go near, before they use their barton for an attack.

When Okoro had tried on many people and saw hom impossible it was, he introduced Rosemary to the road tactics, telling her to use her brains and her picture, when she was in the force, to wark. And he hid just five poles, on the way to Aba. Rosemary knew all of how to drive.

She brought down the minor on the main road, pretending to have been repairing something there.

A whalish man reached there. She glanced at the man and stopped him. The hefty man came out of his car, bringing forward his hand for a warm hand shake. The girl told him, to enter into the minor and see if something was wrong.

The hefty man entered into the minor and got the key from Rosemary. All the time, she was inspecting the car, because he got information about the car and was a detective, on an errand to Aba. He got hold of everything possible to the car and showed Rosemary his picture and quoted the reports all made about the minor. Ros-mary opened her bag and brought out her own picture while in the force.

How they have mistaken themselves was very embarrassing. Tough ain't it? It is a moment for the wise, to win. The detective sergeant Bigbelly didn't know what to do. He was startled. Rose-mary took the key from him, through a tough diploma and informed him that she was speeding up to Aba, to collect people to carry off the taxi, off the road. she went off with the personal hillman car of Sergeant big belly and at the sametime, took the key to the minor taxi, thereby, confusing the issue. She made a brief smile and begged to leave.

The sergeant felt lost and rendered the mind, of countenancing any hazrd. The stratagem was the biggest ever known by man. To toe the way to Aba just seven miles off was quite difficult and to go back a tug of war.

Rosemary had done the game. She not only got the sergeant's car but she managed to get back the key of the taxi which she called" The key of power."

When she rode five poles. as was stated by Okoro, she hollered something off:

" Hello ! " In a tuneful voice. Okoro came out, finishing, at entering the car. He took over and drove at a break neck speed. The car causing a tumult had been left seven miles from Aba. And there was not any possibility of fishing out the car, He later blamed Rosemary for getting the key of the minor. The next day, they stayed quietly in Aba, looking for more undisturbed romance.

Within a forthnight, the owner of the minor was called from Enugu then he managed to come and clear his car. This is not the end gentlemen. The car he drove to Aba, was sergeant big belly's car. It was r e p o r t e d that the car, was given to him two nights ago.The date was evident in the Insurance card. The crime is now another branch, which is unlawful taking over through false pretention sergeant big belly's car. That, counts as a striking rusal ever established. The news went all over the suburbs and towns.

All along, he goes sorrowfully, glaring at man, as a goat and conceiving the empression of hanging any woman police on the neck. The girl couldn't be recognised again. She had done many other illicit crimes in Lagos before she shifted to this place she is now, To trace her must be a vital factor but who is going to bell the cat ?

is now. To trace her must be a vital factor but who is going to bell the cat?

Rosemry and Okoro lodged outside Aba and don't ever dream to enter the town with the car they stole. They loafed about the town and lavish as they wished. They enjoyed the highest strokes and boister into the biggest romance.

The money they have, has got finished. They limited their topping ability and reduced their taste of flavour and joined a moderate boat for life. No being could ever suspect them as offenders, rather they could be noticed through Okoro's tanner. Rosemary had her box with her, but the prank she played would have hit her on the head, if she hadn't got the senses of giving Okoro her boxes the time she hid.

"Anything can happen." Was their motto. It wasn't good in Nigeria, but in Russia. The crime boy and his girl, looked very chicky to life and goy in appearance. Fashionable was Rosemary and startled were her crimes. She had developed her crime waves, at Lagos. Though Lagos isn't for crime, but that it was to Rosemary. It was just a coincidence for both of them to meet and enjoy the same wind of nature blowing.

Soon their money became less and planned to either bend or show them, that its journey with such men, doesn't always seem natural.

Rosemary is a girl who doesn't care. She had many policies of highlife which nature had offorded in her blood.

She could scarcely be in there's a hurry and could rather die than to starve. There is no doubt that the money remains little but she still had of bigness.

She was led into a quandary of dilemma she prattled within herself. She remembered her position in Lagos, or when in the force. She knew that she was doing a sort of smuggling.

She dreamt to leave Okoro. She was badly tightened up to shudder Okoro$\frac{1}{6}$ with a one day pratice. She knew that she could go anytime possible, but the sliding tackle she dreads is one, which is if she could be held on her way back to Lagos. And to fight alone, could pester austerely or may bring an abominable inversion of natural Liberty.

That day, they blamed each other because where there's happiness always, the least disagreement, presents itself as the worst blows of life. Soon they separated from their mournful positions, finding peace and enjoyment again both in the lavatory or in the bathing room under the shower. The evil of this mournful disposition being the scarcity of money with which to-start just like the beginning periods of their love.

CHAPTER FIVE
LOST DAYS OF LOVE.

Now the impecunious attitude Okoro presents became too drastic to welcome Rosemary's consents again.

Infact it was a day for the sully in heart to breath on the air. A sorrowful sigh became a laughter that reigns over the day and sudden shudder at a mere whisper took breed too. To middle up the whole affairs bubbled up in Rosemary's heart of hearts. But in the past days of the week, Okoro read in a local journal about a master detective w h o went out to village chiefs to accuse them and demanded some money from them. He laghed properly at the incidence and believed in his God of crime, to fetch Rosemary money, for a buch of comfort.

He knew that whenever he gets the money, Rosemary must make herself fit again, for inviolable love and tidy romance. She was in no doubt a glamour of a beauty. The elegant beauty type. Exotic, flexible and full of zeals of the West. She is indeed a vital gut to life.

Okoro called her to dress well and stay in the house to wait for any querulous garrulity. She accepted the risky challenge she afforeded herself.

Okoro sped out, asking of a nearby chief and he had understood, that in the past, chiefs, had some people to sell. He didn't believe that slave trade, had stopped. While washing the car of sergeant big belly which they stole, she got his picture, where he dressed in his official uniform, then he determined to show his five stones weight, with the picture. They called him a chief, at a nearby town, but the man was very lazy and old fashioned, just like my grandfather.

Okoro went out, dubiously, doubting if he could succeed. He soon noticed that the little fuel in the car was limited and could rather lead him no where. He soon met another chief whom he believed to have got some treasures. He bumped in and said. " Chief I'm a slave trader. Is there anybody down for the day? "

The chief regretted to have sold one last week. Okoro asked him: " How! "

He replied: " You didn't inform me that you'll require one. "

" This is how I do. "

" Your method is too childish. "

" Look chief, I don't believe you. " Okoro went on: " Let's see the receipt before I believe you. "

" God Almighty!" He mimiced: " Ogbonnaya; bring me that receipt. "

From the beginning, Okoro had in his pocket, sergeant big-belly's picture.

Soon Ogbonnaya got the receipt. In it, the slave trader was sold the slave, at sterling sixty. Okoro had seen his particulars. He told the chief to look at the picture he had, that picture of sergeant big-belly. While he copies down the particulars of the receipt.

The chief hollered: " Are you What? " He glared at him and said: " That uniform in the picture. "

He knew that the chief might notice that he wasn't the actual odd in that p i c t u r e then he snatched it right off from the chief.

"Let's go en ter the car." Okoro told the chife.

The chief was lost. He offered ten guineas but Okoro was what he was, t i l l the chief came in the manner of twenty pounds, till he raised it a bit with ten pounds, making it thirty pounds on the whole.

He left the chief a f t e r he had collected the man through false pretences. He rode off, going to the man who was believed to have bought the boy. He g o t the man quite alright and got the sum of twenty pounds from him. He came back, nearly jamming the traffic police on duty. That night it was a day for the highest love and toping to blast on the air. The highest meal never tasted found its way, journeying down the intestines. They tied up to get into life. The car must not go out, otherwise, their love will be wounded by the police.

Rosemary became what she was. She danced like an Indian dancer and knew the top most style of highlife. She knew the toeing style and the most eyes catching foot demonstration ever, danced with a slide, by any star high life specialist. She was enjoying herself for the last time, but Okoro didn' t know. He thought that she was just happy.

When the dance was over, Okoro and his girlfriend Rosemary went h o m e. The amount Okoro got, had subtracted ten pounds just on the spot of a night. The next morning, Okoro went out with the car. Immediately Rosemary took the remaining money with everything reasonable with her and ran away before Okoro's return.

Rosemary g a v e many informations to the police that she saw a man known as Okoro, riding a car believed to have been stolen, recorded in the detective's diary. She was the girl who stole the car throgh a very high and pranky stratagem of tactic diplomacy.

The only saviour she h a d in the crime was the sergeant didn't recognise her very well. After she gave the information, she fade in onboarding the limited train off to Lagos.

Okoro went out, that was true. He hadn't known of anything that was taking force. He saw many traffic police, flowing on the road. They were mad and red on their two fifty cc., motor jets. He suspected them. H e was scared most, when he saw another set, making harsh, grimy noise of old gears without oil in its gear box.

He manoevred cleverly to get the money, but he didn't know that Rosemary had taken it. When he looked round, he saw her letter and her picture telling him that she had gone back to Lagos. That further more queries, takes hold only in Lagos. Pity, isn't it ? All the horrible helps, which led to crime, are now for nothing Pity !

Sorrowful tears of love rushed down his chin, He was lost in these days of love. He hadn't any hope again. He sat down, forgetting that he was a traffic policeman Soon he lifted up his face and was in a position to see another one, and bumped nto high Olympic game,

He jumped crazily into his car and made way off the town, facing Portharcourt. He nearly finished the speedometre. He was crazy with life and thought of many other bad things.

One of the crudest game he played was to bring out two search lights in the car, already put by sergeant Big belly. When he reached at a narrow junction and wanted to fix the two lights on the road, but the motor cyclists were all bending on the air. He jumped frenzily again speeding very high. He was very lucky to have crossed a very swampy space, before a car sank there.

He looked back but nobody was coming. The big lorry which sank again, caused an obstruction to the policeman. When Okoro couldn't see them, he reached a place where there was a spoilt road.

The road makers had worked on it half way but they placed danger lights on the. dangerous parts. There was a shallow river along the swampy places. He fixed the search light on the side of the road, that is quite bad, allowing a very little space and removed the red lights and put bright lights on the side of the road that was closed and dangerous too.

" Crime Wave "

The worst challenge of it, was that people were riding on the spoilt part of the road before, so it carried away the minds of the policemen. This time, they thought that it had been reconstructed.

It was the highest and toughest plan, ever experienced. All the lines of the detectives all submerged into the river. The time became tough with crime, road and danger. That night, Okoro made way into Portharcouct.

CHAPTER VI
DEF — AMATORY LIBEL

The day a satan was arrested. Okoro is now a satan in the form of a man. He needs to be arrested, no doubt. His crimes were scraping off the typanum of the ear.

Rosemary went away with all the money he got. He rested that night without anything to gulp in, or to masticate. He lay in a hotel. He didn't pack the car there but elsewhere. The next morning, he went out and found the key of the car in its normal position. He went in and started off again to tremor with any style possible. He didn't know that it would be the last days of his enjoyments. He was confident in himself that he must get some money.

He went to a village chief and asked him to sell him a boy, inorder to get the chief and do as usual. They planned to have it out with him. They began to charge prizes themselves, untill they stabled at eighty sterlings. Okoro told the chief to give him receipt. The chief had no receipt. He told him, how he had got him into trouble. And told him to pay him some money but the chief told him to go to any officer and report.

He was lost in his emotional feelings. He didn't know that love had made him to be wanted by the police, with his pictures pested everywhere. He jumped crazily into a police station to r e p o r t. While on the counter, the man on duty began to throw pretty tough questions to him. The picture he had on his hand, was the picture of himself, inside the hillman car with Rosemary. At his surprise, he didn't know how the picture was taken.

As a clever man, he turned the picture. The policeman, knocked something on the counter people jumped in and Okoro became aware of himself. He began by fistal demonstration but his spirit of pugnacity was in exile,

They locked him and parked the car for the lazy sergeant. They telephoned him to come. After reading all his crime reports, the police didn't believe the receipt which misled him because the chief couldn't be held responsible, as a matter of fact, he could deny.

42

The next morning, Sergeant Big belly with big cigar, came to Port—Harcourt, to harcourt the case. Okoro was shown to him but he commented that Okoro wasn't the girl who took it away, till he was knocked a barton by a higher officer there, then he believed.

Okoro must not go in like that he knew something about law. He began to deny the car. It was too tough to impose an arbitration of enforcing him to accept to have stolen the car. Sergeant Big belly was too serious to let Okoro go. The side he had wanted to lay action was against Rosemary.

They got hold of Sergeant Big-belly and put him in for false information. He managed to be liberated again. The car was his own quite well but indeed he was too mild hearted to the boy— Okoro.

The case, became reflexible. It was too tough now to accuse him because as a matter of fact, it was Rosemary who played the game.

The judgement day was fast approaching. No doubt if a drama would be caused in the court or not.

The judge soon called them for their case. A question was thrown to Sergeant Big-belly, if it was Okoro who took the car and or took it must anyhow. He replied: " No: "

Okoro was exonerated. The policemen wanted to hold Sergeant Big belly for false information, he denied it and told them that his report, read a girl. He was out of the fix. Then the police who got hold of him, entered to defamatory libel which led him to three year jail terms. THE END.

THESE LIST OF BOOKS ARE OBTAINABLE FROM

CHINYELU PRINTING PRESS, NO. 1, IWEKA ROAD, ONITSHA.

(1) £75, OOO AND 7 YEARS IMPRISONMENT.

(2) DRUNKARDS BELIEVE BAR AS HEAVEN.

(3) SATURDAY NIGHT DISAPPOINTMENT. (IN PREPARATION.)

(4) LOVE AND ROMANCE. (IN PREPA-RATION.)

MAN

HAS NO

REST

IN HIS LIFE

Since the World has broken into pieces,
truth is not said again.

BY

YOUR POPULAR AUTHOR

THE STRONG MAN OF THE PEN.

Books Obtainable From

B. C. OKARA & SONS.

Net Price 2s 6d

MAN

HAS NO

REST

IN HIS LIFE*

(Since the World has broken into pieces, truth is
not said again.)

BY

Your Popular Author
THE STRONG MAN OF THE PEN.

Copyright reserved.

*excerpt

Contents

Preface

No rest

New Pyschological pamphleis

Why

The Sorrows of life

Question of trust

The devil is at work

Bad news

About love

Marriage

Misunderstanding

Special advice to traders

Special advice to School leavers

Good Citizenship

The children we want

Sayings of the wise

Serious warning

Preface

This pamphlet is the best pamphlet so far written and compilled in order to expose the faults of human being, his difficulties and so on and so forth.

This pamphlet is among things, a pamphlet of wisdom, and it offers intensive advice to the general public.

After going through the pamphlet you will learn much. If I fix the price of the pamphlet according to its value, it will cost you over hundred guineas per copy. It is "a food for thought".
The pamphlet touches many aspects of life.

Okenwa Olisah,

The strong man of the pen.

NO REST

Man has no rest in life. Struggle. every now and then, so that the hand may enter mouth, I mean daily bread.

Not many women have the power to work hard as men but majority of the women eat better things more than the men.

Since the world has broken into pieces, truth is not said again. If you ask a little boy a question, he will not tell you the truth, instead he tells you lies. The same thing with little girls. When little boys and girls could give up the truth, then imagine the degree of the lies with grown ups.

NEW PSYCHOLOGICAL PAMPHLETS

The famous Okenwa Publications have the pleasure to introduce their millions of readers throughout Africa and beyond, their new psychological pamphlets:.

1 **"LIFE TURNS MAN UP AND DOWN"**

2S 6d Per Copy.

2 **"POVERTY MAKES LIFE USELESS"**

2s 6d Per Copy

You cannot afford to miss these pamphlets They are very interesting, advisable and put new life in you. Please reject all imitations and insist on the above original pamphlets at all times.

All communications should be made to

OKENWA PUBLICATIONS

13 Nnewi Street, Onitsha,
Eastern Nigeria.

WHY?

Why did Jay Gould, the Amercian millionaire, exclaim with his dying breath: "I'm the most miserable devil in the world?" because money has no power to satisfy the cravings of the soul. Money cannot buy salvation, nor assure the future.

Why did Alexander the Great, when the whole of the known world lay at his feet, weep that his exploits must cease, there being no more worlds to conquer?

Because success and gratified ambition can never give lasting satisfaction. Alexander, the hero of so many batttles was at last to fail before the grim power of death. Only Christ can fill the heart with joy.

Why did Lord Byron with the laurels of fame on his brow, utter such a wine of despair before he died.?

"My days are in the yellow leaf,
The fruit, the flower of life is gone,
The worm, the canker, and the grief
Are mine alone".

Because genius and popularity are powerless to give us what we must need. A personal knowledge of the love of Christ is worth more than all.

Why did a well known religious professor on his death-bed call out, "I am going to hell?" because he relised at last that Religion without Christ is worse than worthless. Profession of Christianity is a delusion and a snare if not accompained by a personal experience of Christ as S a v i o u r.

Why did a prison warder, alarmed by a severe earthquake, enquire of a prisoner whom he know to be a real Christian:

'What must I do to be saved?' (Acts 16 : 30)

Because he saw that nothing mattered so much as that, to be saved is the most vital thing that can happen to anyone. Jesus Christ said: "These things I say that ye might be saved" (John 5 : 34).

Why, reader, do you not seek the acquaintance of Christ be saved, satisfied, and sure of Heaven?.

THE SORROWS OF LIFE

The world has broken into pieces and things have gone wrong, brother fights against his brother; sister fights against her sister, relative fights against his relative, friend fights against his friend, "Child" fights against his parents, neighbour fights against his neighbour and everybody fights against and poison each other indiscriminately.

Peace, and unity do not exist in many families today. Quarrel, hatred, disunity, enemity and fighting are replaced with peace, love, unity and harmony. I hereby call upon all the wise people to enlighten their people on the advantages of peace, love, unity and help to each other.

QUESTION OF TRUST

Another thing which is very regrettable is this question of "trust". If you trust your brother, he will disappoint you, if you trust your sister she will disappoint you, if you trust your friend, he will disappoint you, if you trust your relative, he will disappoint you, if you trust your very child, he will disappoint you, and anyone you attempt to trust, he will abuse the confidence you have on him or her. In such situation, you should not trust anybody this time. You should replace "Trust" with carefulness.

Instead to trust anybody in the transaction of any business or arrangement you become too careful. However, all the good and trust—worthy people are not dead. Some are still living and realy at all times to honour any agreement you may enter with them. Only that they are few amongst millions of unreliable people.

Life is worse than useless without love, peace, unity, truth, honesty, and reliability. It makes nonsense of gentility to fail to keep to promises or arrangements. However, one may fail to keep to promises or arrangements due to difficultes or eventualities but an information must be sent early telling the other party of the situation.

SAYINGS OF THE WISE

(TO WIDEN YOUR KNOWLEDGE)

1 A wife is like a wooden blanket, if you cover yourself with it, it irritates you, if you take it off, you feel cold.

2 A man who has many wives dies of hunger.

3 Do not wonder how you will do a job, but do it and then wonder how you have done it.

4 Serious sickness reminds us about the severity of HELL.

5 A woman sees more with one eye than a man does with both.

6 If idiots don't go the market, bad wares will not be sold.

7 Even a crazy dog recognises fire.

8 To be understood, you must first understand.

9 It is joy, not poverty, that kills people.

10 A bird thrown up knows its way home.

11 A hungry dog does not play with a well-fed dog.

12 It is not on the day a pit is dug that the frogs go in.

13 A Hen's step does not kill its chickens.

14 If the son of the rich dies of hunger, what will happen to the son of the poor?

15 One who misses a known road gets to know a new one.

16 A Child who wanders about misses his mother's hot meals.

17 Learning makes a wise man wiser.

18 Ambition is the last refuge of failure.

19 Wisdom is never at a height for only the aged to reach.

20 A hen with chickens does not sleep on the tree.

21 Don't judge a child at birthday but on its last day.

22 A Bad woman is better than an empty house.

23 Nothing can induce an old woman to run as when a goat carries away her snuff box.

24 Only the dead have no enemies.

A rich man is not bound to go to hell unless he is proud, bad in life and behavours.

25 Good deeds never go bad.

26 No one can part an article from its shadow.

27 Man is the head of the home, but a woman is the heart.

28 A Cock is never satisfied unless it fights another in the presence of a hen.

29 The Lion that treads softly is the one that eats meat.

30 The tree that bends before the gale does not break.

31 The head of an axe is unless witnout a handle to wield it.

32 Laziness travels so slow that poverty soon overtakes it.

33 One who has been bitten by snake fears the earth worm.

34 **Poverty is no licence to Heaven.**

35 Chameleon can change its colour but never its habits.

36 Much can be known of man's character by what excites to his laughter.

37 Parrots are not expected to keep secrets.

38 It is only the sick who realise the advantage of good health.

39 The dance of the rich never pleases the poor.

40 The value of silence can be worth more than gold.

41 The reward of good work is more work.

42 Being ignorant is not so much a shame as being unwilling to learn.

43 A man without a smilling face cannot run a candy shop.

44 A man's enemy.

45 Guard your honour in the days of your youth.

46 Doing nothing is better than being busy doing nothing.

47 The strenght of a rich man lies in his wealth.

48 Proverbs are the palm oil with which words are eaten.

48   If you find someone sitting on the floor in
     his own house, do not ask him for a chair.

49   The strength of the hoe is tested on the soil.

50   A man becomes rich not because of what he
     earns but because of what he saves.

51   Sleep can only send you to the paradise of
     sweet dreams, but never to heaven.

52   He who must eat the kernel must first crack
     the nut.

52   Gentleness and friendliness have been found to
     be stronger than fury and force.

54   A hungry visitor has no patience to discuss
     the weather until he has been fed.

55   Choose your love, and then love your choice.

56   Those who make the best use of their time
     have none to spare.

57   A thief always prays never to be the victim of
     any theft.

58   If I promise you a smock, first look round
     my neck.

59   What old men see while sitting, young men
     cannot see even if they climb a tree.

60 There is no man in the word with handred per-cent sanity.

61 The only cure for poverty is industry.

62 Fools sometimes ask questions that baffle the wise.

63 Those who want to be rich over night are idle all day and compain all night.

64 He that has two but spends three needs no purse.

65 The same water which makes a man thirsty also drowns him.

66 A fault confessed is half redressed.

67 From the cradle to the grave, life is all a struggle.

68 Life alone would be dull if there were no difficulties.

69 The superior man is great without being proud, the inferior man is proud without being great.

70 Youth lives on hope old age on remembrance.

71 The morning sun shine does not alwrys last the day.

72 The rich live in fear but the poor in safety.

73 Three may keep a secret if two of them are dead.

74 If you want the best prepare yourself for the worst.

75 If nothing else, a poor man has got the, right to look at a rich man's horse.

76 A good woman inspires a man; the beautiful woman fascinates him but a sympathetic woman gets him.

77 Do not wonder how to do a job; do it and wonder afterwards how you did it.

78 No elder ever admits he was a coward in his youth.

79 Avoiding the mud soon clothes one in mud.

80 He who has no enemy is a friend to none.

81 Delay of justice is injustice.

82 No man is really old until his mother stops worring about him.

83 A boaster says, "All my things are sliver and gold, even my copper ketter."

84 When a girl casts her bread upon waters, she expects it back in the form of a wedding cake.

85 No cat can take a mouse as his best frind.

86 It is only the man who owns a head who knows what is inside it.

87 The best kindness to a dead man is the burial of his corpse.

88 Unrequited love breeds hatred.

89 He that is born to be hanged will never down.

90 A blind man does not know when you are sad.

91 The same rain that makes the good farmer's crops grow fast makes the lazy worker's weeds grow faster.

92 Best friends are always bad enemies.

93 No matter how much you turn around your heels will always be behind you.

94 The squirrel consider himself owner of the land and yet fears the farmer.

95 There is nothing in laziness save tattered clothes.

96 One need not put on a light to be able to recognize a friend in the dark.

97 You cannot have a good look into a bottle with both eyes.

98 The pond stands aloof from the stem as though water were not common to both.

99 He who is too proud to ask will be too good to receive.

100 If the world were full of play, then playing would be as tedious as work.

101 A bathroom never awaits rainfall before it gets wet.

102 The black man's gold is cattle.

103 The fowl scratches for another.

104 A stranger is as the dew.

105 A traveller sees more than a climber.

106 A mouse and a cat cannot stay in one room.

107 He that everyone loves has many ways.

108 If your friend's bread catches fire, wait yours in time.

109 Wealth bequeathed to a fool is like water stored in a basket.

110 It's the second helping that makes the stranger smile.

111 A stranger with a better hand entertains the host.

112 A husband never refuses the food cooked by a soft-spoken wife.

113 Secrets should never be told to a busy body.

114 A begger can never refuse any-thing given from his enemy.

115 The eye that sees does not see itself.

116 The devil hurts only those who believe in witch-doctors.

117 In the home of the coward there is no sorrow or suffering.

118 He who destroy's himself needs no pity.

119 A traveller is as large as the bamboo tree. No one can embrance it.

120 It is the lazy man who says, "If I were a tinker no tinker would be able to mend a kettle as well as me."

121 The chick that always keeps close to the mother gets the fat grasshopper.

122 Do not take the advice of one who wants you to spend your money on wine.

123 A foolish man never knows why people thatch their roofs until the rain sets in.

124 By fighting you will never get through, but by yielding, you get more than you expect.

125 It is by the river that we see the pot that surpasses the other.

126 An inefficient workman quarrels with his tools

127 A man with false teeth chews and and laughs with care.

128 A man who habitually laughs at other's misfortunes ought not resent being laughed at in turn.

129 A yaw sufferer cannot be happy save by the permission of flies.

130 An eyelash may be older than a grown up bread.

131 Pay what you owe and you will know what is your own.

132 A well which has many sources never runs dry.

133 While you are cutting the leaxes for medicine, someone else is cutting the roots of same tree for medicine.

134 A dog carrying a dead chicken is blamed, but a chicken moving next to a dead dog is not blamed.

135 Work done by the bettle during the night is easily seen during the day.

136 The drunkard's purse is a bottle.

137 The feathers that the eagle plucks off itself with disregard are the ones people pick up in admiration.

138 The monkey says that the man who killed him did not annoy him more than the one that sold his flesh.

139 Beware of friends who, when they discover new friends, forget old ones.

140 The most valuable thing in life is time.

141 Birds flock together only on trees bearing ripe fruit.

142 When they have sucked the orange they will throw the peel away.

143 Goodwill, like a good name, is found by many actions and lost by one.

144 Cats are honest when the meat is out of reach.

145 Young folk think that the old are fools, but the old know that the young are fools.

146 The love of a young woman lies not truly in her heart, but in her eyes.

147 If you don't get the time to cure your sickness you will have the time to lie.

148 One never makes one's footprints on the sands of time by sitting down.

149 Nobody who want throats to cut, wants his own throat to be cut.

150 It is easy to swim when another holds up your head.

151 There is no day however beautiful that is not followed by night.

152 A mouse with its proud moustache, is nothing compared to a cat.

153 In this atomic age, Lukewarm is the balance of power between the drink and the cold war.

154 He who marries at an old age may not gain much from his children.

155 He who encourages you to embark on a wrong venture is your real enemy.

156 He who waits for a dead man's shoes may long go barefooted.

157 An unmarried woman does not know the pains of widow.

158 A good listener is always a welcome guest, especially when he encourages his host to talk about himself.

159 A beetle on the palm-wine pot says he is intoxicated, and what about the bee which is inside.

160 Autobiographies are often the last throw of the failures.

161 Health is a crown on a healthy man's head that is only seen by the sick.

162 A man who proposes to shake the world will have himself shaken as well.

163　To live a poor life and own nobody is better than riches with many troubles.

164　He who never made a mistake never made a dsicovery

165　Marriage is not like wine which should be tasted before it is entered into.

166　Any person who belives in his own ill luck is an enemy to bis own good luck.

167　Life is like a cup of tea the more hastily we drink it, the sooner we reach its dregs.

168　A Bed is never measured to size, but a coffi n is.

169　A good reformer considers what the result of his reform will be like; before he raises his hammer to destroy he thinks of What will replace what he destroys.

170　If a man deceives you once, shame on him if he deceives you twice, shame twice on you.

171　Wisdom is as large as the baobob tree. Nobody's hand can go round it in full embrace.

172　Without an answer to selfishness no system can create unity.

173　When poverty knocks at the door then love finds the means to fly through the window.

BEWARE AND BE WISE*

BEWARE !

Beware of the words you utter from your mouth.
Beware of your pen not to incriminate you. It is indelible.
Beware of your movement, not to mislead yourself
Beware of your wife, she can do anything any time.
Beware of your husband he may not be faithfull.
Beware of your father, he is a father of many children.
Beware of your son/daughter, once they are matured they disobey
Beware of your boss he has something in mind about you.
Beware of your junior workers they are envious and after you.
Beware of your master's wife she is keen about you.
Beware of those sweet stories, they are false.
Beware of envying great people, it is their fate.
Beware of the taxi you are entering, there are thieves
Beware of those rogues in suits, they are money doublers
Beware of those painted lips, your money will soon go.
Beware of those highly elegant lasses, it is your money they want.
Beware of those friends you trust, they will let you down.
Beware of those fine girls, it is rapery.
Beware of a private affair with another man's wife, it is adultery.
Beware of a forcible intercourse it is fornication.
Beware of fighting with another citizen it is affray and may be criminal.
Beware of that College you are entering/attending it may be illegal.
Beware of giving false information to the Police it is criminal.
Beware of your education, else you will be a servant for ever.
Beware of the application you] wrote, there will no reply
Beware of the house where you live, there are private enimies.
Beware of your Pride, it leads to destruction.
Beware of taking another man's property without his consent, it is stealing.
Beware of taking away another man's child, it is kidnapping.
Beware of setting fire on a house intentionally, it is arson.
Beware of minting counterfeit coins, it is criminal.
Beware of your movement in the street, you will be involved.

*excerpt

Beware of running to another Country to evade Punishment, you will be a Refugee.

Beware of a lazy friend, you too will be lazy.

Beware of certain security fishing businesses, they are false.

Beware of fighting for any legacy, it is dangerous.

Beware of your monthly earnings, your pocket will be empty,

Beware of your dreams, they mean nothing.

Beware of your superstitious fears, they are nothing.

Beware of commiting suicide because of your abject poverty you will still be rich

Beware of your political affiliation, you may be tormented.

Beware of that stranger staying with you temporarily he may be a thief.

Beware of your children going to Schools, they may be kidnapped.

Beware of going out in the night, it is dangerous.

Beware of having many wives, it is deterimental.

Beware of taking your children to the Cinema, it educates beyond expectation and reveals nonsense

Beware of buying those cheap, cheap articles they may be stolen ones.

Beware of what you tell those small children, they may immitate you.

Beware of the Church you attend, there are saints as sinners.

Beware of a sudden noise of thief! thief!! thief!!! you may be mistaken.

Beware of the song you sing, it may be mistranslated.

Beware of over-feeding your children they will be accustomed to it

Beware of a boasting man he is full of word alone.

NO
CONDITION
IS
PERMANENT

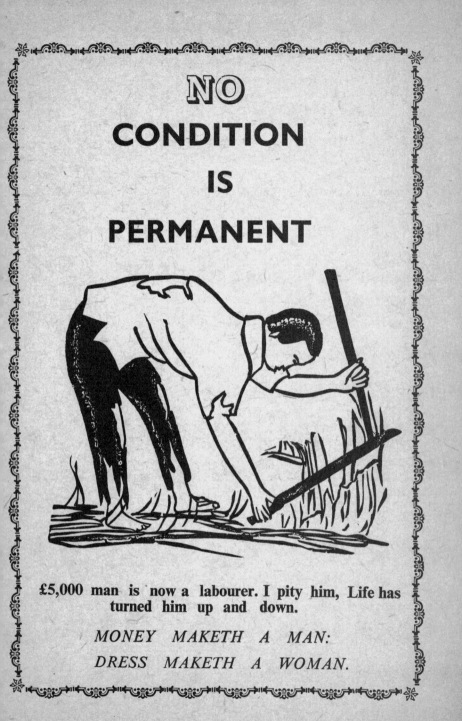

£5,000 man is now a labourer. I pity him, Life has turned him up and down.

MONEY MAKETH A MAN:

DRESS MAKETH A WOMAN.

NO

CONDITION

IS

PERMANENT *

Revised And Enlarged

By

THE MASTER OF LIFE

MONEY MAKETH A MAN:
DRESS MAKETH A WOMAN.

NET PRICE 2/6

ALL ORDERS TO:—

Njoku & Sons Book-shop

C/o No. 11 Arondizuogu Street,

FEGGE—ONITSHA.

Send 3d Stamp for our Catalogue and be one of our customers.

*complete text

THANKS TO:

"NO CONDITION IS PERMANENT"

Sweet things never plenty

Says Mr. Okafor Of Aba;

Why it is that sweet things, like rich food never plenty but give the body the greatest refreshment and strength while the poorly prepared food which fulls the big plate never help the body rather than stop hunger ? I have read a good number of voluminous books, novels and pamphlets but none has slightly advised me better on how to tackle life problems and win them. But see the page nine 'No Condition,' what it has done for me ! By contents worth over £1000 to best knowledge, but by volume, not up to 1|-. You can depend on it. I find it invaluable. Thanks to it.

Above is an article Mr. H. Obuneme Okafor of Aba. If you send yours it will be published.

THE PUBLISHER.

CONTENTS.

Thanks, to No Condition is Permanent
Notice
Gift for people
Life is an empty dream
Human beings
Onitsha market burnt
Things are not what they seem
Advice to men about money
No Condition is permanent
Another advice to young men about money
The troubles by our women
Enjoy her at the moment you see her
Money maketh a man Dress maketh a woman
Life and money
Lack of maintenance
Child and money
Early wealth
Women love me to much
General advice for men and women
Honest is the best policy
Now advice on your life
Live like natives
Now words for commonsense.
Business is gain and loss
Fighting has stoped
Husband and wife
What makes a marriage success?
The mistake you should not make
24 charges against wives
My charges against women are justified
The life of a woman
Poor man has no friend
A poor receives insults
A poor mam is not loved by his people
Poor man is sensible
Women hate poor men
Poor man has no good clothes
Some wives feed their poor husbands
A poor man fears a rich man
Letters to the Author
Here comes the fourth letter from a man
Here comes a letter from a widow
Tough girl Pitakwa
My wife only loves her children
I am tired of this world
My sons are useless
Gift for everybody
The truth about cigarettes:
Public notice
£5000, man is now a Labourer

LIFE IS AN EMPTY DREAM.

No condition is permanent, in the world but fools
do not know. A person could eat on the plate in the
afternoon and eat on the ground in the evening. A
person could also eat on the ground in the afternoon
and eat on the dish in the evening. Things could be
good for you this year and become bad next year.
Things could become bad for you for six years and
become easy in the seventh year. One could rejoice in
the morning and cry in the afternoon. One could also
cry in the morning and rejoice in the afternoon. One
could also cry in the morning and rejoice in the afternoon, because things are not what they seem, and
life you see, is nothing but an empty dream.

HUMAN BEINGS.

The lives of human beings, are like the ones of animals living in the bush, birds living on the tree, fish
living in the sea, and other creatures in the world.
Those creatures are lucky and some times they fall
into traps as human beings. They feel hunger and
pains as human beings. In them there are also ones
that could feed well today and become hungry tomorrow. In them there are also ones that could become hungry today and feed well tomorrow, because
no condition is permanent and things are not what
they seem and life which some people do not
understand, is nothing but an empty dream.

ONITSHA MARKET BURNT

The well known Osha Main Market burnt the third
time on 11th Feb. 1953. A large number of rich traders suddenly lost their riches. Some of them are now
servants, some are truckpushers some are headcarriers.

some are labourers, some are now thieves. some intended to kill themselves in view of critical condition,
some had gone home to do farming business, some
had left Nigeria for another Country in search of new
lives. The said events were grave ones. May God
bless those who suffered the incidents. The events
enriched many headcarriers because b o x e s of big
value were carried for £10, £5, £3 as the case may
be. The events showed us that No Condition Is Permanent in the world and things are not what they
seem and life is nothing but an empty dream.

THINGS ARE NOT WHAT THEY SEEM

You could see a parcel on the street and call it a
bundle of money, when you open it, it becomes a
box of sickness and bad luck. You could see a devil
standing on the street and call him a person, when
you salute him, he shows you wonders. You could
see a stick on the street, and call it a stick, when
you match on it, it changes into a snake, and bites
you. You could see a dirty cup on the street, and
call it a useless cup, when you cpen it, it becomes
a pocket of money and wisdom. An informant could
befriend you and you call him a good friend, after
some days of friendship, he puts you into trouble.
You could born a thief, and call him a good son,
when he grows, he spoils your name. Y o u could
born a devil and call him a merciful child. He could
become ill with his mother, he could die when he
sees that all your money has finished ; you naked
and begin to borrow money. You could see a good
person, and call him a bad person. You could see
a bad person, and call him a good person. You
could have a big amount and boast of it, within
a short time, it runs away without giving notice or
sign as a harlot you keep in your house. Y o u
could believe when you are deceived and disagree
when you are

told the truth. You could practise because your neighbour had practised and succeded without trouble, and you fall into trouble because destinies are not the same Your kindness could bring trouble to you and jail you, as well as the truth you talk could be turned into lie. Though God will bless you. What you hope on it could disappoint you at the last moment. You can memorize what to talk, when it is time, you forget all. You could see a man and think that he has small power when you abuse him he turns you down and disgrace you with your boasts Thereforer things are not what they seem and life is nothing but an empty dream.

ADVICE TO YOUNG MEN ABOUT MONEY.

When you are poor, be an industrious man. Don't sit idle. You cannot win raffle when you do not sign it, it is when you sign it you will watch what will be the result. That is, you cannot become rich when you do not work, it is when you work that you will begin to watch what your labour will produce. To be rich is very very hard, but some people do not know. Some people think it totally a thing of chance. God cannot send you a parcel of food or money from Heaven. He can only bless and protect you. Don't immitate when you have no money. You know that a hungry man who does not take care will eat poison, as well as a poor man who immitates will steal.

NO CONDITION IS PERMANENT

The phrase No Condition Is Permanent affect poor, rich, sick health, temptation, happy and other conditions in the world. Poor condition is not the worst one in the world nor a comfortable one. A poor man acts almost sometime like a woman who has no child. She goes to many places and consults so many Doctors to know why and what she could do to have a child. As poor man goes to many places and consults many native doctors to know why he has no good luck and what should be done for him to be rich. Richness is not the greatest position in the world nor unpleasant one. To be rich is a thing which almost everybody wants. Money is not a trustworthy thing, it is a devil and acts like harlot you keep in your house. S h e could move away at a sudden time and lodge again at your neighbour's house.

ANOTHER ADVICE TO MEN ABOUT MONEY :

When you have money these misbehaviours could drive it and you fall woefully.

1 Pride

2 Reckless talk

3 Carelessness

4 Highlife

5 Excess Happiness

6 Chasing Badly

7 Drunkenness

8 Wickedness

9 Envious

10 Unnecessary Economicals

11 Having confidence in every one

12 Deceit and fraud

13 Pretence

14 Claiming too know and Superiourity

15 Forgetting God.

THE TROUBLES BY OUR WOMEN

Women of nowadays have a number of tricks they use to arrest the attention of our young men, ruin their pocket and run away.

1. Their "show skin" fashion is magnet.

2. The styles of their walking has a big amount of attraction and admiration.

3. Their learned methods of looking and smilling are love and are active traps.

4. They can offer you themselves in a very enjoyable way so that you will spend your last penny.

This man is suffering from Gonorrhea causes by woman. He is crying, I am dying.

5. They can offer you petty things like Handkerchiefs. table cloths, pillow cases, and oranges. Their offers give them a very big gain when you reward. A woman's offer is like the corn offered to a hen by a thief in oder to catch it, make use of its feathers and sell it at the later part of the day.

6. The contents of their letters are insincere and could scatter one's brain

7. They can swear before you that you are the only person they love.

8. They could come one morning to you and deceive you that they dreamt of you and then wanted to see you.

When you befriend a woman she will tell you that many handsome young men had appiled and promised her a sewing machine, Iron beds, gold and to take over all her responsibilities. She could lie to you that she insulted them. She could tell you this to commit you to befriend her, when you ask her about the person you met. She could tell you "don't mind he is my cousin." Your woman friend doesn't care to press until you offer her last penny you have. tomorrow when she sees you pushing a truck, she will scarcely greet you thinking it to be too degrading for her.

ENJOY HER AT THE MOMENT YOU SEE HER

Enjoy your woman friend at the moment you see her and forget her the moment she leaves you because women of nowadays have no natural love for men but for private ends. If you have a brother or son who has no saving because of troubles by women, offer him a copy of this book he will begin to make savings.

Know yourself else you endanger your future. Prison yard is the home of a person who misleads his life. Know yourself else y o u endanger your future. Think over and over before you do anything otherwise you regret. It is as easy as A B C to have supporters who would encourage you to attack somebody or to do any other thing. But it is very hard to have supporters who could support you with their money or ever agree to appear for you as eye witness, if your actions bring troubles for you. Labour hard when your nerves are healthy so that you might have something to eat when you become old. Protect your lips, else harmattan dries them. Before you get money you must call yourself a boy. Never you remember women when it is time to sow what you could reap in future, otherwise you go home with empty pockets.

One who puts his mind on women goes h o m e without a penny and tells his people that thives had stolen him. Numerous diseases in public women had developed chronic diseases in the bodies of many young men, don't spend because others spent, you do not know how they manage to get their own money. Don't show appettite in all things, otherwise you eat poison. Don't show that you have no money when honour is being given to you. Don't publicise a news as soon as you hear it else you will be called upon to explain. Respect yourself so that people can regard you as somebody. Don't argue when you have no point.

Venture not to tell your opponent "What can you do" or "Deliver wasps let me see". These sayings can make your opponent to lose his temper and fire you "Double Barreled knock out blows" Hunger raises the anger of a poor man, while over feeding causes reckless talks. When a foolish man marries a foolish woman, peace and love go out of the door ; quarrel and devil comes in. Advice and show your Son good examples when he is young otherwise he will rest in prison. Don't borrow if you have no source to pay to pay. Don't love who does not love you or hate who does not hate you. Study the characters of someone before you fall into deep love with him or her. One who does not owe debt is a rich man. A debtor's p r i d e and boasting is nothing. Fear God and be prepared to receive blessing.

MONEY MAKETH A MAN DRESS MAKETH A WOMAN.

Money is man. Dress maketh a woman. Be ye the most handsome man in this world, or fashionable one, if you have money the world could call you "Angle of my Street." Be ye the ugliest man in the world if there is a money you gain love and respect. Be ye the biggest man in the world, if there is no money it is a "Penny big" Be the smallest man in world, if there is money, people will begin to fear you. Be ye the most fool in the world if you have money you are a reasonable some body Be ye a man of commonsense, if there is no money a boy could throw sand in your mouth. Keep yourself hungry live in the cheapest room, work day and night if you don't succeed people will say that you are womaniser and drunkard. When you have no money, people would call you old man but if you have money you are a boy of yesterday. The world has broken into pieces. Money could make an accused to be the complaint as well make complaint to be the accused.

be a good man because he has money. A good man could be a bad man because he has no money. When a girl marries you because of your handsomeness when you have no sufficient money to maintain her, the love she has for you could fade, and she has to look for rich friends. Is it good for a human being, to gain the whole world and loose his own soul? No, Is it good to practice bad things, so as to have money? No sir, straight your canoe, follow the ways of God. Be ye a man of your words leave the people with their good and bad. Let them mock you. God's time is the best. Oh! God gives us the sense to live together. Bless the poor, rich, and the sick.

LIFE AND MONEY

Some men prefer to become very rich and die untimely. But some like to have moderate money and live longer. I myself, the Great Master of life prefer to have moderate money and live longer because life is precious and money is money.

LACK OF MAINTENANCE

Some people earn 4/- a day and eat only 9d and save 3/3. But some people have 4/- a day and eat 1/6 and save 2/6d. I myself will like to eat belly full because bad economy is sickness and lack of maintanance weakens the nerves and brings premature death. I do not advice you to eat all you have but too much of everything is dangerous.

CHILD AND MONEY

Many men particularly women, l o v e children exceeds thousands of pounds. But some love money greater than children. I myself the Great Master of

Life uphold that human being irrespective of sex is greater than money in value, and at the same time advice you to accept any one God gives you................. children or money.

EARLY WEALTH

A great number of people like to have money in their youth and become any thing in their old age. But some prefer to be alright in their old age instead of having money in their Youth and eat on the ground in the evening. I myself the great master of Life will thank God when ever he gives me.

WOMEN LOVED ME TOO MUCH.

A confession by boy of love who gave all his time to women affairs later suffered the consiquence of such habit.

Women loved me too much, because I was extravagant rascal and entirely too much over their responsibilities. My real name was Mr. Belgian but women did not like this name and stopped me answering the name. They gave me two titles, one was M. W. which meant Master of women. The other one was B. L. which meant Boy of Love. I accepted these strange titles and meant business with women. I forgot myself and my people and did have them at heart every second I also took to drinking. I used to finish 2 dozens of deer daily. Dancing was also my hobby.

Within few weeks of my dealings with women my pockets dried up. I never knew that the world is deep and full of wonders until my girl friends bycotted me because I could no longer secure them. I am now living miserious life. Please my readers know yourselves lest you regret like me.

GENERAL ADVICE FOR MEN AND WOMEN :

1 You should be well off before you dream of marriage.
2 You should bring the news to the knowledge of your parents because a fatherly and motherly advice is nearer to God's instructions.
3 You should not be boastful in the presence of your would-be wife.
4 Try to marry a girl from your town so as to know the exact genealogy of the girl.
5 You should always maintain y o u r intergrity, decorum, and gentility before her.
6 When the girl arrives to your residence, treat her with the greatest respect. Do not show her your colour immediately.
7 Don't show any sign of flexibility before her.
8 Visit y o u r inlaws regularly and endevour to compromise with them.
9 You should never be seen at randomly in the bars and try to secede from the prostitutes because they will jeopardise the harmony of your family.
10 Do not promise your wife heaven and earth and be ready to accomplish none.
11 You should try to be Christians and God chosen family worthy of emulation.
12 Lay a good foundation for your children.
13 Let your wife be labourious but n o t to the extend that she becomes an object of ridicule.
14 Do not beat your wife animalestically, treat her like a human being with the same equality.
15 Women should not be a sort of canopy to their husband by over-shadowing t h e i r husband's intergrity.
16 Do not abuse your wife publically, because public abuse hardens the heart.
17 Do not be controlled by your temper but let your irritability be abstemious.
18 You shouldn't allow your wife to be loquacious, she should not be cantankerous. Let her keep her tongue within her teeth.

19 Do not overshadow her deficency with canopy.

20 Do not praise her in her presence if her attitude is impressive.

21 You should not be close fisted but not to be highly extravagant.

22 Try to be up and doing.

23 Look before you leap; do not take for granted because certainty is better than possibility.

24 Always hear your parents' advice.

25 You should always mind your P's and Q's taking for granted that as you are married the whole deeds are done.

26 You should send your children to school.

HONEST IS THE BEST POLICY:

First impression in an important thing. When starting to associate with somebody, one first of all impress him. This shall make you win him. Anything started with poor impression cannot succeed, because the interest of your intending associate shall be killed, he shall think that further communications would in like manners be the same. Therefore when ever you start to deal with any person, man or woman, first of all impress the one that you are honesty. You know that "Honesty is the best policy."

NOW ADVICE ON YOUR LIFE:

What do you think of yourself? Are you a bad smoker, a drunkard, a womanizer, a liar, a thief slave trader or a general wicked man? God forbid, but if you are one of the above I am sorry, don't hesitate the change. It is never paying. It will do you more harm, than good. What type of life are you living, strange life or usual life? When I say "strange" life, I mean life which your fellow town's people or tribe's people never like or play in their area. Life which does not agree with their custom and tradition,

Some people like to live like Hausas and some Hausas like to live like Ibos. Hausas shave their heads entirely without one single hair remaining but Ibos do not shave like these. They shave with styles, namely: 'Senior Service Cumba' Baby face' 'Police style' 'Ajilo' 'Sugar baby' 'Lagos style' etc.

Hausas have no style other than the one called here 'Mala' which means entire shaving off the hairs. If you are an Ibo, do you shave like Hausas? If you are a Hausa, do you shave like Ibos? It is what I mean by strange life different from the ones of your people.

I must make you know that natives can criticise you if you are living strange life. They can dislike you for it. Shaving the hairs in contrary, however is not serious offence but I have just mentioned it as an instance. It is never serious, there are other things which carry weight and which can certainly earn you bad name and hatred before your fellow tribe's people or town's people.

LIVE LIKE NATIVES

Many people say that is very wise that a stranger should change and commence to act like the natives he is like in their place in order to sign their love. I myself I suggest that a stranger should only just be social to the people he is living in their place but will not eat what is forbidden in his town in other to please them and do injustice to himself.

NOW WORDS FOR COMMON-SENSE

Copy nobody's ways than yours. Not that the son it tall is power. Do not do to somebody what you will not like him to do you. Your near-rest neighbour is your nearest brother. Life is but an empty dream. Honesty is the best policy Nearly never kills a bird A shilling in the hand is greater than the £1 in debt. This world is not a simple world it is full of hardships, worries, pains, troubles.

Respect your father and mother for your days to be long. Your elders are also inclusive. A wise man receives no disgrace in the public. You should know that you can make out hell or paradise out of your life, it is possible what you make it.

BUSINESS IS GAIN AND LOST

Endeavour to avoid too much enemity with people. It is bad. Business is gain and lost. He who lacks patience cannot do it. He who knows not and claims that he knows is a first class fool. Beware of people. Every carefulness should applied in all you do. The more one looks, less he sees. Another man's like is another man's dislike. Hunger puts fire in the misery of a poor man. When a cunning man is dead, it is a cunning man that will burry him. What you don't know is older than you. "Knock the door shall be opened for you, seek ye shall find" are biblical sayings. When two wise men meet, "battle of sense" begins. It has been said that fools make lawyers rich, "I will kill you and hang what have I says poor man whenever you annoys him. He is not afraid of death. He has no plot, lorry, other simple properties and does not feed regularly. Big men are sometimes afraid of poor men. When a big man remembers his cars, lorries, monies and, properties, he will tell a poor man, please take your trouble go. He is afraid of murder by the angry poor man who has not taken his past meal and not sure of the next one.

FIGHTING HAS STOPPED :

Nowadays fighting has stopped. Many are internally sick, if you heavily beat any, he dies and no doubt you shall be charged of murder. Some people in this world, are bodily human beings but spiritually and behaviously animals. They talk without senses and act really like beasts. I cannot have any dealings with these half animals, half human-beings.

It is very risky. To cut some body with knife and do other harms are simple things for them. They have no respect, or fear. They are not afraid of prison or death, they call these things nothing.

HUSBAND AND WIFE

Marriage is a good thing. It sweets at the beginning and sometimes bitters as time goes on. Some people have not developed the ideas with which to bear its bitterness or difficulties. They give up the marriage. Marriage requires some look-over and tolerance. Not all the things that will annoy you. You should over-look and endure certain things. If you cannot endure or over-look the slightest thing, failure in your marriage will be your lot. The relationship between husband and wife is so delicate. Love today and hatred tomorrow. Peace today, quarrel tomorrow. Both the husband and wife have respect in the house. Both parties should respect each other. Husband should not disregard his wife either because she is a woman or that he paid some pounds on her head. These were old unwise ideas.

The wife should also not disregard her husband either because he has no money, or that you see another man who is more handsome. Is it bad for a husband to attend dance with his wife ? There is no bad thing in it. It is a n enjoyment of life. Dances are not only made for men I know that some people would have some objections, but it will be agumentally defeated.

Should a husband tell his wife his secret ? Yes a husband should tell his wife his secret, though, not all. If your wife discovers that you hide things too much for her, how do you expect that she can tell you her own secrets.

But I don't surpport that you tell your wife your secrets if you know that she is a talkative, can't keep secrets. Secret should not be disclosed to those who can't hide things.

Has a wife the right to oppose an instruction given to her by her husband ? Yes the wife has right to oppose an instruction by her husband if such an instruction is not good. A wife is subjected to agree all the instructions from her husband and these are not disobedience. Only genuine instructions that you would expect your wife to comply with and not any type of instruction.

Has a husband the right to restrict the movement of his wife ? I may say that "Fundamental human right" makes this impossible. It is only government or other legal authorities that have the power or right to restrict the movement of someone with a strong reason. Individual have no right or power to arrest the previledge of anybody. As I have said, only legal bodies have this right. For instance, the government of a prisoner is restricted because he is in the hand of a legal authorities.

What rights has a husband over his wife? A husband has the right to divorce his wife when he is no longer wants the marriage of the woman with reasons. He has the right to warn his wife when she starts to live immoral life or delicerately become disobedient to him. A husband has no right to beat his wife. It is unlawful. And a woman cannot be displined by beating. Women are afraid not of beating. When you for the habit of beating your wife one day she starts to revenge. Next time, the least hand you touch her she takes up fire wood, or the nearest stick and knock you.

Fighting brings disrespect and hatred between husband and wife. Therefore stop fighting. There are other displinary measures you may use to displine her; when she commences to open strange eyes.

Has a wife the right to go or move as she likes? She has it a fundamental human right, but she can be warned when her foot-steps are no longer good. She can be also advised, places she would not go, obviously bad places. Is it not good to move badly. Certainly, a wife has no right to travel to another place without the permission of her husband.

Has a wife the right to fall in love with another man, when she is in marriage? She has no right for that. If she does this, she invites trouble to the house. The husband can be annoyed and divorce her for this. It is not good, unless the husband likes it. I have been informed that in some places, wives make friends and not forbiden.

Has a wife the right to beat her husband? She has never the right. If she dreams it, she has committed an offence. Has a wife the right to claim the money and other properties of her hus, when the husband is dead? She has the right to do such. Provided the law protects her. She must be a legitimate wife having a male child as an advantage. Some times when husband dies, his relatives come to drive away the wife in order to share the properties of the dead man. This is regretable and should be stoped forth-with.

Husband and wife who is greater in the house? Husband is greater. He manages the house. The wife is the deputy manager. When the husband is away the wife takes over the management of the house.

What spoils marriage? First is gossip. Inability to endure the smallest thing, and too much poverty contribute to the failure of marriage. A man who wants his house to be in peace should never believe gossipers. He should work hard to avoid poverty.

WHAT MAKES A MARRIAGE A SUCCESS ?

Love is number one, then, money follows. Endurance and non-ear to gossipers contribute to the success of a marriage. How will you know that your wife loves you? She will be respecting me. She will obey me and will not like me to be unhappy. When ever I become unhappy, she will try to make me happy. She will be taking less before me. She will like my own people, especially my dad and mum.

How will you know that your wife hates you? She will have no respect for me, She will never care my money. She antagonize with any body, called my relatives. When I become annoyed, she puts fire in it. She will never like to do anything, intentionally to please me. She will be giving my money to boys she loves. She will be associating with my enemies, knowing it to be dangerous to my life, Anything which I tell her "don't do" is what she will be doing in order to suffer me mentally.

What will you do when you discover that your wife hates you and shows love to another man? I will withdraw my own love for her. I will do her nothing in the respect of the love being shown by her to another man though I will do some thing when the love develops to another thing immorally or conspiracy against me.

How will you know that your husband loves you? He will treat me kindly and will not be hard on me. If I annoy him, and apologise, he will easily forgive me, and forget. He will give me my own respect and tells me his mind. He will not be too secretive to me. If I become sick, he pets like a child and struggle for the regaining of my normal health at all cost. If I become annoyed with him he begins to please me, I will not lack clothes, he will see, if there is money that I dress all the times as other wives.

How will you know that your husband hates you? He will not be sympathetic with me, he will be hard on me and punishes me at the smallest offence. If I offend him, he cannot forgive me, he will be talking the thing always even before strangers. He will not cloth me. When I become sick, he will know that I am s i c k. My life will not be important to him. Before he brings out his penny to cure me, it becomes tug of war. He will not be visiting my parents, and will not formally welcome any of my relatives who comes to pay us a visit.

THE MISTAKE YOU SHOULD NOT MAKE :

It is one of the greatest mistake to marry a wrong somebody. Marry with love, Marry n o t a girl because she is beautiful but necessarily because she is a good girl. You cannot eat her beauty. You will enjoy her manners more than her beauty. Therefore make no mistake in marriage, it is one of the greatest mistakes in like one should make. It is regretable too much. If you have not married. When you will be ready for marriage don't make serious mistake.

24 CHARGES AGAINST WIVES

Many wives today are doing very bad things. I am annoyed with those type of wives and declare wordy war against them. Below are my 24 strong charges against them.

1. Some do not wake up in the morning to cook what their husband shall eat before g o i n g to market or work.

2. Some wives do not cook afternoon food in time.

3. Some wives quarrel with their husbands over chop money.
They demand chop money too much in order to make gain out of it.

4. Some wives do not clean their houses instead they follow children to soil every place.

5. Some business-wives do not help their husband in chop money and other expenses. They have money but would not bring it out, instead they persist to worry their husbands to give them money.

6. Some wives cook bad things and present to their husbands.

7. Some wives are very careless, they rough handle things, break plates spoil other things in the house due to carelessness.

8. Some wives do not know how to please their husbands, instead they do annoying things.

9. Some wives would never one day by "mistake" wash the clothes of their husbands.

10 Some wives tell lies to their husbands. When they wish to visit their lovers, they tell their husbands that they are going to meetings.

11 Some wives receive poisons and give to their husband. This is an unforgivable sin.

12 Some wives fight their husbands. This is a very big disrespect and lack of fear. Wives who fight their husbands are irresponsible and do not come from good families, where respect, honour, a n d fear are in existance.

13 Some wives are very wicked, dangerious and take their husbands to court.

14 Some wives steal the money of their husbands and send to their people.

15 Some wives are very lazy and can't just struggle to get a penny of their own. They depend entirely on their husbands.

16 Some wives are very much after dresses, When they get money, they lavish all in buying clothes.

17 Some wives have long 'throat' and appetite for every things.

18 Some wives do not look well after their husbands during their sickness. They pray that their husbands die so that they m a y become Governors of the house and have all the properties of their husbands,

19.   Some wives are not satisfied with whatever their husbands give them. They want the whole world to be given to them before they would be satisfied.

20.   Some wives are disobedient. They can't just obey any order. What their husbands tell them not to do, they do it, and what their husbands tell them to do they can never do it. They do whatever they like and please themselves.

21.   Some wives are cunning. Their husbands can not trace out their foot-steps. They are deep in their ways.

22.   Some wives love the money of their husbands and hate their husbands.

23.   Some wives are too dirty. They don't wash their clothes, their bodies and even extends their dirtiness to the food they chop.

24.   Some wives are attempting to control their husbands, and they want to be too free and go where ever they like, and return to the house at any hour that they like.

The above are the 24 strong charges which I have levelled against some wives. I know that there are many good wives. I even know some of them, but the bad ones are by far greater in number than the good ones. It is the duty of sensible women to call meetings of women where the sensible women would deliver lectures to less-sensible women on husbandary, and other domestic affairs.

MONEY HARD

To Get But Easy To

SPEND

These two gentlemen are Lavishing money here
But money is still hard to get

BY OKENWA OLISAH
Author:- No Condition Is Permanent

PRICE 2/6

Money Hard To Get *

But Easy To Spend

BY

Okenwa Olisah

DEDICATED TO

Okenwa Olisah the Author, who died on 12th
December 1964,

May His Soul Rest In Peace

All enquiries and orders should be addressed to;

J. O. Nnadozie

17 Okwuenu Street,
Fegge — Onitsha

Price 2s 6d

Copy right Reserved

*excerpt

ANY THING YOU DO

PEOPLE MUST SAY AGAINST YOU

Any thing you do in this world whether good or bad people must say against you. Nothing you will do, that they will praise you for that instead they find out fault in it and say against you. Please my friend, when they say against you, show them not that. you are worried, reply them not because silence is the best answer to a fool.

These Two Genttlemen Are Lavishing Money Here.

I n t r o d u c t i o n

Money is hard to get but easy to spend. You will see that things are very hard nowadays. No business moves as it was in the past. Things were better in olden days, when people were in darkness no civilization by then, but now people are civilised wise and educated, you cannot deceive any person again.

I have written this booklet, for it to act as a guide to you. If you read it with care, I hope it will help you much.

Master Of Life

MY IMPORTANT WORDS TO THE PUBLIC

Jealousy is too much nowadays, whatever you do, people must jealous you for that and say against you.

Go home and build a house, big or small it is important, there is nothing like house, how small it is.

One wife, one trouble, Two wives two troubles. Not the person who calls Police do win, but the person who is right.

Money is hard to get but easy to spend, Big man, big trouble, Small man, small trouble. Time is money and waits no body, Law is no respecter of any person, whether rich or poor,

Not only to get money is hard but also to save it. You do good, your enemy meant it bad, Don't marry only because she is beautiful but also that he has good manners. He who married an ugly and mannerless woman will know that he did not marry, but he bought a useless thing with his money. No man is above death.

ONE DAY VISIT THE HOSPITAL OR THE LEPER SETTLEMENT AND SEE HOW GOD LOVES YOU

Sound health is far greater than money, but if you doubt it, or think that you are an unlucky man in this world or hated by God, simply because you have no money, visit the Hospital or the leper Settlement, there you will see with your two eyes men and women, boys and girls, who never talk about money but talk only about how to get good health which you have, but does not take as some thing, simply because you have no money yet.

110

Labourer Works Under A Heavy Sun

"Too Hard To Cut, Too Hard To Cut" He Says

In fact money is hard to get, and heavy rain and sun must beat you before you get it. Look at this 3s-per-day labourer doing his hard job under a heavy sun. He is cutting down a strong tree. He cannot go unless the tree is down. If he goes because of the heaviness of the sun, his appointment will be terminated.

MONEY IS HARD AND SWEET TO SPEND

Give me 12 bottles of beer. ''Say This man. The labourer has dressed up and has recevied his payment and he now spend one third of his salary.

He is buying from the shop 12 bottles of beer. The cost is £1 10s. His salary is £4 10s per month 3s per day. It takes 10 tough days to get £1 10s but takes him only 5 minutes to to spend it.

Put Better Records!

These type of men and women dancing, are the type of people who spend money too much. They can get £5 a day and spend all on useless things. Give me 12 bottles of beer give me one roasted fowl, Tune to Congo: Tune to Nigeria: Tune to Ghana: put better records," is what their body wanted.

The Big Man Who Never Wanted To Die.

This man is a rich man, but he is sick. He is afraid of death and never wanted to die. If one can buy everlasting life with money, this man can buy it no matter what will be the cost. He is on his sick bed praying to God to take all his property and money and give him good health.

BUY

Money Hard To

GET BUT EASY

To Spend

And Present It As A kola

To your Visitor,   It

Entertains More than 2

Bottles Of Beer.

LACK OF MONEY
IS NOT LACK OF SENSE*

PREFACE.

This is an African novel, written by an African and for the people of the vast continent of the blacks. In the main, it gives comfort to any person in dismay and contains a great rehearsal of various types of experiences, suitable for use, by both the young and the aged.

It is in all forms an imaginary story and all the characters herein contained are fictitious, bearing no type of relationship, to any existing people.

Like my other adventure writings, I have no doubt, that my usual readers, will find this, very interesting and educative.

The wise saying towards the end, are originally African ans serve as pieces of advice to each and every individual.

FELIX N. STEPHEN.

(*Novelist*)

*excerpt

CONTENTS

Man in the world of money

The woman Duper

The money monger

A happy Terminus

The Beginning of A long Journey

The change of fortune

The Control

The Ambition and Determination

The Turning point

MAN IN THE WORLD OF MONEY

Money is a double-edged sword. It can both destroy and save. Its numerous uses in all fields of life, cannot easily be gainsaid. People who have it, always look for more. Those who do not have it, feel that they are the most unfavoured.

It is such a wonderful confusionist, that no person can with safety and certainty, admit that it can be relied upon. There is always a very hot race for it. But the paths leading to it are on many occasions, barricaded by many odds. It gains recognition, from all classes of the community - men, women and children. Atheists, feel that it is their own god.

Mammon or infact. the desire for it, can stimulate a quarrel or even a bloody struggle, between one brother and the other; father and son; husband and wife and a man and his friend. It can give rise to untold atrocities which when perpetrated, might not be regretted, provided the objective, is attained.

Women, seem to be twin born with money. They love it very much and will always, like to go near to a person, who has it. This they do, inorder to see if there will be any possible means of extracting some, from him. Really, those days seem to have gone, when free women in particular, admired a man, for his physique or qualities, when he is without the cash. But they will like to go to a monster, on the understanding, that they will be well rewarded, financially.

Many people do not actually like to steal. But, it is the desire for wealth, that pushes them, into the detested business. When they succeed, the past is often forgotten. When they fail, they are hooted and shamed at as if they are wizareds.

Thus, life at once, makes fun of them. In some cases, where the law intervenes, they are subjected to penal servitude.

More often than not, people who have no money are not heeded, even when they make valuable suggestions. They may not be invited to all functions. In many cases, those, below them in age, try to regard them as their own equals. But however young a person is, when once he has the cash, he is respected. People term him a sensible fellow. Many poor people are thought to be foolish. So then, is this a life of mankind.

Money is capable of doing many things. Where some unscrupulous judges exist, it might even be used as a means of perverting the right course of justice. Where there is no money, feeding, education, housing, marriage, maintenance, enjoyment and business, all become difficult. They might only seem just like the wishes of a beggar and a tale, told by an idiot. Life looks very dull and man, looks like a very helpless and forgotten imp of misfortune.

In the pursuit of it however, discretion, ought to be applied, if possible, to the very last. Where this is neglected, then, life might be lost and some bitter stories might remain, to be told. Infact, the biographies of very wealthy men, always reveal some moments, awful ones too, when the barriers of misfortune, were penetrated through and finally the goal, reached.

If money were easy to get, people could have remained in their houses, with their arms folded everyday. But whosoever tries this, must surely regret, when he will be tortured by, both hunger and distress. At any rate, if people can only realise the fact, that things done gently, can bring about good results, then, life would be a pleasure.

MISS COMFORT'S HEART
CRIES FOR
TONNY'S LOVE.

MISS COMFORT'S HEART
CRIES FOR TONNY'S LOVE*

RESPONSE TO THE TOAST.

Response to the Toast of the Bride and Bridegroom by the Bridegroom.

Ladies and Gentlemen,

My wife and I are, quite happily to begin one weded life by starting with an agreement with my inlaw. I thank Mr. Alex for the very mind and pleasant manner in which he has proposed our health, and to you all for the hearty manner in which you have responded by to the good wishes so eloquently expressed by our friend. I do not deserve all the goods things that have been said of me, but I will try to deserve them, and to be worthy of my wife. I am sincerely grateful to you all for your kindness in so cheerily drinking to our health. I stop so far. Thank you.

After the response to the toast of bride and bridegroom, one old man was called to give the audience the history of palm wine.

THE HISTORY OF PALM WINE.

The history read as follows:—

The history of wine and the value of ashiboko needs no more emphasis or any appropriate description than this I am going to tell you now.

The more our natives do talk of wine it takes the name(mmanya) When it first steps into the Church it is known as Biba. Got its Baptismal name as Aligwe.

*excerpt

123

Assumed, it has got its comfirmation name with over night stay by, then it is known as Ashiboko. While couple with all marriage alliance, having cups as servants. By then, again it is known as Ashiboko Npi Agbos.

Being a nick name Father Bacus. Then comes the Blessings. *Ergo te consicreto et benedicto Ashiboku.* Thou art the Spirit that act in the palm tree. Let thy affection Nche be mild. Give us this day our normal beverage. Be in our belly as you were in the pot which was attached to the palm tree.

Forgive us our abusive languages as we forgive the sellers of Ashiboko who annoy us every day with their palm wine. Let those who drink you go to heaven and drink with God the Father. O, Father Bacus. Bless the tappers and their ropes so that their ropes must cling tite to palm trees for more wine. May Lord give us this day our daily wine and bread Amen. The marriage feast closed.

Then Tonny and his wife lived for a month after wedding quarrel entered the house through the window, because she neglected her duty as a house wife. My Advise to the married couple. Man does not live for himself alone. He lives for the good of others as well as of himself. Every one has his duties to perform the richest as well as the poorest. To some, life is pleasure, to other surferings. But the best do not leave self-enjoyment, or even for fame. Please never marry for money sake or for things that money can buy. If there is no money the lady overlooks the husband.

DRUNKARDS BELIEVE BAR
AS HEAVEN *

The guitar players and the bottle knockers are one of the groups of "high life players" who used to sell their properties by auctions before leaving the township. When they are in "Bar" or Restaurants" drinking and performing their musics they used to insult God through the words they pronounced.

They believe no place again like paradise or heaven than music halls. A great number of rich men who were among the company of this group of "guitar players" and "bottle knockers" have for the sake of this misleading life. Sold their plots, and other costly properties, because of falling automatically. This dangerous musical parties closed their business so early and enter bars by 6 30 p.m. daily. Returned home by 12 mid night with soacked cloths vomitting wine along the way falling side by side of the road as a mad man trying to be naked.

When they reach home they begin to make noise in the mid night ready to destroy the life of any body that comes out of room. The readers of this book should take this story into their hearts. The end of it carry the advice that irresponsible people should avoid disgracing fair people in the town.

*excerpt

If you wish to drink native wine, what you will do, is to send your boy to the bar with gallon to collect how many bottles required. But if you do not want like that, you have every freedom to enter any bar. If you reach and sit down, you vote how many bottles you want, and drink it politely and go back to your respective house at the proper hour. So many people's wives have rejected their husbands when after discovered their husbands are drunkards, because of fearing that they would one night be stabbed.

24 CHARGES AGAINST HARLOTS

Since the harlots have refused to abandon prostitution and begin to live clean lives. I have decided to declear wordy war against them. Here under are my strong charges against them:—

(1) The harlots live dirty and dangerous live

(2) They corrupt young men, make them live immoral lives and 'feed' them with chronic disease.

(3) They show bad example to the women who are not harlots.

(4) Almost all that had married, left their husbands without sufficient reasons, and the unmarried ones have refused to marry in preference to harlotism.

(5) They associate with ruffians, holigans and particularly thieves. When the thieves, steal something, the stolen property is handed over to the harlots to hide.

(6) The harlots smoke "India Hemp" otherwise, called 'Gay' and this make them to act as mad people sometimes, when they take 'Gay', they become stronger and satanic, as a result they fight without provocation.

*excerpt

7. The harlots steal the money of strangers.

8. The harlots tell lies and take false oath.

6. All the harlots are money mongers.

10. The harlots don't go medical examination regularly. They suppose to meet doctors constantly for examination treatment. They never do this bocause they are too much after money.

11. No single harlots is healthy in this world, that is why they are smelling.

12. The harlots drink beer too much and some smoke cigarettes in like manners, and no single harlot is beautiful that is why they always paint themselves with beauty make up's and yet you can easily know them Wash a pig, comb a pig, dress a pig, it must be a pig.

13 The harlots are spoiling the world and make no contribution to the progress and high moral standard of their respective countries.

14. Harlots get plenty money every day. But where do they save money? They have no savings. They have lavished all on unnecessary things.

15. Harlots have no plans for the future, and do not think what their condition may be in the future.

16. The harlots are dishonest, bad and untrustworthy people.

17. The harlots are wicked people. They have mastered all tricks to get money from men, but have no idea to make the least saving.

18. They love money more than their lives

19. They like bachelors and dislike married men and women.

20 Harlots cause disgrace to our lovely country

21 The harlots do not attend Church or mospue

22 The harlots are wicked and insultive.

23 They lack fear, respect, manners, truth and sincere love for men.

24 The harlots love evil ways and hate Godly ways.

So, beware of harlots. They are 'satan.'

Above are my twenty four serious charges against harlots. I deserve congratulation, because I have done what "Napoleon could not do." Have you heard that working class of men who are friends to harlots, always go home with pillow cases only, instead of carrying with them, things worth money as their counterparts who are not friends of harlots?

HOW TO AVOID
CORNER CORNER
LOVE
AND WIN GOOD
LOVE FROM GIRLS.

HOW TO AVOID CORNER CORNER LOVE AND WIN GOOD LOVE FROM GIRLS*

Raymond: Do you know Veronica Okoro?

Baby. Yes she is my friend.

Oliaku. Palaver don finish now, Go callam for we if she ask you who dey callam, tellam say na me.

Baby. Yes ma. (Exit Baby)

Chief John. Look Raymond. when she come make you brainam proper. Come, tellam say if she do as una tellam, she go be your wife the time wey you go be king.

Raymond. That is an easy job for me for I have been playing such game before. She must surely fall into the trap for with money, man can buy any thing—even his father's head.

Oliaku. But na which day una talk say dem go make dan boy king?

Chief John. Which boy?

Oliaku. I mean dan one wey dey think say him go be king.

Chief John. Oho, dem talk say na for fifteen this moon. But abeg una make una no gree any body sabi say my hand dey for this thing.

Raymond. You must know we are no longer chiidren sir.

Oliaku. Unless say na dan two people wey we bee meet for your house dan day wey we come to talkam. But for we, you no fit hearam for another place.

Chief John. Dan people no go talk because dem dey support Johnson. Even before una come dey day, na the thing wey we go do Johnson I been dey talk with them.

(Enter Baby and Veronica)

Oliaku. Welcome my pickin, how you people dem wellam?

*excerpt

133

Veronica. They are all sound in health maa.

Oliaku Look my pickin, I want make you do something for me. But before I tell you dan thing hold this money. Na five hundred pounds. (She gives her the money.)

Veronica. What is the money for. I'm confused you know.

Raymond. Hold it yet Vero for she is coming. Hold it. But to start with you are in love with Johnson my junior brother?

Veronica: Yes.

Raymond. And of course, he promised you marriage?

Veronica. Yes, but I don't think he is serious for he has been playing me game about it for some time now.

Raymond. Very good. I'm happy you know he is not serious. Now listen, that throne to which Johnson told you he wil ascend is mine, because being his senior by three years. And he with the support of king makers wants to instal himself the King of our Town on the flimsy excuse that our dad said that he—Johnson should be made king when he was dying. So that being the case, I, being the right person to take my father's place, now want to fight Johnson to a finish that he might not usurp my right. If you help me in this struggle, I promise to take you as a wife.

Veronica. Is that so! What will be nature of the fight?

Raymond: It must of course be a bloody one.

Oliaku. Look my daughter if dan money wey I gave you no do, tell me make I put more on top.

Chief John. I think you sabi me Veronica.

Veronica. Yes sir, I know you as the second in Command to the OBI.

Chief John. Very good, so the thing wey we want you to do be make you put some poison for him chop so that he go sick.

Raymond. Give her two hundred pounds more mama so that she may know that we are very serious. (Oliaku gives her the two hundred pounds)

Veronica. I don't think I can do it ma. No, I can't.

Oliaku. Wetin be say you no fit. Nobi money dey you for hand so. As you say Johnson love you true. true, how many money he don give you since una begin make love ?

Raymond: Am I not as handsome as Johnson Vero ? don't you know that Johnson only pretends to love you because you satisfy his sexual emotions ?

Veronica. I quite agree with you in this point but—

Chief John. But wetin ?

Veronica. If I administer the poison to Johnson, are you sure you will be instatlled the OBI ?

Raymond. I am thousand times sure.

Veronica. Are you sure that your promise of wed-ding me is not a window dressing designed to deceive me ?

Raymond. I am not like that, Vero. If you care I can give you a promising note to that effect

Veronica: Alright Raymond, I shall do the job for Johnson has never been of any use to me even since we fell in love.

Oliaku: If you doam my pickin you go see say we no dey talk lie.

Veronica. When do you want me to do it ?

Oliaku. I wantam today today today.

Veronica. I will do it ma where the poison ?

Oliaku. Make I bringam. (she enters the house) after which she came out with it.)

Oliaku. Lookam but no agreeam touch your mouth

Veronica. How will I give it to him ?

WHY HARLOTS HATE MARRIED MEN AND LOVE BACHELORS*

INTRODUCTION

IT seems to me as if the readers of some certain pamphlets of Money-hard will share this view with me that these pamphlets help to add knowledge to growing youths; and readers of this book will read it with interest and the facts it contains.

THIS book as it is entitled "Why Harlots Hate Married Men And Love Bachelors" is a newly edited pamphlet in its first edition and readers should mind very little of the poor English it contains, which is hope to be amended when this book will celebrate her puplication.

Port Harcourt   C. N. O. Money-hard

16th Edition

*excerpt

C. N. O.   MONEYHARD
(The Author.)

WHY HARLOTS HATE MARRIED MEN
AND LOVE BACHELORS

The reason why harlots, independent women, mostly lip painted ladies hate married men is only because they know that as they have married, they will have no time again to see them or to take care of their pride. Also married men will not care to come to their houses any longer and even if they come, they are only coming to show themselves not to spend for them as they were doing before.

Why harlots, independent women, mostly the lip painted ladies love bachelors, is because they know that the bachelors have a long way to go with them, and they will have to see them, and also will take care of their pride. They come to remember what they use to get from the bachelors and also the money they get from them to buy their needs such as rekiy-rekiy, popo-cloth, velvet, ejecombe lawyer, sasarobia scent, fine pomade, gold and silver, head-tie, handkerchiefs, umbrella, shoes, skirt and blouse, sandals, iron beds, blankets and bed-sheets, pillows and pillow cases, sleeping gowns, cushion chairs and covers, door blinds window blinds, mosquito nets, tables and table cloths carpets, bed curtains, ladies hand watches, lookidg glass, powder, ladies sewing machine, portmanteaux, trunk box, bicycle, gramophone and so many other things that a woman could use.

To be a customer everywhere, is to be a friend to everybody and that is why they are free to everybody and can do anything they like. There is nothing women want from men than their money inorder to enable them to get all what they want. That is why I said that money is hard but women do not know.

Really, it is a pity for harlots to act in this way bacause when they are demanding all these things they forget to remember that the most important thing a woman could want is child and without the child the woman is useless to the man.

Money mongers shall soon lead themselves to the prison yard. Who are the money mongers in the world? Ok! Let me tell you if you don't know. Do you really see with me that the rich men are the most money mongers in this country? The world has been spoilt by the so called rich men. Really, money has spoilt the world and has shown herself that she is the greatest evil of the world so that people could not live without money.

The evil that men do lives after them. Once I was a friend to so many money mongers but I have now known their ways and I was afraid of them because their ways are not true as I saw them. They could not tell you the truth or tell you how they manage to get their money. So beware of those men who are not straight-forward in their ways.

❖❖❖❖❖❖❖❖❖❖❖❖❖❖❖❖❖❖❖❖❖❖❖

Now my dear fellow readers, I am going to tell you the story of what money mongers are doing. So many of my friends who are money mongers have been to prison yard, when they return instead they will tell me the correct story and how they suffered in the prison yard, they started to tell me that prison yard is a paradise. Which of you could believe this false story?

FRIENDS OF THE WORLD

Oh! Friends of the world, friends today enemies tomorrow. It is very wonderful of course, why I am still making some friends up till today is according to what the fowl said "let it be, I am going to bed because night has come" but not because she has eaten sufficiently for the day. I wonder why a poor man's debt can make a great noise, but a rich man's debt is a rumour in the ear.

Can cheating prosper? Oh no, not at-all. Infact to choose a woman on Saturday night while going to cinema or ball room dance, is just like you are marrying through photograph because the woman will be so beautiful that you cannot control your temper. A poor man could steal in the night because he is poor and needy but you rich man what do you find before seeing the poor man? Any rich man who did a bad thing in his life is planting an evil seed in his family for which they will reap as time goes on. So you must beware.

Rich men always hope on their wealth but they forget that they can die and leave their money for others to use. Infact, however you are rich do not boast of your riches because riches are just like water which comes and goes.

Oh! rich men with their great debts. Infact some of those whom we call the richest men are the most senior debtors too. Hardly they believe that there is God, therefore you should beware of such people who claim to be all in all.

Such people only believe on their money because as soon as they get the money they feel they have even got the life of a man. Money men fear to go into the dark. They don't know that women and money are evils of the world. They are more foolish when they see women than when they see their way of life. Please, I say beware of them.

A man who hopes for nothing can never be disappointed at all. You should be better be short of money than to be senseless. There is no righteous man in this world. Rich men and women are all money mongers. An educated man without money is like a new man in another country.

A man who helps his brother saves him from danger. Please listen well as you may know what to decide on this issue. So listen to me now.

Could you see with me that half education is dangerous in life and a poor man's certificate is a hard labour but an educated man's certificate is written paper? Women education ends in smoke. What do you say about those things gentlemen ?

THE STORY ABOUT MONEY-HARD AND HIS INDIAN LADY.

Now, I am Mr. C. N. O. Money-hard, the money commander, master of money and small man with great value. Now, I want to tell you a story which you have never heard before, it is very interesting. It was the time I went to war time victory under the famous German war side by side we fell like devils till the evening of the day,

When the bullet struck my congress which made me to say take my girl to Eunice because she is the only lady that I love and tell her that she can never see her jolly boy any more and if I die in action I am fighting for the crown and every linger of my jolly boy belongs to freedom jack.

Every person wondered about in the field because of me which made me to say by singing "take my gun when I die". Every body was singing this with a very strong mind then until I saw a person who took me up and said to me that he was a cowboy and he was in army co-operation plane to French land. Then I took my bayonet and my gun and followed him.

As we reached there my life came back to me again in full swing then I began to sing. "Take my bullets when I die cowboy, take my bullets when I die cowboy." If I die while I am fighting for the crown, I can never forget cowboys' life.

After sometimes I fell in love with an Indian lady by name Rosaline, we were living in peace and harmony. We never thought that we would depart in life because the lady so loved me that I nearly forgot my blessed land of Africa. Life is precious.

About two months after, one Saturday evening I got a telegram from my home town which read that I should prepare to leave tomorrow morning to the blessed land of Africa. A big lorry will be waiting for me tomorrow morning to take me away.

After reading the telegram in the presence of my lady friend, the lady wept bitterly which made me to sing "My Indian lady don't you worry for me no more, tomorrow I am going home, for there is a big lorry waiting for me tomorrow 8 o'clock I am going home.

Then she asked me to give her the gold and silver I promised her and immediately I dipped my hand into my pocket and gave her anything that she wanted from me. Immediately the lorry carried me away to my blessed land of Africa where I enjoyed with friends, parents and fellow cowboys.

Really, many battles have been fought and won by the British Navy Protection through the assistance of the Africans.

As I reached the blessed land of Africa I got another lady friend called "This and That" as you know. One day I was in her house playing with her, she called me dollar boy, money commander and master of money.

After she had called me these names then I asked her whether should I command money or money to command me? she answered and said, you are to command money and not money to command you because you are master of money, and you can produce money at any time.

After she had finished her talks people began to call me "Master of M o n e y." The reason why they are calling me by that name was because my original name was Money-hard.

Love the women at the time they love you and hate them at the very moment they hate you because their love is to eat you dry and run away to another man. Beware of such women for they are very dangerous.

If you want to be rich, don't try to rob another man's property to make up yours, because such habit can make somebody die.

One day, I was in my girl's house, a certain young man came in with his car and met us and we started to play. After some times, I asked the man, Hello! Mr Man may I know whom you are?

He replied and said, "I am one of the money mongers." I asked him again is there a man of your type who is also a money monger? And I asked him again that he should call their names for me.

He replied again that all big men as you see them are all money mongers, because any place where people think there is money but very hard to get, and if we big men go there we can make business that people may not suspect us at-all.

From there we can get plenty of money to buy cars, build fine houses and many things that will make us richer than before.

After he said this then my lady friend said, let me introduce the young man to you. I was afraid when I heard these words from the man, then I told my lady friend to introduce the young man to me.

She said this man is one of the money mongers in this country, those who can drink another man's tombo but cannot buy their own. Then I laughed at him and he went away. So beware of such money mongers.

After the man has gone away, a certain young lady came in and said to me, hello! Mr. C. N. O. Money-hard, the master of money and money commander are you here?

You are a small man with great value and I am here to monger out money from your pocket. Then I asked her please may I know whom you are?

She replied and said, I am one of the lip painted ladies and the money mongers. I laughed at her and told her that she cannot monger out any money from my pocket because I am the man called money-hard. As I told her this, she said I know you are Money-hard, but don't forget that you are also the money commander.

After she had said that then she started to tell me so many stories how she went to one of my poor friends who was having nothing to eat and monger out money from him and so many others too.

She started to tell me that some rich men are very dangerous because they have the money but they cannot spend it. Even it will be very hard for them to use the money to buy the food they will eat.

They are even offended with the medicine they will buy for themselves when they are sick. When she told me these things, I was afraid of the so-called big men.

She started to tell me that even the big men who drink others tombo but could not buy for others, I monger out money from them how much more a money commander of your type. Infact I must monger out something from your pocket. Wait and see.

I still told her that it will be very hard for you to get something from my pocket because I am money-hard as I have told you before. Really women are wonderful.

As I said this, the woman immediately began to loose her cloth and her gown so that she will attract me to fall into temptation. She powdered her face and became more beautiful than before.

As soon as I saw her bobpy, I was attracted and I fell into temptation. After we had ended our secret intercourse, I was advised to give her something and I did accordingly.

After the woman got up from the bed she laughed at me and said I told you that I will monger out money from your pocket and I have done so. After she had spoken this she went away to her house.

It is true that apart from natural beauty of a woman, I can definitely say that all women are one because the same thing I enjoyed from that woman is the same thing I enjoyed from other women too.

Please my dear fellow men let me tell you the money which you will give to harlots you better use it for dressing or to use it for food because giving it to them has no profit rather you lose your money and energy.

Infact, they are butterflies and we are their flowers. They can come and suck us at any time they feel like doing so, not minding us whether we are dying or not.

Another thing is this, however a woman is rich unless she gets a penny from the man she will never be satisfied in her life. You know women are pests and they are bent on sucking the man until he becomes tired if he doesn't take care.

When will it be good for us to marry? Now listen. It is not good for us to marry at a very old age, and at the youngest age. Really we should marry at the ripe age so that we may enjoy the benefit of marriage.

It is good for us to marry between the age of thrity and thirty-five years, by that time we might have got some dresses and some few shillings to manage the family.

Really to marry an expensive lady is a risk because the woman can never think of helping the man in any way at-all. Rather she will be interested at remaining in the house from morning till night because her husband has money and can maintain her very well.

Ofcourse really, women are very fond of pride also with their sweet mouth and beauty are, just like dead bodies of which if you keep on crying according to how they keep their faces, you will be tired of crying.

WHAT ARE LADIES LOVE TOWARDS MEN?

Ladies love towards men is only to eat them and get their needs from them, mostly to get clothes and money because as you know without clothes the women cannot be regarded.

Now I want to tell you that apart from natural beauty of a woman's appearance and dressing all women are one, whether tall or short because they all have the same natural body and shape.

This is another advice to boys and girls, ladies and gentlemen, men and women, those who are interested in love and friendship.

Please lend me your ears, do not love because of cushion chairs and iron beds let not yourselves to be tempted.

Really, there are some women who are very fond of that by going to a mans's house telling him I love you and thereby snatching every penny from him. When they come they sit on the chair drinking the man's penny.

MABEL
THE
SWEET HONEY

THAT POURED AWAY.

Her Skin would make your blood flow in the wrong direction. She was so sweet and sexy, knew how to romance. She married at sixteen. But she wanted more fun. Yet it ended at seventeen, And what an-end?   **SO THRILLING.**

MABEL

THE

SWEET HONEY

THAT POURED AWAY *

Her skin would make your blood flow in the wrong direction. She was so sweet and sexy, knew how to romance. She married at sixteen. But she wanted more fun. Yet it ended at seventeen. And what an end? So thrilling.

BY

SPEEDY ERIC

Obtainable from:

MEMBERSHIP BOOKSHOP

87 Upper New Market Road
P. O. BOX 214,

ONITSHA E. C. S. NIGERIA.

*complete text

5/– Net Price

CONTENTS

A look at girl's skin

The effects sight on Mabel

The Young man in the Pleasure Home

What Mabel did in the next early morning

Comfort to Mabel's incident

Mabel and Margie to close the Hotel

The Sweet honey was engaged to Gilbert

Mabel in full Romance

Mabel in her mother's home

Mabe'l belonging to the Pleasure Home

CHAPTER ONE

Have you ever looked at a girl's skin and felt that if you pinched her she would shed blood. A skin as smooth as glass and also round and plumpy. No trace of nerves or bone on the skin.

Add to these an underformed and elegant structure hips that would raise temperature of every full-blooded young man, an oval face, full lips, high cheek bones a pointed nose: black eye lashes, under pencilled eye-brows within which you have two sparkling eyes, set a bit deep in the eye sockets.

And when the sugary lips open there are two rows of equal and well-sized teeth. Can your imagination travel and gather all these qualities and then combine them at one place? Then you have a picture of Mabel. The picture of seventeen year-old Mabel. The daughter of Mrs. Helen Ojina from Orlu town. Mr. Ojina unfortunately had died in a car crash when Mabel was eleven. The family then were living at Onitsha in a two-storey plot of Mr. Ojina. After the death of Mr. Ojina, Helen and her daughter gave up the whole rooms to tenants and took up a bungalow at Moore Street. Helen being a very good cook decided to convert the whole bungalow into an eating house with Mabel to help her.

Helen was very industrious and had over-flowing energy; she was then thirty-two, though she looked twenty five. She loved Mabel tenderly and gave the eleven years old girl every thing she wanted. You know that Mabel was her only child. Inveitably Helen had to spoil her with kindness add care.

At the age of eleven Mabel knew practically every thing a woman could know. Though she had not yet met her first man. But one could see the desire in her eyes. The terrible desire to taste a young man. The business progressed immensely. There was so much work that at the end of the first year Mrs. Helen was forced to employ another helper other than Mabel. The new employee was a girl of eighteen and a girl who had seen the world and even tasted her first man and more. Mrs. Helen hoped that the new girl-Margie-would keep Mabel company also, for Mabel was really lonely.

Margie had to help in preparing the food while Mabel would be serving it to the customers. Mabel was more beautiful than Margie but if you look at Margie from the back when she's walking you must surely lose your head. The girl had a special way of shaking her waist so that a young man's blood would flow in the wrong direction. And do you know what? Margie was a great taser. Her right place was in the kitchen but at odd time you would see her in the dining-room. For what?

Some times she would come to collect the plates or switch on the fan or even look around. If you were lucky to be there when she comes to collect the plates you would know how she teases. She would go to your back and, pressing her two sharp breasts on your hunch, expend her hand to pick up the plates on the table. Infact your temperature will so rise that you would wish to hold her there for hours.

That was Margie, the girl that Mabel had for companion. The girl she copied her manners from. Margie loved the body of men and she did not hide this from Mabel. She told Mabel fantastic stories of how the THING was. She fed Mabel's mind with news and lectures about men. Mabel had the greatest desire to meet a real adult of about twenty one or two, for according to Margie, they knew how to do the thing at that age. Mabel was only twelve years old, yet she was five feet four inches and plumpy and round. Her breasts were conical and had needle points.

One day she saw something which robbed her of a whole night's sleep. It was by about seven p. m. one Friday evening. Mabel's mother had gone to collect rents from the tenants in their plot at—, Bright Street. There was only one young man in the dining-room. Mabel and Margie were conversing in the kitchen, talking about men.

Then Margie left to go and collect plates in the dining-room. For six minutes Mabel waited in the dining-room but Margie did not come back. At last she decided to go and find out what was holding her. But before she reached the door of the eating room she saw something through the window which stopped her from going forward.

She saw it entirely. She trembled. But could not tear her eyes away from the sight. She saw the youny man pressing Margie against the wall. Margie was not strugglign at all. She put he arms round the young man. The man took Margie's head in his hands, then he bent down and put his own lips on Margie's lips. They stayed like that for about seven good minutes. The young man was moving his body this way and that. He held Margie very tight............

It was wonderful. Margie was enjoying it greatly. While Mabel was shaking with desire. She tip-toed to the side of the window and peeped and peeped and peeped. At long last Margie shook slightly. The young-man left her and with satisfaction. They eyed each other for some seconds then they smiled. Margie took the plates.

At that Mabel slipped away and ran back to the kitchen before Margie could come out of the dining-room. Throughout the whole night Mabel did not wink. She tossed and turned and sighed. At one time Margie, whose bed was near to Mabel's own asked her. 'Mabel, what is wrong?'

"Nothing" Mabel replied. "Is there anybody in that bed with you?" Margie asked her.

"What do you mean?" 'The sound from your bed seems to suggest that............................' 'Oh! shut up Margie!' Mabel stopped her.

'Alright' Margie said, 'but give me chance to have some sleep.'

But there was no sleep for Mabel through out the night. She kept on picturing the scene in her mind. The way the young man shook his waist around Margie's own waist. How Margie clung to the young man. How their lips pressed together tight. And after that the sweet way that the man eyed Margie. As she thought of all these things she was working herself up terribly, she lay there tossing and sighing.

CHAPTER TWO

The effects of that sight on Mabel lasted a life time. In the first place she began to desire the touch of a man. She longed to be held as Margie had been

158

held by that man. Whenever people came to eat she would look hungrily at them, though she would threw away her eyes if they look back at her.

Then on another occassion she saw Margie collecting the plates in her teasing style. She saw how she pressed her breast on the back of some young men and she saw how the face of the men turned purple.

It was wonderful. Margie was a wicked girl and Mabel told her so one day.

'Why do you think I am a wicked girl?' Margie asked her.

'Why do you collect plates like that from the back of the men?' Mabel told her.

'How do you mean?'

You press your breast on the back of the men and they turned purple and then stared at you when you leave, Mabel asked her.

Oh! Margie laughed, so you watch me? Infact it is a great fun, Mab. I enjoy it terribly and I know the men would wish I never left them at all.

'Please don't talk like that Margie. I am burning like a flame,' Mabel said.

'Infact you are missing a great deal, Margie said. 'You don't seem to like to go near the men. But I see them look hungrily at you every time.' 'You are talking rubbish. Nobody cares for me,' Okay you shall see,' Margie said and went back to the kitchen. Mrs. Helen Ojina's business was p r o s p e r i n g rapidly. She was making much money. Mabel, her only child, had anything just for the asking. She had a special dress-maker and a special hair dresser. She had everything that a young girl could need. Any time she wanted she could leave the home and see something of Onitsha township and come back again.

She had extensive freedom. Her mother rarely shouted at her. She was never hungry and anytime she had some illness, great care would be lavished on her.

Yet she never appeared very happy as the days went by She was never as cheerful as Margie. Helen had told her daughter of this gloominess for many times, but it seemed that Mabel could not help herself.

But it was not long before things began to change much to the fear of Mrs. Helen.

Mabel was now fourteen years old. But she looked as sexy as a girl of eighteen, though she had not yet met her first man.

Mrs. Helen's eating house was now very popular and was known as 'Pleasure Home'

It was becoming the most popular eating house in the town. If you wanted to eat the best of food and asked someone to tell you where to go he would not waste time to direct you to 'Pleasure Home.'

The hotel was full every time of the day; but especially in the evenings more seats were brought in to accommodate the customers. Some times Mabel's room was used to receive the customers. But they were always warned to make sure that they leave the room as neatly as they found it.

That young man of Margie's attended frequently at the hotel but Mabel had not caught them again.

Many other young men were then attending the hotel and Mabel had begun to catch their eyes.

One day as she was serving food to the customers it happened that she had to pass behind one man to go out of the room.

You know what happened? As she went between this man and the wall, the man threw himself back a little and pressed Mabel into the wall, intentionally. She struggled for two minutes and freed herself; everybody was laughing, the sight was so funny, the young man enjoying the thing and Mabel squirming and blushing.

When she was free she glared at the young man who winked at her and said: "Do not pretend that you dislike me, sugar baby,' Everybody laughed again. With a thumping heart Mabel left the room. But surely the warmth from that man's body was working havoc inside her. The young man was so handsome and looked so strong yet he had sweet and kind eyes.

Back at the kitchen Mabel could not take her mind off the man and the incident.

But when she came back into the room to serve food, the young man had gone. Oh God! she nearly cried.

Throughout that day she prayed that the man would turn back, but he didn't. For a greater part of that night she tossed again and sighed her bed.

Again Margie's sleep was disturbed and she camplained. What is in your mind Mabel? Margie asked her. "It is nothing."

"You said disturbing me again. Infact something

must be wrong" Margie reached for the wire and switched on the light.

"Come now Mabel, tell me, who is breaking your heart?' she asked her. 'What do you mean?' Mabel asked, sitting up in her bed opposite Margie.

'I mean that this your tossing is not without cause There must be a man in those sighs and tosses.' 'Shut up, silly girl. Wetin e dey talk sef?', Mabel was trying to look serious and hurt.

'Look Mabel' Margie began cooly, 'I was once fourteen years. You must remember I tossed for some while too. Till I knew what to do. Spending sleepless nihgts will solve it. If you don"t know it, let me tell you that you are very beautiful, very juicy and appetising..... ——........

Margie are you mad! Mabel jumped up and went across to her bed. Do you know what followed? Margie caught the virgin - girl by the waist and lay her on her bed and jumped on top of poor Mabel. At the same time shaking her waist in such suggestive way that Mabel screamed and kicked in her excitement.

It was about one o'clock in the night. The noise woke Mrs. Helen who jumped up from her bed and came racing to Mabel's room. She banged at the door and shouted; 'Mabel! Mabel! na wetin' Nothing mamma, Margie replied. Mabel de dream-o. "So na him make she de make such noise for the middle night?" said Mrs. Helen. Angrily she went back to her room at the other end of the long house.

When she left, they begin to laugh, though softly. "I beg, Margie, no do me like this again," Mabel said.

'But na you wake me up. I lie?' Margie asked softly, 'And I been want satisfy you. 'Idiot, you think say woman de satisfy woman?' Mabel asked.

'Okay no wake again, now,' Margie said, to-morrow I go find one young man for you. E hear?

'You fool like sheep, Margie' Mabel said. 'Alright I fool but you go suffer so tee you tire' Margie said.

They went back to sleep. But Mabel kept wait-ing every hour and tossing. Something kept pinching her inside and she kept on thinking of that young man who had pressed her against the wall. Some times she prayed that the man might turn up the following morning.

The following morning Mabel took special care in dressing herself. It took her seven minutes to take her bath. something she used to do in three minutes before.

Then in her room she rubbed two different pomades. After that she went to the mirror and pencilled her eye brows and eyelashes - they became even blacker. Her eyes were twinkling and clear.

Then instead of putting on her brown working dress she took her flowered Sunday tight-fitting gown and put it on. She abandoned her working slippers and stepped into an expensive high heeled Italian bally shoes.

When she appeared in the kitchin by about nine a.m, her mother glared at her. 'Mabel, where are you going?, her mother asked her. 'How mamma?' Mabel asked.

'As you go put your best dress now' 'I no de go anywhere-o. I no wan the customer to explain of a dirty girl wey de serve them. One de say na yesterday' she said. She had caught her mother who always liked to please her customers.

'So they complain of your dress before?' her mother asked.

'Yes mamma and I no want any person make that noise again,' she said and sat down. Then Margie came in. But just at the door her eyes caught Mabel. She stopped short and stared at her.

Mabel turned and saw her 'Na wetin e de look me so?' she asked Margie.

'To God I no sabi say na you-o' Margie said. 'I been wonder if mamma don bring another young lady to work here. Infact Mabel you be like queen,' she said.

Mrs. Helen laughed and Margie laughed too. Mabel was just blushing 'No de talk so to me Margie,' Mabel said and went into the dining room.

There was no customers yet. But she was expecting to find that young man. She sighed and went back to the kitchen.

Mrs Helen left them together and went to the market. After a while Margie said, 'Mabel' 'Na wetin?' she answered. 'To God, if that young man see you today e go mad. The time when I enter this kitchen I been wonder which kind beauty been come for our house this morning,' Margie stopped.

Which kind young man you mean?' Mabel asked her, fearing that Margie knew the man who pushed her on the wall yesterday. But it proved that Margie was just guessing.

'I mean that man way no de gree you sleep for night,' Margie said. 'Rubbish,' Mabel said 'who tell you say na man de worry me for night'?

'Okey' Magie said, but I been wan tell you one thing wey happen to me this morning.' Mabel was anxious. 'Tell me, I beg, she pleaded. You remember that time when I been come out to buy pepper?' Margie asked Yes'

'Some person been meet me at the passage and gave me this,' Margie brought out a paper from her pocket and held it towards Mabel. 'It was from a young boy who say him de come here every day and that him sabi two of us. Mabel took the letter and opened it.

Juicy Margie,

Trully I cannot tell how I fell every-time I come to chop for that your hotel. Every time I see you something moves uneasily inside my body and I wsih I could hold you in my arms and press you close to me.

Infact I like you very much and if you give me a piece of your love, I think I will be the happiest boy on earth. We live at No......Moore Street and I see you from my window every time you pass to the market. Please Margie say you will like me little and I will do anything for you once you say the word.

I shall come to eat in your home this afternoon and I am hoping to get your answer-oral or written.

I love you greatly.

I am,

Your Own,

Edward Uzor.

This letter was meant for Margie alone but when Mabel finished reading it her inside began to sweat. She looked at Margie then at the letter,

Mabel you know, doesn't know what is a boy friend or love letter. Because of her intelligence she had been able to finish school life before she was eleven and you know at that age she had not developed enough to desire boys.

Margie's letter was the first love letter that Mabel saw. You can see that it was a simple letter but Mabel could not contain herself with excitement.

"Margie, swear that a boy wrote you this!" "True for God, I got it this morning at the passage from Edward's own hand", she swore. I have been seeing that boy everyday that I pass to the market. With the tail of my eye I always see him watch me as I pass. And to God the boy is an angel. His shoulders wide. He has strong arms and his eyes are sweet, He is not quite black and he is up to five feet ten. O! God, Margie was passionately killing her companion 'Infact Mabel', Margie continued, 'you must see this boy. When he comes today I go show you' Mabel sighed and put her chins on her palms. "But

Make e no take the boy from me-o Margie said smilling proudly, 'Don't be silly', Mabel shouted "them tell you say I dey craze for boys?

Aha! make you de pretend, now, And make the thing dey pepper you inside there', Margie said,

Mabel could not hear it any longer, she left the kitchen and walked towards the dining - room.

'Hey Mabel,' Margie called, 'bring back that letter! 'No', Mabel continued to the dining - room. 'I beg bring it', Margie left her work in the kitchen and pursued Mabel, who ran into her bed-room. But before she could lock the door, Margie had met her.

'I think e don readam. Make you givam back to me now', Margie pleaded.

Margie laughed. 'But you de make like you no like boys' she accused Mabel. 'Na lie' Mabel said, 'I like boys but them no de care care for me.

'Wait Margie', said Mabel, 'I wan readam again. The thing dey sweet plenty.

Margie laughed, Wait small, Mabel, the THING go belle-full you, But I beg no take my own boy from me-o! she said, Mabel promise not to seduce Margie's boy friend.

BUT YOU SHALL SEE WHAT FOLLOWED

CHAPTER THREE

By about two p.m. a young man came into Pleasure Home for lunch. Mabel was serving some other customers then, and had her back to the door, then somebody said behind her 'Hey baby, you are getting sweeter as the day goes by When Mabel turned round, do you know whom she saw? No other than the young man who had pressed her on the wall yesterday.

He was smiling down at her. Her heart missed two beats. The man was tall and strongly built. His shoulders were broad and masculine, Mabel was losing her head. She served the other customers quickly and turned to face him.

What will you eat, please? She asked him, trying to hide her desire as far as possible.

'You', especially, the man replied looking very sincere. Some men nearby began to laugh. It was very amusing.

'But you cannot eat me,' Mabel said seriously. 'Please tell me quickly.

'Okay, juicy baby if you won't allow me eat you, then give me some eba and meat stew,' he dipped his hand in his pocket and brought out two shillings. Privately Mabel was wishing to hold that young man in her arms. That was the very man who had made her toss and twist in bed last night. Yet she was pretending she did not know him. This kind of word She took the man's money from him and went to the kitchen to collect his orders.

When she came back with the food she saw that the man was looking at her at a particular place around the waist. She was quite uneasy then their eyes met. She blinked at him. He just smiled and took the food and started eating.

Mabel went to a far corner of the dining room and surveyed the young man for long.

At one time the man caught her looking at him. She threw away her eyes immediately. The man smiled. Without any need for it she cried, 'salt please'. Mabel raced down with the salt and hold it out to him.

But he held both the salt and Mabel's fingers. The girl for a minute looked at him, not struggling to free her fingers. He looked deep into her eyes, a look that seemed to spell intense hunger and desire. Mabel who had long fallen for the man gave the same amorous look.

Somebody called for water at the other end. Mabel freed herself and went to attend. But some thing had been registered between her and the man.

'The young man finihed his meal and went out of the passage Mabel went out too. Pretending she was heading to the kitchen. As she tried to pass the man he he,d her by the arm.

'What's wrong? she asked the man softly, looking into his eyes.

'You, and nothing more', the man said tremulously. He was about twenty one years or less. But he was full and complete and healthy looking. 'I don't understand you please,' she said trying to continue on her way. But his hand held her strongly.

'Please Mabel won't you give me a chance?' he pleaded. Good God! who told you my name? he looked very crossed. But she so like the way he called her. 'I know you very well', he said, 'it's only you that don't know me. I come here everyday and I long and long for you', he stopped.

But Mrs. Helen called from the kitchen 'Maa-bel! Ma-be-el!

'Ma-a-h', she answered. 'Please I must go and answer' she told the man trying to free her arm. The man clung to her. 'Tell me first that you will like me a little' the man insisted.

'I cannot tell you like that. But who are you. You know my name but I don't know yours? 'I am Gilbert Eric. Gil for short', he said. 'Okay Gil, I shall see you tomorrow when you come back,' she said. Gilbert's heart was singing with joy.

'Promise you must, he insisted. I promise it she said softly looking at the floor. Gilbert left her and she ran down to the kitchen. Gil also left the 'Please Home' feeling very pleased. But his pleasure could not equal one quarter of Mabel's own.

When she appeared before her mother she was bright and smiling. Mrs. Helen noticed it, being that Mabel was always looking very gloomy and dejected. Even she could not help comenting on it. 'You look cheerful this afternoon, Mabel' her mother said, smiling too.

'Thank you for that mamma said Mabel!' I think it is because no customer has called me a dirty girl today, she lied. I am glad of that, her mother said. Go to No. 4 stall in the market and buy some meat. Meat worth about fifteen shillings. Take this pound note.

Mabel took the money and speed to the market. She kept on looking this way and to see if she would find Gil, but she did'nt. But on her way home somebody halted her 'Please are you not living at

Pleasure Home hotel?' the man asked, a man of about twenty six or more. 'Yes I am,' Mabel replied "Please can you do me a little service?" "Say it,' Mabel urged her, ' Kindly deliver this envelope to Margie who works for your mother,' he held out an envelope to her. She took it. "But who is it from?' She asked him.

"The sender's address is at the back,' he said. She turned the envelope and read the sender—Edie Uzor then she smiled. What's wrong the boy asked: Nothing she said and ran away with the envelope, So that was Margie's boy friend? She decided to keep the letter till they were in bed.

Things went by slowly till about five o'clock in the evening Customers began to crowd in. Margie and Mabel were absorbed in attending them. By about seven p m. it became necessary to use Mabel's room again. She agreed grudgingly to the use of it Three men were taken into the room to be served. Nothing happened till they finished eating, then one of them did something exciting to Mabel.

When she was leaving the room the man walked faster before her and went up to the door. As Mabel approached him he raised his hand and switched off the light.

Before anybody could tell what was happening he caught Mabel by waist and pulled her to himself. Then he kissed her cheeks strongly. She screamed. He left her and again switched on the light laughing. She glared at him. "I am sorry baby,' he pleaded but I couldn't help myself, you look so juicy that my blood flows in the wrong direction the other men laughed at that.

Mabel in her embarrassment rushed out of the room. But she did not tell anybody what had happened: how could she?

But one thing was becoming clear to her in that single—day. That was this. She had something the men could like.

It was dangerous for her to think so. But she did, under the influence of romantic touches she was getting. She began to feel wanted You know that such a feeling can have a disastrous effect on anybody. When you feel so needed, you have to do one of two things Either you give yourself, or bluff for ever those that yearn for you.

WE SHALL SEE WHAT MABEL DID IN HER OWN CASE READ ON, DEAR

By about twelve Mid—night Mrs. Helen closed down and Mabel and Margie retired to thier room. It had been a very busy day, especially in the second half of the day. But Mabel had never had a happier day.

Margie, however, surprised her, "Hah Mabel, you know I saw you this afternoon.?'

"Doing what?' Mabel asked, in surprise.

"Talking to your young man in the passage' Margie said.

"What? So you saw? Where were you peeping from? Mabel asked her.

"I was not peeping.' Margie said "I saw you through the window in the kitchen. That window faces the passage. you know' Mabel laughed. "But we did not do anything' 'I know,' Margie said.

"You were making a beginning. But I like the way the young man held your arms and the way he pleaded with his eyes. Please do not refuse him"

'Don't be silly.' Mabel scolded. 'By the way do you know that I met your Edie today?'

"Rubbish, said Margie" 'You say it's rubbish?' Then look at this, Mabel brough out the 'etter that she had received in the afternoon and handed it over to Margie.

Margie stared at the letter in wonder. "When did you get this, Mabel?' She asked, 'Aha! you believe me now?' Mabel asked. "You see I couldn't believe you before.

"I got it when I went to buy meat for mama' she said.

Margie, with shaking hands open the letter and read:

My Sweetest,

This is to tell you that I receieved your vital letter this morning. As my heart is now, I think I can go without food for a week and yet never care, as long as I know you are mine.

Please Margie, there is one thing I will beg you. Kindly tell me the day I will come and take you to my home.

You know that the hotel is always full of people and we will not be able to make true love and do that thing I told you about.

Tomorrow I shall come to the hotel and if your heart is as ture as mine, you shall follow me home.

I dream about you,
Your own,
Eaie Uzor.

"What have you read from your letter, Margie?' "He is inviting me to come tomorrow evening,' Margie replied.

There was a long silence. Mabel broke it at last 'And you shall go?' Mabel asked her.
'If I get one important thing, I will go,' she answered.

"What is it?' Mabel asked anxiously.
"Do you want me to tell you?' 'Please do.'

"Well it is something I shall use if I am going to let him do the thing he wants with me,' Margie said. "But what is that something?' Mabel asked.

'Bring wine before I tell you.'

"Do not tease me Margie, please tell me, I may need it one day, 'Mabel was pleading.

"Okay if you want to know it, I will tell you that it is medicine in tablets. Are you alright?" Margie asked. "But what is the name of the tablet?' Mabel asked.

That I must not tell you. If you want to have some, simply give me money tomorrow and I will buy for you. "How much is the cost?" Mabel asked. Margie told her.

Alright when you are going to buy tomorrow I will give you money, Mabel.

Dear reader you watch for yourself how the only daughter of Mrs. Helen for even the only child is drifting slowly to her ruin.

This is the child on whom great amount of money and care is lavished. The child that Mrs. Helen is expecting to marry one day and take the wealth of Ojina's family for the training of her children.

One may say that Margie was corrupting her but one thing is certain—she is predisposed for corruption. She had an unhealthy desire for sexual matters.

The first time she saw some people kissing, she tossed and tossed in her bed during the night.

Now she has decided to buy contraceptives to help her achieve her ends uninterruption.

But when they finished this conversation, Mabel had another thought which kept her awake for the greater part of the remaining night.

She thought of her Gilbert who had promised to come the following afternoon. She remembered how Gilbert had looked appealingly into her eyes. At once something stirred inside her. She felt some sweat gather around her body.

Again she began to toss in her bed. The time how ever she did not wake Margie. She just kept on wishing that morning had come and she would dress up well again in readiness for Gil. It was about three a. m. before she was quite enough and had some sleep. But some thing crazy happened by about five in the morning.

May be some devilish desire came into Margie's head. She slipped out of her bed and in groped her way to Mabel's own bed. By groping too she found out that Mabel was lying on her back with her belly upwards and with legs thrown carelessly apart.

You know what Margie did? Cool down and hear. She mounted on top of Mabel exactly in the normal position and began to push and push.

Remember that Mabel had gone to bed thinking of man and sex. So may be she thought it was in a dream and what she did was to throw her arms around Margie and hold her tight and push too. But after some minutes she felt that she couldn't be dreaming and more over she sensed that it was a woman's body that she was holding. She stopped pushing, but the body on top of her kept pushing and pushing.

She called in a low voice "Margie"
Margie framed a man's voice and said, "Sweet Mabel" But she could not deceive Mabel who shouted: "if you don't come down now, I will bite you to pieces.'

"Wait, wait" Margie said going on with her business. But Mabel, with force, reared on the bed and dumped Margie on the floor.

She sat up and began to giggle. "But why, Mabel, you were enjoying it at the beginning?" Margie said.

"Because I thought that it was just a dream" Mabel said, "But let me tell you the THING IS SWEETER than this, Margie said.
"It doesn't matter, but don't disturb my sleep any more, you hear?" Mabel warned and went back to sleep.

CHAPTER FOUR

The next morning Mabel woke up early and went to the bathroom.

This time it took her about ten minutes to take her. She used the soap for more than four times. Out in her room she changed the dress she had yesterday and put on another new one.

More care was even taken on her face she used two powders on it, then she used the eyebrow pencils. What she saw at the mirror pleased her greatly. When she appeared in the kitchen again at about nine her mother could not help commenting.

"Boh! Mabel. But e de change too much these days, Na you sabi—o,' her mother stopped.

"I wonder what you mean mamma!" she said. 'As you de change dress everyday it be like you know say somebody de watch you.

"Oh mamma stop that', Mabel said. But when Margie came in too she could not take her eyes off from her. When she caught Mabel's eyes. She simply smile, cleared her throat and went about her business.

The day was hot one. The sun came out very early and beat mercilessly on everything exposed to its rays. By about one o'clock evey place was warm and people were carrying beads of sweet on their foreheads

Business was not very heavy at the Pleasure Home. By two p. m. when nobody was watching Margie slipped of the hotel and went to the chemist and bought the tablets.

By about two thirty she was back. But Mabel had noticed that she went away and she asked her.

Where are you from Margie?

"I go tell you but no be now,' she replied. Mabel urged her on but she refused to tell her. She gave up for the time being. Customers began to mill in by about three o'clock. Mabel had eyes here and there for her Gil. But he did not appear.

By about four thirty when she was giving up all hopes of ever seing him she saw him in a blue suit walking majestically up the passage. Her heart missed a beat then another beat.

As he approached her in the passage she smiled. He smiled too. 'Good-evening, Mabel' he greeted. 'Good-evening Gil' she responded. Let me have some rice please, Gil said 'Again when you reach, give my greetings to your mamma' Mabel agreed and with a singing heart she went into the kitchen.

'Mamma one young man say make I greet you', Mabel told her mother.

'Hmm! who can that be?' Mrs. Helen asked. Mabel began to describe Gil: He is tall and strong looking He is wearing a blue suit. He will not be over twenty years. Her mother smelt a rat. She thought that might be the young man who was responsible for Mabel's constant changing of clothes.

'Go call that young man here, Mabel' her mother said: 'Okay mamma', she raced out to the dining-room. At the kitchen Mrs Helen hinted to Margie; 'Sometimes na this man wey de make Mabel change dress everyday'.

Margie laughed and said that she had one day seen Mabel standing with the young man at the passage.
Mrs Helen cleared her throat 'Bo-o so Mabel don begin de see me? E go hard - o.'

After some more seconds Mrs Helen saw Mabel coming back to the kitchen with the young man following behind. 'Good evening ma, Gilbert greeted cheerlly. Good even son', Mrs Helen replied, you be regular customer here I think.
'Yes ma,' Gilbert replied, My name is Gilbert Eric. We are from Oilu. But we are living at Moore Street.

178

I go to School at C. K. C. I shall finish this year."
All the time he introduced himself Mabel stood
gazing at him in admiration. A thousand things were
passing through her mind. Sometimes she saw herself being pressed 'against the wall as Margie was
once pressed. Again she saw her lips being kissed
for a long time.

But her mother interrupted Mabel's thinking.
'So you are from Orlu? We are from there too. How
long have you been in this town?' Mrs Helen asked
him.

'Oh! since I was ten years old.' Gil replied 'But
why do you take your lunch here everyday while
you are living with your parents?' Mrs Helen asked
Gil. He had not expected that question but he told
her the truth of it.

'You see, my parents are traders and my junior
sister has married. Nobody keeps lunch when I return
from School: so what I do is to come here,' he
explained. 'I see' Mrs Helen said 'how do you like
the place, Gilbert?'
Infact ma, everybody knows this place and they
praise your meals greatly. With me I do not think
my own mother cooks as good as you do. Everybody laughed at that.

'And this your daughter, ma, I think she is
doing very good service. She is always clean and
serves the customers quickly and correctly' Gil said.
Mrs Helen looked at her daughter. Mabel was
looking at the floor, blushing. Margie was smiling.
'Ma, make I go chop, Gilbert said, walking out
from the kitchen. 'Okay my son' she said 'Mabel
have you served his meals?'
'Yes mamma' Mabel answered going up to the
dining room with him also.
Mrs Helen watched them go in. Then she turned
to Margie: 'Don't you think that this is the man?'

"Aha! I saw him yesterday" replied Margie, 'he is the person'.

'Anyway I no go mind if he no spoil her. But the boy fine I no go lie,' said Mrs Helen.

'Na true mamma' Margie agreed.

It was getting to six o'clock. Margie's boy had not turned up

But he came by about seven p m. Margie saw him standing at the passage, waiting. She did not know what to do because there was too much work in the kitchen.

Then she saw Mabel coming from the dining room and greeted him. He greeted her and asked her some question. Margie saw Mabel pointing towards the kitchen. It was certain that Mabel was telling him where Margie was.

But with Mrs Helen there in the kitchen she did not know what to do.

After some seconds Mabel came down into the kitchen and asked to help Margie as there were no more customers to serve.

Margie understood and went out to take some air. Instead of staying in the open place she went into the dim passage where Edie had been waiting for her.

'What have you been doing since?' she asked him

'I wanted to come when nobody can see me,' he said. 'Lets go to my house,' he suggested, taking her hands.

'No! we are still working' Margie said.
'What do you mean. Simply let us slip away. You can make any excuse when you come back.

'No! no!' she refused Mrs Helen will fire me. 'Her daughter could tell her where I have been.' 'What shall we do now?' Edie asked her. 'You come back another day. Before then I will think of how to deceive Mrs Helen,' she replied. 'But when do you stop work here?' he asked her. Like today as we have few customers we will close by eleven.

'Usually we close by twelve when business is heavy'
'I shall come back by eleven thirty and we will go back to my home' he said.
"Oh no! we cannot Edie! I do not sleep alone. That girl shall see us go," she said.

'Look just leave that for me. Leave the door open I shall come and take you away with me and she will not know,' He said.

Margie could not say anything more. She simply stood there in silence. Then, without warning, Edie put his arms around her waist and pulled her to his body, He pressed her breast against his chest then he tilled up her head and kissed her lips strongly.
Margie flung her arms on his shoulders and held him close to her.

Their lips were together for about four minutes. Then Margie short him gently and freed herself. 'Go home now,' for..........she urged him.

"Okay honey but now," remember I must be here by eleven thirty he said.
Margie said nothing. She watched Edie walking down the passage and disappear in the street. She turned too and walked back to the kitchen. "You don waste plenty time, Margie' said Mrs Helen.
'I been de watch see if any customer go come,' she lied.

Mrs Helen took her for her word, But Mabel who knew what was going on stared at Magie who stared back at her also.

The hotel closed ealier that day by 10 p. m. This was because their ready supply ran down.

When they came into their rooms Margie asked Mabel what had gone between her and the young man from the college.

"The boy likes me plenty,' Mabel said He took me by the waist and pulled me to his body. I put my arms on his shoulder and begged him not to do rough. I know he didn't hear me at all. He pressed me tight on his body Then he kissed my neck, then my breast. It touched me greatly. I was flaming inside, I held his neck tight. He kissed my lips strongly and for a long time" she stopped, she had began to toss again in her bed.

Margie laughed heartily and stared at her. Then she asked. 'If he asks you to givam the thing, I think you go givam?'

'Infact I don't know what I will do. He is so sweet and beautiful' Mabel answered.

'Look e never answer my question, I ask if he wan take the thing from you, you go givam or not?' Margie asked her again.

Don't ask me again. E never ask for the thing. When e ask for-am, I go know wetin go happen, Mabel said. 'Do you know say I don get that medicine?' Margie asked.

You need to have seen how Mabel jumped out of her bed and rushed to Margie. She put her arms round Margie's waist and pleaded 'I beg show me how it looks like. Please show me I beg you' Mabel said.

"Ah! ah! Na wetin? So you like the thing so?' Margie teased.

'Please show me now. You know I go need the thing shortly' said Mabel.

'Okay, wait for a minute' Mabel was told. Margie reached under her pillow and brought out two tubes of tablets. Mabel had eyes for nothing but the tubes. She glared and glared.

'How do you use it?' Mabel asked.
'Now watch me,' said Margie, 'I may be needing

one today and I am going to use it now. Watch me. So saying Margie started to apply the tablet while Mabel glared at her, gasping now and then.

"You see?" Margie asked when she has finished with the application.

Mabel nodded and gasped.

'For two hours from now' Margie said 'I am entirely free from pregnancy, I can even be taking the thing twenty times."

Mabel stared at her instructors. "But how do you know that you shall need this thing within this for two hours?"

"Just watch and see" Margie said.

It was almost eleven fifteen then. They were silent for some munites. Then there was an inaudible tap at the door. Mabel glared at Margie. She put her finger to her lips motioning Mabel to lie down and pretend to be fast asleep

With a thumping heart Mabel obeyed. Margie tiptoed to the door and there, for sure, was Edie dressed in grey Agbada.

"Let's go quick' he said trying to take her hand. "No, we shall wait for some minutes. The people have not slept properly yet" Margie said.

"What shall we do now?' asked Edie.

"Come in here and wait for some minutes' Margie suggested. "Okay' said Edie. He had an idea too. To go in there and force her to give him.

So they went into Mabel's room, where Margie had her bed by the corner. Edie locked the door. They sat down on Mabel's room. The light was still on.

Edie carried Margie and placed her on his laps. He kissed her breast. Then he put his hand into her frock, it was very warm. He started to unbotton her dress,

She held his hand and pointed at the other bed. "Oh! don't worry sh's sleeping," he whispered.

Margie who was far sleep heard the whisper and knew that they were talking about her. She lay still there but her heart beat and beat.

Edie continued to work on Margie's dress. He had opened all the buttons which reached the hem of the dress. Margie was making some inffectual struggles.

Then he draged off his own dress and tore away the baggy trousers. He was boiling inside him like water on a great hot stove.

Margie glared at him. But he had no eyes any more. He flattened her on the bed.

"Please Edie" she began to mumble, "don't hurt me! don't hurt me please" Then she changed her request, "hurt me! hurt‗ ‗‗‗‗"

Mabel's legs were trembling, her head was spining round and round. She was having the greastest difficulty in controlling herself. Beads of sweet were dropping from her forehead.

At times she wished could turn round and look but it was impossible.

In about ten minutes they were okay and Edie picked up his trouser and put it on.

"We shall still go home, Margie" he whispered. "What do you mean?"

"I mean I still long for you." Edie said, "No please," Margie said, "till next time." Look take this, Edie gave her ten shillings note. She took it and said nothing.

Edie put his arms around her waist and pulled her towards the door. She was a beat yielding. They tip toed out of the room. Magie switched off the light and carefully closed the door.

When they left Mabel jumped out of her bed and switched on the light and stood gazing at Margie's bed.

184

"So here was where she had been enjoying herself" Mabel thought to herself. She wished ten times that she was Margie.

She reeled and gasped and coughed. It was the greatest emotional stres she had ever suffered in her lift.

She went back and slumped down on her bed. But there was no sleep to come. She thought about Gilbert. But that inflamed her desire the more.

She tossed and mumbled under her breath. At one time she bit her pillow with her teeth and tore away some part of it. Poor girl, her insides were running riot.

She managed to close her eyes by about two a. m to have some sleep. But the sleep was packed full with evil dreams. At one time she dreamt of Gil come up to her and pressing her against the wall of dining-room and there pressing her lips to his own and sucking and sucking while something kept burning hot inside her.

It was terrific, the agony a girl could suffer. But Mabel's own was very great. Because why? She helped to agument her passion and worst of all she had an experienced girl who feeds her emotional life more than required.

Sometimes that night she lay on her belly and pushed and pushed.
"Tomorrow," she said, 'I must make that my Gil do the thing with me.

By about five thirty Margie opened the door gently and slipped in. Mabel was lying on her belly, her cloth throw away. She had only a short blouse on, no pant, nothing and she was snoring.

The mischievious Margie went over and with her palm began to rub the sleeping girl's waist and hips. Mabel stirred uneasily but responded to romantic touch.

Some second later she jumped up from her bed and glared at Margie who sat there giggle

"Have you come again, Margie" she asked. ,I sorry," Margie said but you see when I saw you lying naked like that I wished I were a man to come and............. — .... — ....

"Shut up Margie," Mabel said, "when did you come back from your Edie?"

I am just returning What? You have been there since eleven thirty? Mabel stared a her,

O! yes. It was so sweet that we could not stop, Margie said.

Mabel glared at her; Margie you are spoilt,

And you are spoiling, Margie retorted. Go to your own bed I want to sleep, Mabel said.

No, I shall sleep with you till morning Margie said lying down by Mabel's side. Mabel tried to go out but Margie caught her and pinned her down. Then unexpectedly she took Mabel's head and pressed her own lips on hers. It was abnormal but somehow Mabel liked the taste of it and so she clung to her and responded to the kiss.

They clung and kissed and sucked and rubbed. To Mabel it was terrific. She threw her legs on Margie and ruffled her hair and twisted. They clung so for minutes and minutes.

The two girls left the bed by about seven o'clock and began to dress up for the day,

Mabel again refused to put on a working dress. She put on another new dress and took much time again working on her dress and face.

When she appeared this time her mother just

looked her up and down and smiled. No comment. But deep down in her heart Mrs. Helen had a great fear of something deadly approaching.

The early hours were not crowded. A customer walked in now and then, ate his meal silently paid and walk away. But nearly everybody who came in would stare at the juicy Mabel.

One cheerful man who came in by eleven a.m. smacked Mabel on the buttocks and exclaimed; "Hah! If them give me this one I no go ask for food any more', Mabel glared at the man who must not be less than thirty years. He had a squarish face but his arms were full of muscles. He was dark black but his skin was shining and clean as if it had been polished.

"Please, don't do that," Mabel said seriously ' Okay juice, the man replied, "but you are so much like honey that a man with a healthy appetite cannot help but try to dig his finger into it and lick and lick.

Mabel simply stared at him while he poured out his mind. There was no other customer in the dining room. The man felt he could take another lick from the honey. So he said: "Come here baby. Mabel stood by the door and asked, "What do you need?" "Just come over, I will wishper it in your ear' he said, his temperature was surely rising.

Mabel walked nearer to the man. "Tell me your need," she said.

The man reached out and took her hand. She allowed him "Look, sweet sugar, I am mad with your beauty." "And what shall follow? Mabel asked.

"You shall allow me simply to kiss your neck and no more" he said.

"Nonsense" Mabel scorned, why my neck and no other place?" Look, baby," he pleaded "there is a certain sexual honey about your own neck. The thing is so smooth and shining. I can not see it from here

187

"Please stop talking like that. Leave me," Mabel said, but deep down in her heart and some where again in her insides something was sizzling and heating up

The man gave her no time to think but caught her by the waist and placed her on his laps. She made some sincere struggle but the man had iron muscles. She hit his head but he seemed to enjoy it the more.

With one hand he turned her head one side and pressed his lips on her neck just below the left chin. Some how the thing was very sweet and Mabel gave up her struggle and closed her eyes.

The man sucked and sucked. Mabel was lost Then some one cleared her throat at the door of the dining-room. They started Mabel struggled to free from the muscle man and jumped up.

Margaret was standing at the door. She glared from Mabel to the man and from the man back to Mabel. Mabel glared back at her.

"Anything wrong, Margie?" Mabel was bold to ask.

"But you know that this is not the time and place for this. Anyway mamma wants to see you" she left the door.

The man appeared very silly "I am sorry baby, but never mind. Nobody fit beat you" he soothed.

That word put some beans into her. Nobody can beat her, for sure.

"Goodbye customer," she said and went out to the kitchen.

CHAPTER FIVE

Much to her comfort her mother was not calling her because of the incident.

But Margie kept on eyeing her. But she never bothered. After all Margie had spent a whole night taking the thing from Edie.

"You go help Margie, because I wan go to Aba now and if I no return today I go return tomorrow. We are expecting to buy a taxi from there" her mother said.

"What a taxi?" Mabel asked her mother. Mrs. Helen was very enterprising. She wanted to use some part of her savings to purchase a taxi. The taxi would be serving dual puppose. It would be making money yet it would be used for travelling.

"Yes, Maybe" her mother said, "It shall prove very useful you know. We have need of a vehicle and the best thing will be to buy a taxi which shall make some money while it helps us too".

"Okay mamma," said Mabel "It is only that I never knew you had so much money to buy a car."

They laughed over that. But there was one thing that Mabel was extremely happy about. It was her mother's going away. That meant that when Gil came they could do anything without fear of being caught.

Mrs. Helen left the Pleasure Home, by one p.m. and went to Aba. It was plain to see that she would not come back that very day.

Mabel had never been so plesased before in her life. She had full liberty for almost two days. And one thing more, she had some medicine to use.

WE SHALL SEE WHAT HAPPENED TO OUR MABEL

The day was Friday, somehow unexpectedly, business was very heavy that day. People came in great numbers. But Mabel never missed the stare of every man that came in.

She was just fourteen and half years. But she was real sweet honey. The mere looking at her would hold up the flow of your blood for sixty seconds. Mabel had became aware of her power over men.

189

And when ever somebody looked steadily at her she would blink and make such soft eyes that your temperature would speed up to hundred degrees farehiet.

It was disastrous. But Mabel enjoyed it Sometimes when one thought of it one would turn around to pity Mabel insteed of condemn, seeing that she had not her full time to live.

But to our story, Mabel kept on looking out when her Gil would come in. She was serving the customers with her hands only. Her heart was miles away from 'Pleasure Home' and the customers

In her anxiety she broke two tumblers that after pouring water on some of the customers but she was full of apologies.

"I am sorry please," she said rubbing off the water on the laps of one of the men. But the touch of the young virgin was even enough without her modulated voice, to work him up terribly. Impulsively he seized the girl who was cleaning him and kissed her cheeks. She glared at him.

He looked at her and said: "I am sorry too, please" It was very amusing and the customers began to laugh. Mabel ran out of the room. Just at the door she jumped into who? Her Gil. He took her by the waist and pulled her to him. For a second she was turned. Then she recognised who was holding her. Then she put one arm on his neck and gazed into his eyes.

"Come and sit down here," Mabel led the way to her own room.

"Sit on this one" she pointed to her own bed, "Where's mamma? Gil asked her.

"She's not at home" "Where has she gone?" he asked.

"To Aba" Mabel told him. You need to have seen how Gil's face brightened at the information. Mabel just smiled.

"So it means you are the boss here today,"

he asked her.

"I don't know" she said.

"Is your mother returning today? he asked.

"She will be back either tomorrow or Monday. But why do you ask?"

Gil answered that in a different way. He took her by the middle and lay her on the bed, face up. Mabel was smiling in silence. Clothes on, he climbed on top and astride of her and levelled his whole body on her own. She murmured some inaudible words which did not disturb Gil in anyway

He put his lips squarely on neck just below the chin and sucked avaricously. That was not enough. He opened two buttons on her blous exposing her conical breasts. He placed his lips just at the tip of the thing and began to suck her. Infact the girl began to quiver all her body began to dance frantically. She threw her arms on his neck and held him down to her tight. At the same time their waists were making marvellous gestures.

After that he raised his lips to her own lips and kissed her so strong that she screamed without knowing. Yet her arms had gone round Gil's waist holding him down to her trembling body. Her legs were kicking wildly with excitement.

It was terrific. Mabel forget her entire self. She gave up her entire self. Her eyes were closed. She was breathing fast. And Gil? I wish my brains were good enough to allow me give you a full and fitting description of his wildness. His entire frame was dancing like jelly-fish; to see his eyes, you would swear that he had been drinking alchoholics for the past four hours.

Margie had been wondernning where Mabel had been for the past thirty minutes. Fortunately no fresh customer had come yet she wondered what could beholding the girl.

She left the kitchen and went into the dining-room to know what Mabel had been doing. There was no Mabel in the dining-room.

Margie began to suspect that Gil must have come. So she raced her room. She tired the door. It was looked inside.

She knocked. No response. She knocked again No answer.

She called, 'Mabel!' Nobody answered.

Meanwhile Gil had taken away Mabel's dress from her but the girl refused to pull her pant. She was desiring the thing even more than Gil but remember that she was a pure virginphysically and however she tired she could not bear to be naked in that broad daylight.

Gil had already stripped himself to the pant. He had been pleading with Mabel to remove her pant since the past three minutes but she could not do it even though she was sizzling inside with desire.

It was when he lifted the girl to his laps to tear away the pant that Margie began to knock on the door.

They two jumped up and out of the bed. Mabel put her hands to her lips motioning Gil to make no noise. At the sametime they began to dress up in fasted style imaginable.

When Mabel finished dressing purposely sat down on the bed in order to do two things. First to regain the control of her voice and her breath and second to tease Margie a little longer.

Margie continued to knock and call from the other side.

At last Mabel rose up and went to the door.

Gil was still sitting on the edge of the bed.

"What is on your mind, Margie? Mabel asked her without opening the door.

Margie stopped knocking but said nothing. She could hardly contain herself with anger.

"Please go back to your work I am busy now. I will come out later on" Mabel said.

"What the hell are you doing there?' Margie barked. "It is best known to me. Go to your work, I am coming" "Okay" Margie said, "but open the door I wan take something."

"No please I can't" Mabel said. Gilbert was now feeling like a trapped rabbit. Looking very silly and foolish.

"Ma-bel what do you say that you are donig?" Margie asked.

"I won't tell you. Simply mind your business. I will come out when you go away to the kitchen. Mabel answered.

Margie knew that a man must be inside there with Mabel. Somehow the thought stirred something in her. She walked away from the door and went back to the kitchen.

Mabel who had heard her footsteps as she walked away, opened the door slightly and watched her as she walked heavily down the passage and out the yard into the kitchen.

Then Mabel turned to Gil and motioned him to come out of the room.

He stood up with a question on his lips. Mabel cut him short.

"Please don't delay. Let it be another time" "Okay I shall come when you finish work today," he said, his insides still burning with desire He walked out of the room feeling very sour and unsatisfied.

When Mabel went down to the kitchen there

193

was hell to do with Margie.

"You are spoilt too. Ma-bel, she warned. "You have spoiling already. Mabel reported. They glared at each other for about two munites "Just tell me Mabel, who be that lucky man wey break that your thing for you this afternoon?" Margie asked.

"You fool, Margie, Mabel said. "Na you been disturb him from breaking the thing."

'So the thing still de pepper you?' Margie asked,

'But why did you come there to disturb?' Mabel asked, "Who tell you say na for afternoon them de doam?" Margie asked.

Mabel stared at her 'You forget say I no disturb you last night when you been stay here with your Edie. You no know say I been suffer that night when you de take the thing?" Mabel was serious.

Their querrel was interrupted by the call of a customer from the dining room.

Mabel ran out to answer the call.

A short time later a little girl of about seven years came into the hotel. She saw Mabel at the passage.

"Please miss" the girl began, "who be Mabel for this hotel?" Mabel laughed "You are talking to her" she told the little girl. The child laughed. Then she brought out a blue envelope from her side pocket and held it out for Mabel who took it from her and saw that it had not come from the post, who givan to you?' She asked the little girl.

"Na my brother' the child said. "Thank you' said Mabel. E say make you readam now and give me another letter wey I go bring foram. The little girl said Mabel knew that it must surely be from Gilbert, who had been greatly disappointed that afternoon.

Mabel laughed. "Okay, come wait for me here,' She took the little girl into her bed room and sat her down on one of the two beds.

194

Then she ran back to the kitchen to read the letter in Margie's presence.

"What have you?" Margie asked when she saw the letter.

"Something from my honey" she replied boastfully 'Look how e dey talk am as if I no get honey,' Margie jeered 'I beg read am quick and tell me.

Mabel was already working on the envelope. She opened it and took out the letter. The first thing that cought her eyes was the picture of a heart pierced with arrow.

MY SWEET
HONEY,

No tongue can speak

What I have suffered this afternoon.
Despite the fact that we were disturbed, the way you delayed and teased me, while I suffered and burned like a flame inside me, it was so painful. Oh! I don't think I can forgive you.

Look I promise you everything you can choose to ask of me. Even I will give you my life willingly, provided you first let me before I die. What are you afraid of? I have sworn that you won't have any trouble.

Please my honey, I am coming down there by seven this evening and as your mother is away we can go out and see a picture or to another hotel or even walk about and back.

Please reply this letter through the bearer.
I am longing terribly for you.

GILBERT.

Mabel did not know whether to laugh or cry She herself desired the boy terribly but it was hard to show it.

She gave the letter to Margie who read it
hungrily and then gave out a mischievous cough.

Mabel looked at her. "What do you think of it?"
'So the boy no take the thing from you?' Margie
asked. 'Na you cousam' Mabel said, feeling quite
sad.

'Well e no bad plenty. Mamma no de for house.
You fit go him house sleep till morning; nobody go
bother you' Margie said sincerely.

'Bo make we dey look now.' She took the letter
and went back to reply it.

She wrote also on a blue envelope. She drew a
heart which this time was pierced with two swords.

My Sugar,

You think you are suffering more than I do.
But you are wrong The thing is this: my heart is
strong for you but my body is weak.

I love you three times more than you love me.
But there is one thing wrong. I do not know how we
shall do that thing. You know it will be my first
time and that is why I don't know how to start.

That afternoon I wanted it more than you but
I was very much afraid.

Don't blame me for what you say you suffered

for I was not free from agony.

I wait for you.
Your Sweet Honey,
Mabel.

She folded the letter and put it into the blue envelope and address the letter to Gil. Then she handed it to the little girl.

CHAPTER SIX

Nine p. m. Friday night. Mabel and Margie decided to close the Hotel.

Gil had called by something past seven and was told to repeat by nine. Nine fifteen he was back with two tickets of the Broadway Cinema.

Mabel was waiting at the door when he came in. She was already dressed up to kill. A look at her sent Gil's blood runnig this way and that inside his body.

"Oh! baby, you are sweeter than honey this evening," Gil said.

She smiled and leered at him. 'Come let's look for a taxi' he said laking her hand. She followed him.

They entered a taxi and drove to Broadway. In the taxi Gil put his palm on Mabel's lap and rubbed and rubbed. Mabel stared and looked at him.

'I nearly die in the afternoon,' he told her. 'What of me?' Mabel reported. 'It didn't affeot you as it did me,' he said and tried to put his hand into her blouse. She recoiled and held back his searching fingers.

The taxi slowed to a stop at the Cinema. The

romance was interrupted.

Gil came out and held the door for her to follow. Then he paid the cabman. They linked hands and walked into the building. They never cared was who looking at them.

The picture was a good one called ROCK PRETTY BABY: It was a musical sensation. They enjoyed it greatly. But they were more absorbed in themselves. For the whole time. Gil's left arm was round Mabel's waist with his fingers making funny gestures about her waist.

Mabel had shoulder and head resting on Gil. The warmth that passed from one body to the other was causing havoc. Gil was at boiling point for the whole period. What Mabel felt inside would rather be imagined by the reader that explained by the writer.

By eleven fifteen the film ended. Gil again faced another problem. That of persuading Mabel to follow him to his own house.

"But your sister is living with you" Mabel reminded him. 'Yes but she dosen't sleep in my room,' said Gil. Mabel did not know another excuse to make. She stood there outside the Cinema building. Gil stood in front of her, waiting for her to decide.

"But Gil———" she stopped. However that was enough for Gilbert, who was an eperienced young man with women.

'Okay, I understand my sugar' he said and took her hand. They entered another taxi.

"No———, Moore Street," Gil called the number of his own home. Mabel looked at him. He did not see her. The car moved.

The inside of the car was dark and Gil found

it a very favourable condition. He carried Mabe and put her head on his laps. Then he bent down and pressed his lips on her own and sucked her passionately.

The highly aroused girl entivined her arms on his neck sucking his lips too At the same time Gil had his fingers in her hair ruffling the thing passionately. When they stopped at Gil's door there was a hell of trouble persuading Mabel to enter the room. Gil pleaded and pleaded and pleaded and pleaded. Mabel could have been deaf. She didn't seem to have heard Gil at all

The boy was tired of begging. But he also knew he was standing with a complete virgin. That made him resolve to take her in, even if he had to die after.

So he simply lifted the girl to his shoulder and with one hand fished for his key in his trouser pocket. He did'nt even know that the girl was tearing away the hair on his head. He even never knew that his shirt had been torn. Mabel beat and beat. But Gil's body had turned to steel.

Gil found his key and opened his door. The girl then fought as she had never fought before. But Gil had a wild passion, a flaming desire that rendered him strong and blind and cruel.

Stiffly he carried his meat into his room and then put her down, locking the door immediately. Mabel's eyes now were red with fear which some time changed to desire and then back again to fear. She glared at her boy-friend as if she had never seen him before.

Gil came closer to her but did not touch her. He knew he could have to be tactful. It is no simple matter to BREAK a virgin. You are a lucky man if you have a virgin to break but you must taste pepper in doing it. The first pepper you taste is that of making your virgin yield and that was where Gilbert was then.

"But are you not going to marry me any more, Mabel?" he asked her. At those words the blood left her eyes a little but she asked. "When have you ever asked me to marry you?" Gil saw that he was succeeding.

"Well my honey, I thought you would understand." he said. He took her hand, she was still. He threw in another bomb to explode away her fears and leave bare her desire.

"Look, my sweetest, if you are going to marry me in a month or two now, it is not bad for you to give it to me now, I love you and I long very much for you,' he stopped and drew her close to him; she was yielding.

"Wait, Gil,' she said, stiffening, are you going to marry me truly?'

"Good heavens, Look honey, if you don't marry me yourself, I think I will like to stop living', he said. Mabel smiled and placed her head on his chest.

Hell was burning inside Gilbert now. In a second he dragged off his shirt and in another his trousers and shoes were send flying about the soom. Mabel stared at him from where she stood in the centre of the room.

He knew she would not take away her dress by herself, so he came to her and started working on it. Mabel continued to beat away his hand. But that did not disturb him in the least. In about twenty seconds he had stripped the girl to her pant.

There again she used some real force to prevent him but he put more force himself and dragged that off too. She quivered and trembled.

But he carried her fighting, into his bed, and

there too he had more trouble. There real trouble in breaking a virgin.

Look dear reader, for the sake of my mother and father who may come across this book, I am ashamed to tell you the rest of how Gil overcame the second part of this trouble. Imagine it for yourself. But I must tell you this, he did overcome it, but his body was covered with sweat and he was breathing as if he had done cross—country run. But Mabel too, how she scremed at one point!

Mabel stayed at Gil's room for the whole night.

It was such a night better experienced than heart. They agree to tell Mrs. Helen when she returned of their intention to be married. Before six a. m. Gil escorted her back to 'Pleasure Home.'

"When shall I see you again?' asked Mabel. 'So you will like to see me again upon all the beatings you gave me last night? Gilbert asked her. She reered at him romantically. 'Answer my question dear.' She said. Okay my baby, when would you like to see me again?

"Come in the evening today, she said, Alright you see me by four thirty, said Gilbert. Then he kissed her cheek and went home. Mabel walked through the passage to her room. Margie was still sleeping. She did not wake her but just jumped into her bed and started sleeping when it was well over six in the morning.

'Oga! they tell me that women do not ever forget their first men. Look, there's no lie in that. But saying it that way is just a mild way of putting the obvious fact into light.

Mabel had made a beginning. She has had her first man. But she did not stop nor did she go a slow pace. The thing could not have been sweeter. She was thoroughly mad and for the first week. I think she did betray Gilbert a great deal. Whenever she saw him around she made such glad eyes at him that even a fool could tell w' at was between them.

But coming back to Saturday morning—Mabel was in bed till nine thirty, sleeping and sleeping. For one time in her life Margie acted reasonably. She understood and allowed her to rest.

The first thing that escaped her mouth when she woke was 'Gil,' Margie was in the room then and she laughed and laughed!

"Oga!" Margie began "this,' please no be him place—o!' Then Mabel rose up from the bed and stared at Margie. In about three minutes she realised that she was turly at her mother's hotel. But what surprised her more was that the time was more than seven a. m.

"How be the thing?' Margie asked her. "No ask me—o,' she replied, "at one time I nearly die, I tell you.

Margie laughed again, and laughed. By about ten a. m. Mabel was ready for work. She put on again a quite different dress from the ones she had been using before. The blouse was pink blue, but the skirt was pink with flowers of various colours.

She was again overcareful about her face. She rubbed and rubbed, then penciled the brows and lashes after that she tied a broad belt in the middle. The shoes were also fitting.

Ask me why does she lavish so much care on her person. You know the answer under the eyes of young and admiring men. But this time she had a particular man in view—her Gilbert.

Inspite of the fact that Gil. had told her that he would come by four—thirty she yet was looking.

out for him from twelve noon.

Business was too heavy that day for it was Saturday. Some people had come in from other towns and villages to Onitsha and were crowding the hotels.

Some very hungry customers wou'd take their plates and rush down to the kitchen to be served quickly. Others were patient to wait till Mabel had brought their food to the table. But mar, the girl can serve. She was quick and careful and accurate. She knew who had called for yam with meat stew yam with fried oil only, rice with yam and meat stew, yam or 'Garri' and stew with some fresh fish. She served and smiled. Many customers would leave the hotel well feed and satisfied.

But the young men only quenched one hunger to get another one immediately, the hunger and unquenched desire for Mabel.

By about one p. m. the hotel became less crowded for the next two hours. Mabel went to sit with Margie in the kitchen.

"Young lady you have not told me how you went through the thing last night,' Margie asked her. Mabel told her as much as she could. It was interesting. After that Margie laughed and said: So you don become a full woman now? Hah you don chop—o. Wetin go give that man wey show you how the thing be first?"

"My heart and my whole being,' Mabel answered. Margie smiled. "But that go be for some weeks, I tell you.' "Why,?' Because no be him alone de hungry for you. Margie said. Mabel stared at her.

"How do you know?' she asked. "You go see now' Margie said.

Their conversation was interrupted by the call of a customer. Mabel rushed in to attend.

Whom did she see? No other than the ebony black man who had kissed her neck some two days ago. For some seconds they looked at each other in silence. Then the man spoke.

'But baby you de grow sweeter everyday,' he said. Mabel smiled. "Tell me what you will eat she asked him. "You wan make I tell you wetin de hungry me?"

"Do' Mabel urged.

"Na only one thing,' he said.

"Wetin be that?'

"You alone,' he said. Mabel stared at him. The man made glad eyes at her, she smiled,

'But you chop some food first,' Mabel said. "Okav, bring me rice and plenty meat,' he ordered. Mabel went to the kitchen and brought the food: As she placed the plates before the man, he gripped her by the middle and sat her on his laps. Then she titled her face and kissed her on the lips. She kicked and kicked but the man sucked and sucked. Then she cooled down a little and kissed the muscle—man's back. When the man puts his hand into her skirt, she jumped like a wounded lion and ran out from the room. The man who had been worked up, simply there, his breath coming fast.

After some minutes he cooled down enough to bend on his meal. He was eating but his mind was drench in thought about how to get Mabel. He had an idea. He ate quickly and when he finished, he called Mabel, she appeared at the door but did not go in.

The man, who had paid for the food since, put his hand in his pocket and brought out a bundle of pound notes. From that he detched out two pounds and held it out to Mabel. She could not believe her eyes.

"Take it,' the man urged. She shook her head but inside she was full of 'Yes.' The man persuaded her to take the money. She came forward and took the two pounds Then she looked at the man.

"Let's go to your room.' he suggested. For some seconds she was baffled and at a loss what to do.

Then her hand was seized by the man. He drew her out of the room and they started walking up the passage- 'Which is it?' the burning man asked her. She pointed at the door of her bed room.

The man pushed open the door and forced her in. Then he bolted it from the inside. He looked at Mabel. He looked at the oily skin and at her lips. She was pure honey.

He took her by the waist and pulled her to his body. She was shaking. He put his hands into her blouse, it was quite warm and good: Then he opened the buttons. And pressed his lips on the point of her chest. Her legs were making left right, left right on the ground. The man carried her to bed and loosed her belt. He took away his own shorts in a flash.

Mabel was drembling. The man tilted her head and pressed his lips against her own. For many minutes they kissed and kissed. Then they changed from kissing to the real thing.

Mabel's eyes were closed for almost for the time at last she slipped from under the man after about thirty minutes.

The she dressed up quickly and ran out to the

kitchen. There she flung the two pounds at Margie who stared at her. 'I got it now,' she said proudly "who gave you?' Margie asked. 'He's gone!

"Hah' I been tell you before. You fine and plenty men go de hungry for you, Margie said. That was it, Mabel realised that she was beautiful and that the men were full of desire for her. That realisation was the begining of her ruin. She began to but on the best of her dresses and began to choose costly cosmetic.

CHAPTER SEVEN

Our sweet honey by now was engaged to Gilbert when Mrs Helen returned from Aba her duaghter told her of the engagement. "Hmm! But do you know that you are barely sixteen years?' Mrs. Helen asked her.

But I am big enough to marry, said Mabel. Her mother looked at her, surprised, it was not the sort of reply she expected from Mabel.

When did you know about your business? Since last year, Mabel answered boldly. Are you still a virgin! Mabel? her mother asked. I was last year, she answered. So you are not today? asked Mrs. Helen No I am too old for that, she answered. Mrs. Helen had not been suspecting her daughter, But it was not much of a shock for her to learn that Mabel was broken. After all there have been too many men coming up and down. And Gil., the way Mabel looks at him can tell anybody.

"Okay, Mabel, till your young man comes around," her mother told her. That evening Mabel

went to Gilbert and asked him to go and announce
their engement to her mother·

By seven thirty Gil dressed up in his blue wool-
suit and went to pleasure Home. He walked right
in to the kitchen where Mrs Helen was. Margie was
there too but Mabel was not.

'Good evening ma', he greeted. Mrs Helen
responded then they conversed on 'trival matters for
somewhile. Mrs Helen asked of his work at the
Allied Brothers Company. He told her that all were
well. You know that Gil had finished with the
Secondary since the past two years and was working
in one rich Trading Company—The Allied Brothers.

'Ma, please I go like to talk to you', Gil said
after some minutes of silence. 'You wan talk here
or for any room?' Mrs Helen asked him.
'I think we better go for your room' he answered.
'Okay' she replied 'I beg Margie make you and
Mabel deserve the customers, I de come', she walked
to her room with Gilbert covering her steps behind.

At the passage he caught sight of Mabel who
was serving the customers in the dining - room.
They exchanged broad smiles. Inside Mrs. Helen's
room Gil began his talk: 'Ma, you know well that
me and Mabel be strong friend. Every time when I
de come e no be for chop I de come. But to see
Mabel and talk to am. True for God I like the girl
plenty. And I know she likes me too.

Na him make I come ask you make you gree
me marry-am, he stpoed. Mrs. Helen cleared throat
then she began, 'Bo Gil I no go lie. I been de
see you and that my daughter talk and talk plenty
time and I been wonder wetin result go be
Plenty time on Sundays I no de see Mabel for

207

house and them de tell me say e come for your place. To ta'k, I for say Mabel na small pikin. But e de worry me every time, say him go marry you. So my son, if you too gree say una go marry, na you sabi.'

Thank you, ma-a thank you plenty. Tomorrow or so I go bring my parents make una settle for money' Gil was very happy. So he went home after seeing Mabel and telling her that every thing was working well.

Three days later on Wednesday Mr. and Mrs. Eric with their son Gilbert came to 'Pleasure Home' to see Mrs. Helen. The two lovers were present also. In the presence of their parents they agreed to marry each other.

Native kola nuts were brought and according to tradition they were broken and served round. Some native wines were also served. After observing these customs, the bride price was settled and without moving an inch, Mr. Eric put his hands in his pocket and from a great bundle of pound notes he counted out the hundred pounds. What remained in the bundle still was apparently more than a hundred pounds.

Gilbert was smiling. Mabel was blushing. Mrs. Helen's face shoed blank. It was arranged that the wedding would take place on the following Saturday.

All necessaries were bought for the wedding day. Bridal gown was bought, invitation was sent out to a handful of guests. It was not intended that the wedding should be very public.

On saturday Gilbert dressed in a black suit, with an immaculate white shirt inside and a tie to match, drove to the Central Church. Some minutes later Mabel arrived accompanied by her parents and the brother of her mother who was to take her away. By about ten a. m. the ceremonies were ended. And Gil took his wife into his own car and they drove to No _ Moore Street. Mabel was so happy.

BUT WHO EVER SUSPECTED HOW SHORT THE MARRIAGE WOULD LAST

Gil was a very considerable husband, always trying to understand. Mabel? she had the brain of a hare. That Saturday night there was fiery romance. Mabel and Gil first went to 'Pleasure Home' where they look for their supper.

They conversed for long with Mrs. Helen and Margie. Margie was very sad and did not hide it. She told Mabel how she miss her. At one stage of their talk there were real tears in Margie's eyes.

Mabel tried to console her as far as possible, By about nine thirty the young couple left the hotel. Remember that Gil was only twenty two and Mabel was just over sixteen.

At Gil's home people were playing and dancing for the wedding. But they had started to disperse by about ten p. m, By ten thirty the place was quiet and normal. Gil took Mabel's hand and drew her into his room. He locked the door behind them. He put his arms round her and whispered: 'Hello! Mrs Gil Eric. She looked at him and smiled: then she called him Hello! Mr Eric. Then he put his right hand into her blouse and opened it. He kissed the point of her breast and sucked and sucked and sucked. Mabel put her arms to his neck and dipped her fingers into his hair.

Then he opened all the buttons of her dress and took it out. Mabel quivered_She had only her pant on. Gil lifted her up and carried her on his arms to his bed. There he put her to his laps and turned her to face him· He tilted her head and put his lips on her neck and pressed it hard· Then he kissed her forehead then her eyes and then came down to her mouth. He pressed his lips on her own and sucked to madness.

Mabel was holding him tight and close. She was scratching his back passionately and tossing and tossing. When Gil was full of fire he tore away his own clothes like lightening and level the girl, face up, on his bed went on her and _ ....

CHAPTER EIGHT

Day after day there was romance full of fire Mabel had learnt how to raise a man's temperature. She practised her learning on Gil who was running mad at every point of the affair. But the romance did no last long on Mabel's side. After the first month the insatiable taste for man in her was beginning to show,

One morning she tried a ruse she had been thinking of long since, 'Gilbert" she called. "Ye baby Gil replied 'I have been thinking, you know,' she said. Gilbert whose love was genuine asked 'what's in your mind, baby?' he asked coming up to her. 'I have been thinking of my mother for a long time now,' she said, looking very sad. 'You want to see her honey?' he asked her. 'Yes I want to go and stay with her for some weeks,' 'Okay baby if you are ready I can take you over even now' he said, She was singing with joy inside her. She had tricked her husband. But little did she know that she had to pay for it in a bad way. They packed some clothes in a box and left in a taxi for 'Pleasure Home'.

Mrs. Helen welcome them so warmly. When Margie learnt that Mabel would stay for some days she was so happy and clapped Mabel to her body. They laughed and talked. Gil stayed for some minutes and then left to be about his business. This was the beginning of the END. Mabel came home not just to see her mother. She wanted her liberty. Liberty to live and enjoy herself to the full. She wanted a change of man. But we shall see what followed.

Mabel took up her former job of serving the guests. Margie went back to the kitch. Previously, she had been working at both places helping in the kitchen and serving the guests.

That day Tuesday, nothing spectacular happened. The customers came and were attended by Mabel. She had not grown less pretty. Her lips were still bulging and appetising, her face had yet showed no change at all. Unless you were told you can never imagine that she had married. Even something had increased in her desire for man and sexual grafitation.

The next day was more eventful. Mabel woke by about six thirty and spent fifteen minutes in her bathroom. In her dressing room she spent even more minutes. She has got many clothes since her wedding and she was out to dress to kill.

Infact you can never believe, how Mabel dressed, that she would be entering the kitchen at all. The expensive flowered dress and the Nylon handkerchief then the sportless shoes and plastic belt to match. It was wonderful. By about three p. m. somebody walked into the hotel The black muscle-man. You remember? The one that had once given Mabel two pounds. Mabel was in the dining - room serving some people when he entered, 'Hey! juicy baby', he called at Mabel who turned and on seeing him nearlly droped the breakable plate he was holding.

'O! Mr————————' Mabel did not know his name 'Mr Eze please' he completed for her, 'Hah Mr. Eze, I no de see you here anymore! she said, holding out her hand to greet the man, 'Na you I no dey see-o' he said shaking her hand, Who say you go for three months now? he asked her. Mabel did not want to inform him of her marriage,

'I been go home-o' she said, blushing, Ah-a, I been talk now. I de come here every day to find you, but I no de see you the man said. It is surprising that this man of about thirty two years or more attracted Mabel so much, even much more than her husband who was just a little over twenty two.

The man who had been dreaming of Mabel with his eyes said to her: 'I beg Mabel I go like talk to you small.' Mabel looked into his eyes and saw something she could not explain But she said 'Hmm? Okay give me two minutes to attend that customer'

'Okay' said the man, and he walked into the passage to wait. For four minutes he waited for Mabel. She then appeared and walked up to him at the far end of the passage. 'How baby?' the man asked her. 'Fine' she replied. 'I no like this place we are standing, said Mr. Eze, 'make we go inside your room'.

Mabel sighed. 'Okay' she said and led the way to her bed-room. When they entered the man turned round and locked the door. Mabel graped at him, mouth wide open. 'Never mind baby,' he said, gripping her waist. Then he drew her against his body. She mumbled. She turned her face one side and kissed her neck just below the chain. Mabel liked it and held down his head to the place. The excited man opened her frock and sucked her nipple passionately. She trembled and made a kind of mad dance against the body of Eze.

Then he worked on her belt. She shook her head negatively. 'Please don't my mother is around,' she said. But J wonder if the man heard her at all. He took off her belt and unbuttoned her dress.

Mabel continued to say 'no' 'no' Mr. Eze continued to be deaf and to work on her dress. At last he removed it. Then he carried the girl to her bed and lay her flat on it. She kept on grumbling and protesting But a kid could have seen that she never meant her protests to be taken seriously.

He pinned her to the bed and went over her and in another second her pant was gone. And Eze plucked the apple he had been dieing for since the past three months.

Mabel kept Eze from leaving after the first five minutes. She asked him to stay back in her room while she went to do some work in the dining-room. So keeping her man in her room, she locked her door from the outside and went back to the dining-room to attend the customers.

Back at the kitchen she behaved as naturally as possible and saw that neither Margie nor her mother had taken note of what she had been doing for the past ten minutes.

A few customers came in and she attended them. But her soul was in her room where a romance of the highest order was waiting for her, when the customers left she raced back to her bed room.

213

Eze was reading a little book when she entered. She locked the door inside, walked over to Eze and tore away the book from him.

He looked up at her and smiled. Her eyes were burning with passion and desire. He grasped her waist and put her into his laps. She flung her arms round his neck and lucked up into his eyes romantically. He bent down and kissed her nipple passionately, she wriggled and waggled. It was so sweet. Then he k ssed her lips and she sucked his mouth passionately.

Then he said to her: 'Please pull off your dress.' She did willingly, leaving only her pant. He carried her to his bed once more and helped to pull out her pant. Again he got the thing. But I wonder if she got it half as much as Mabel. When they were gratified Mabel locked her man in once more and went to see the customers

Don't ask me how Eze was feeling, for I can't tell myself. But I may think that the pleasure of having a sweet honey eclipsed the fear of being stung by the bee. He had some moments of fear as to what he would do if they were caught. But the fear could not be compared with the pleasure of having the sixteen years old beauty.

After about fifteen minutes Mabel came back again and drenched her-self in the pleasure of the body. Trust to say the thought of Gilbert never came into her mind for a second. She was blinded by a mad desire. She even never knew that her mother was some where around the hotel.

The affair continued with Mr. Eze for many times and ended by about five thirty in the evening when he left Mabel's room. He came to the dining-

room and had some fine dish of yam foo-foo. Mabel
prevented him from paying anything He find his
meal and went with a promise to come back two
days later.

CHAPTER NINE

Mabel has stayed at her mother's house for about
two months now. One day Gil came to take her home.
No, Gil I think I need to have more days of rest
here she told him. "But I need you so and I miss
you everyday,' her husband said.

'Don't worry dear, I shall come later' she said.
"It seems your love for me is wining" he said
Hhmm when did that began to get into your head?
she asked her husband. 'You can see for yourself,'
he said 'imagine it, a married woman leaving her
husband for over two months and never even wanting to come back.'

"Don't talk like that Gilbert. I have told you
that I shall be back in a week's time." Gilbert went
back home feeling that something was going wrong
somewhere. Surely something was wrong. Mabel was
making money and moreover she was having great
fun as she made the money.

Besides Mr. Eze there were a handful of other
men who she had made romance with. Her purse was
increasing day by day. She had more cloths than
she could ever wear. She got to know many of the
best hotels in the township. She had learnt how to
dance very well and was a regular picture goer.

One evening her mother took her to her room
'My daughter, Mabel' s h e began 'yes mamma'
replied Mabel. Don't you think it is time you go

215

back to your husband and stay with him for some months?" "You are not driving me away from home mamma?" she asked her mother.

"No my child, but the poor boy longs for you greatly" her mother replied. Alright mamma I will go when this month ends, Mabel said. "Oh! but today is only 5th. By the way did you querrel with him?' Mrs. Helen asked Please I did not querrel with him. But I like this place and I want to be here for some time.

Her mother gave up the argument and waited for things to see what course they would take Two days later after Margie caught Mabel being kissed by a strange man in the passage by about seven thirty.

The man pinned Mabel on the wall behind the door. Mabel held her arms on his neck. Margie was walking in when she heard some whispering behind the door. She stopped dead and listened. She heard Mabel say "kiss me here just on the neck," Then there was some sizzling noise from Mabel as the man kissed her.

Margie could not bear it any longer. She drew back a little from the door and then cleared her throat loudly as she came nearer. Mabel took the warning and quickly disengaged herself from the man who also walked away into the dining-room from where he ordered some food.

"When he had finished and left, Margie called Mabel into the passage. Mabel," she began "you seem to forget that you are a married woman" "What do you mean by that?" she asked Margie. 'You have spoilt more than I expected you would,' said Margie.

'I don't understand you,' she said. 'Do you know I caught you kissing that man behind the door some ten minutes ago?' she asked Mabel stared at her. "Infact, as a married woman I am expecting you to be very reserved and stop this nasty way you mix up with men. For two times I have come to open our bedroom and found the door belted from the inside. And............."

Before she could finished that sentence Mabel had went across her face 'sla-ap' Margie saw real fire. Instantly she threw herself on Mabel and there was a lot of scratching and slapping.

Two men in the dining-room heard the noise and went to see what was going on. They saw Margie pinning Mabel against the wall and panting and slapping. They ran to the rescue and drew them apart before Margie could do much damage to the oily plumpy skin of Mabel.

"What's the matter," the rescuers asked, looking from one girl to the other. But none said a word Margie and Mabel glared at each other with blooded eyes.

Then Margie walked back to the kitchen. Mabel also turned into the bedroom. She was some how sorry for having slapped Margie, for after all she was her very good friend. However she was feeling very sour and without waiting for the day's business to finish she went into her bed and slept off her sadness.

The next morning she woke Margie up by about six a. m. "Yes Mabel, what do you want?" "I am sorry for last night," she told her. "Oh! forget it my honey," Margie said Mabel left her own bed and went over to Margie's. She put her arms on Margie and began to rub her back. Margie responded and put her leg on Mabel. 'When shall you go back to your husband?' Mabel asked.

I am not going back, Margie, she said hurtly, 'I am not quite seventeen and I am married. I don't get what I want out of life by trying myself down to Gilbert. Margie sighed.

By about eight a. m. they were ready for the days work. Mabel, judging by the way she dressed, had not been changed by what she had with Margie yesterday evening.

She was quite dressed up to her best again. She had another new dress. Customers were coming and going. Mabel was working hard. Things were going on normally. The early hours were not crow.

Then it was about by three thirty that it exploded. It was then that Mr. Eze walked into the hotel. Mabel was in the kitchen when he came. He therefore entered the dining-room and called for attention. Mabel had always seen him. So she rushed up under the pretext of serving a customer.

They exchanged romantic glances. He orderded food that he barely needed. After the meal, he took her key and went into the bed-room to wait for her as usual. Mabel went back to kitchen as if the customer had gone.

Some other people came in and Mabel went up to attend them. That was the time to escape to her bed-room too. So immediately she had served the people she went to her lover. They started again and immersed themselves in theri honey.

But they weren't as lucky as usual. It was just at the beginning of their forth stage. In their hurry they had not remembered to bolt the door inside. May be that the heavens wanted to punish them or

Mabel especially. They were still on the thing when suddenly there was a tap at the door followed immediately by the entry of Gilbert!!

Mabel was under Eze and did not see Gil till he walked right up the bed. When she saw him she screamed and pushed away Eze with all her force. Gilbert could not stand the sight. He acted like a mad man. Eze was already weak and tired. Gilbert full of force and hatred grabbed him by the neck and jammed his head against the wall.

Mabel had struggled to put on her gown and was rushing towards the door when Gil grabbed her by the neck and pushed her to the bed.

She cowered there and was full of entreaties, trembling all over. Mrs. Helen and Margie had heard the scream in the bed-room and they rushed to find out. In the bed-room and they saw everything with their eyes there was no need for words.

CHAPTER TEN

The following day, Gil packed the whole of Mabel's belongings and brought them down to 'Pleasure-Home.' He did not even asked for the refund of the bride-price.

Mrs. Helen tried to plead for her daughter, but Gil could not even speak. His heart was so full. Mabel was lying in her bed the whole day. She never even took her bath. She refuse to see anybody or to hear anything. She would not allow her mother to come to her. For four days she lay in her bed and sobbed, not that she missed her Gil but because of the shame she had been exposed before her mother and Margie.

She decided on one thing. To leave home as quickly as possible. She never cared where she would go to. One important thing was to leave home.

The next day she packed her things in the privacy of her room, and hid the two boxes under her bed. Her mother spent a great deal of time trying to bring her mind down but it was useless.

Margie soothed and soothed but to no use. She was set and with her kind of mind there was no going back. She simply waited for the night to come.

It was by about eight p. m. now. Mrs. Helen and Margie were in kitchen. Margie slipped out of the room and went up the street to fetch a taxi. She saw one in some seconds and asked the driver to follow her. They tip toed into the room and with the aid of the driver she carried away her boxes into the booth of the car.

Margie was in the passage she saw Mabel packing her boxes into the car. She ran towards her but before she could reach her Mabel went into the car and asked the driver to run. He did and Margie just stood there with her hand in her mouth.

By about nine p. m. She had boarded a car to Port-Harcourt. The car reached Port-Harcourt by four thirty in the morning. She took a taxi to Palace Hotel.

The next morning she washed up and dressed up in her best. She had become a different woman. Yet she was just seventeen, sweet and innocent looking.

Mabel's desire was still at its zenith. She has decided to live a free life. She had it. But for how long? The sweet honey which everybody was longing to drink poured away so soon.

She lasted only three months at Palace Hotel. But within that three months many young men had left the town unable to continue their business, having been sucked to the bare-bone by Mabel. Others were owing so much money which would take them more than a whole year to pay.

How did the sweet honey pour away? Within two months of her arrival in Port-Harcourt Mabel found out that she was to expect a baby in the next six months.

It was horrible. She thought how she could afford to keep a baby in her own type of life. Getting a child would surely put her out of business for more than a year. Who then would look after her for all this time?

She decided on one thing. Do away with the child! But inexperienced and young as she was she did not know that the third month was a dangerous one for expectant women.

She took her contraceptives and overdose too. The next day the result come. In the middle of the day the arbotion took place, but a hell of blood followed.

There was no mother or sister to help. No friend like Margie to come and carry her to the hospital.

No one even took notice of her agony. She was in the lavatory. From eleven a. m. she began to have the colie aches and went into the lavatory.

There she wriggled and moaned in pain. The rest of the outside world went on moving without even feeling that something had missed. At the Palace Hotel music was going on merrily in the bar up at the third floor.

Inside the lavatory our seventeen years old sweet honey was pouring away. The agony lasted from that eleven a. m. till four thirty p. m. Mabel prayed and moaned. For the first time in the life she asked for forgiveness of her sin from God. She knew she had a patron saint, she prayed and prayed.

The blood flowed freely unchecked, by about four thirty the last drop that held her together flowed away. And she colapsed and died.

THE END

A. N ONWUDIWE

The Managing Director of

MEMBERSHIP BOOK-SHOP

No. 87 Upper New Market Road,
P. O. 214,
ONITSHA, E. C. S. NIGERIA

BOOKS PUBLISHED
BY
A. N. ONWUDIWE

Love is Infallible	5s	**Net**
Tshombe of Katanga	5s	,,
The way to make friends with Girls	5s	,,
The Labour of Man	4/6	,,
Boys and Girls of Nowadays	5s	,,
Mabel the Sweet Honey that drops Away	5s	,,
To Rule is a Trouble	4s	,,
Agnes in the Game of Love	4s	,,
Miss Rosy in the Romance of True Love	4s	,,
Family Birth Register	4/6	,,
Dr. Zik in the battle for Freedom	5s	,,
The Disappointed Lover	5s	,,
The Last Days of Lumumba	5s	,,
The Sorrows of Love	5s	,,
How to Write Love Letters Toasts and Business Letters	5/6	,,
How to write Successful Letters and Applications	5s	,,
Elizabeth my Lover	4/6	,,
How to know who Loves you	5s	,,
The Bitterness of Politics and Awolowo's Last Appeal	4/6	,,
A Dictionary of Current Affairs and many things worth knowing	5/6	,,
Comprehensive Questions and Answers on Economics for R. S. A. Inter and Advance and G. C. E. Ordinary Lavel	5/6	,,
A New Guide to Good English and Correct Letter writing	6/6	,,

Others in Preparation

❖❖❖❖❖❖❖❖❖❖❖❖❖❖❖❖❖❖❖❖❖❖❖❖❖❖❖❖❖❖

Printed By
ALL STAR PRINTERS
P. O. BOX 52 NNEWI.

HOW TO WRITE
FAMOUS
LOVE LETTERS,
Love Stories, and Make
FRIEND WITH GIRLS

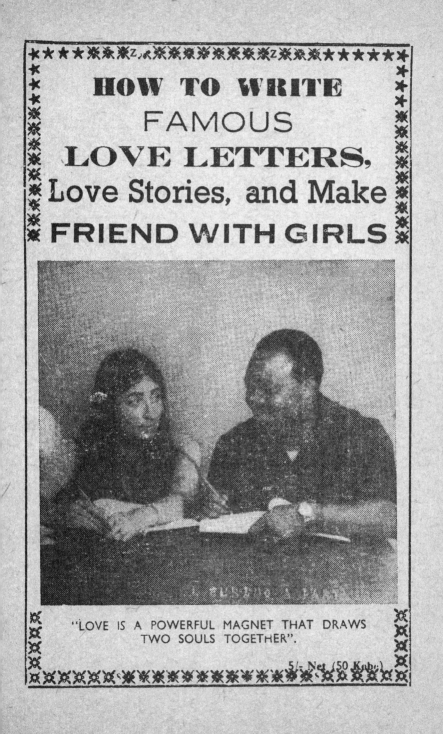

"LOVE IS A POWERFUL MAGNET THAT DRAWS
TWO SOULS TOGETHER".

5/- Net (50 Kobo)

NIGERIA'S DECIMAL NOTES AND COINS

COINS		KOBO
½d		½
1d		1
3d		2½
6d		5
1/-		10
2/-		20
2/-6d		25
5/-		50

NOTES		NAIRA
10/-		1
£1		2
£2: 10/-		5
£5		10

These will be in use as from the 1st. day of January 1973. So try to master all before the time.

HOW TO WRITE FAMOUS LOVE LETTERS, LOVE STORIES, AND MAKE FRIENDS WITH GIRLS*

LOVE STORY

WHY I KILLED MY WHITE LOVER
BY EASTHER JOHNSON:

FROM THE IKOYI JAIL, WHERE SHE IS SERVING A
LIFE SENTENCE FOR THE MURDER OF MAURICE
HALL, A LOCOMOTIVE INSPECTOR ON THE
NIGERIAN RAILWAYS.

That I'm still alive is a miracle. I ought to be dead,
I was on June 18th 1953, sentenced to death by the
Ibadan Assixes for the murder of Mr.

*excerpt

227

Hall, my European boy friend. I appealed against the death sentence, not because I was not responsible for his death, but because I was not satisfied that the Trial Judge appreciated the mental wound on Maurice.

Today I'm still alive, serving life imprisonment. May be that the crime I committed earned me my present suffering. At least, this is how many people will take it.

I GIVE HIM £400

But let me make one thing plain. I did not know that I was about to commit a crime the morning I had a quarrel with Maurice. At least, I had no intention of causing his death. It all started too suddenly.

I have lived happily with Maurice for seven years. On the eve of his departure to the United Kingdom on leave, he suggested that the two of us should find money to buy taxi to play the Ibadan Street. I saw that as a good business, proposal and gave him my life savings of £400.

He did not buy the car before he left for his leave. Four days after he has returned to Nigeria, I raised the question of the car. I did this as we were dining together. His reply to my question was to tell me: 'Pack and go away I have married an European woman while on leave" I was staggered but did not believe him. It was quite shocking to me to hear him saying that. But I soon found, he was quite serious. Then, I asked him to give me back my £400, before I pack away. His only reply was: "which money? You can't have it!" I lost my temper and threatened that I would report him to the police and get him out of Nigeria, not only because he had refused to return my money, but because he was a disgrace to his race for failing to keep a love promise to marry me. Maurice was very angry. But he did not do anything at about 5 a m. Maurice got out of the bed and woke me. He asked me to repeat what I had said to him last night. I repeated all I had said. Without saying a word, he opened a table drawer and got out a revolver, and waving this at me menacingly, he said; "My, my! I'm going to to finish you now, Rose and shoot myself! Then he proceeded to load the revolver calmly. His calm rattled me a great deal.

And—then—I lost my head. There was a faint but a commanding voice in me telling me to defend myself or die. I could not resist the voice.

I THREW A KNIFE.

I turned towards the dining table and got hold of a knife with which we had opened tinned milk the night before. I threw it at Maurice and it pierced his side. He cried out and fell to the ground against the knife, and it went deeper and pierced either his stomach or the intestines. I do not remember which the doctor who performed the post-morten operation on him said it pierced. I did not mean to kill Maurice. I only wanted to scare him off, from drawing the trigger. When I touched him I knew he was died. What had I I done?

Then I became confused. I ran off the house to the street. I saw a lorry and asked its driver to take me to the police station. But I did not know that the lorry was coming to Lagos until we had gone very far, and I could no longer stop the driver. I did not mind. The driver could take me to hell for all I cared then, there were two desires in me to put many miles between me and scene of the incident, and to give my story to the police. In a Matter of hours I found myself at the Central Police station, Tinibu, Lagos.

TREATED LIKE ROYALTY.

Then my case become worse, I found out I had no money on with which to pay the driver. But I was in no mood to argue and plead with the driver. I gave him my wrist watch in hire of payment, and he drove away. When I entered the police charge office I met Inspector Pepple and gave him. Immediately I was surrounded myself by the police treated, as far as their number went, like visiting royalty. I was conveyed to Ibadan by the police to face my trial.

It had since occurred to me that I did a very foolish thing by going to the police. I ought to have done quite a different thing. I ought to have killed myself immediately I found out that Maurice was dead. The world would have appreciated my case better if I had taken my own life at the same spot and gone away with Maurice away to wherever the dead go away from my present phcaly suffering, away from pricks of conscience, away from the jeers and misunderstand of the living.

There is only one thought that is often very consoling. I firmly believe that Maurice, if the dead are left with any sense, must have forgiven me the fatal wound I inflicted on him. I firmly believe that he must have appreciate why I did it. I'm sure he must have known that I never meant to kill him and I'm sure it must have occured to him that he left me down very completely. It is this belief that has given me courrage to continue to eling to life—a life without meaning, without purpose and without sense, Yes, I believe Maurice has completely forgiven us. That he is today even sorry that I am still suffering because of our foolishness—because of his faithlessness and my own mad anger and jealousy.

But Maurice is not the only one to forgive me have writen this with one purpose only: to let my own people and country know that I'm sorry for the crime I committed; to let them know also that I would live and die happy, if only I could know that they have forgiven me.

AT 30—I HAVE LOST ALL

I'm 30 years old now, and I have lost everything. I have lost my youth and, worst still I have lost my case of conscience. And who knows how long I will continue to rot away in prison.

But how long my phyisical suffering will continue is not very important to me. What is more important to me is to ensure that my people and all those who may read me will appreciate that I'm not only sorry for having been resposnible for the death of the man I love, but also for having committed a crime against the laws of God and State.

QUESTIONS

In what circumstances does a women kill a man she loves? And how does she feel afterwards? And if her death sentence is reduced to life imprisonment, does she lead the life thus given with a perpetual feeling of guilt, with a death-wish as the only agreeable companion? These questions are answered here, in the story of a Nigerian woman who, in a fit of anger, dis-appointment and jealousy, murdered a man she loved. It is the story of a baffled lover who killed in a fit of trantrums and then surrendered to the police. It is the story of a woman who feels the urgent need to confess. It is the story of a 30 years old woman, Adaocha (Rose) N t u, f r o m N s u k w a, in Uguashi—Uki District, who is known to most as

EASTHER JOHNSON.

SATURDAY NIGHT DISAPPOINTMENT

By

Miller O. Albert

(Author & Journalist.)

Published by

CHINYELU PRINTING PRESS,

No. 1, Iweka Road, Onitsha.

Price: — **2'-**

Chinyelu Printing Press, 1, Iweka Road, Onitsha.

SATURDAY NIGHT DISAPPOINTMENT*

CHAPTER 111

MY HELP TO A MURDERER IS TO RUN INTO THE BUSH.

It was just like all the other moments. They glared at the hotel hoping to enjoy nice drinks, before they leave for fair. It was a very beautiful house even in its wreck, it looked

*Excerpt

strong and wonderful. It had flowery passages along the corridor, the air breezing seemed much perfumed. That serened, sweet night, mellowed into beauty and romance.

Before they took some steps into the room, lilies and scarlet leaves drove round the hotel, winding over the rooms, making appal dins, with exotic scents.

They hadn't got ready, they were just on their grim commence, when there came a full engine of human derelict, in the form of the waitress. There was no mud, for an immediate flounder, even a nice cave, for an immediate cover. Flounder too, to shun the derelict, sprinting madly from the kitchen. All along in her blue tanner, she had been a black eyed type of girl, the glamorous elegant type, the black hair type and a bandle of commemorative beauty. She was suspected, to have been the wife of the land lord, till she tendered the manner of " ***What sort do you prefer-Ladies — Gents***! "

'Well what sort are you; apearing in this form?'

" That ain't a tough saying. Things with me, are matter of war, with Russia. If you can form a nation and fight Russia, I can be able to answer it, if it wouldn't pull down this house. "

" So long a sentence?'   'Yes.'

" Why then came you— in this modern of such malicious glee?

"They have had my life, like that of the crocodile. My head, that of a rat. My rump like that of expectant mother! what more again, of beauty conception, could I render to a beast? My help to a murderer, is to run into the bush!"

" You are aware I'm sure " Ike said—
" I can tilt you up to a peak and hurl you into an
abyss." "That can gain mastery, if I don't first
hurl you msyelf" she went on "into an oblivion"

" Well meal first, before more topics "

"Thank you!" she went off. With her were
rice and rat meats, distorting the whole show of
broth and taste. All mellowed into a five day oxo.
They were in a course, to meddle to a change of
diet, when a mad uproar started. It was a heavy-
tempest. At the slightest whim, they rumpled into
a mad stampede. The glistening face of **Gentle
Elizah,** fade.

Her scarlet lips turned to yellowish brown.
Beautiful things w e r e marred just d o w n,
bringing t h e spirit o f creative designs debased.
Debased too, were the honours and glories of the
proprietor. Not him alone, even the manager. It
was a heavy war of inversive disposition.

The couse of the uproar, was yet unknown, rather
a race for life must become prevalent, before the
karma law officials appear w i t h their hoods.
Everybody thought of larceny and tort, even Indian criminal law. The bats even were included
in the sleepless night. It could have caused much
epidemic of child death or even a continuous belly
ache. I'm sure women couldn't have conceived.
The surgeons could have complained of exhaus-
tion of drugs.

THANK God, It never shone, as It was proposed.

After this what next?'

Come and see where God is wrestling with

Mr. Satan and Angel Michael, trying to take over the fight from God!
Myself, I hadn't the zeal to wait, even the zeal to help God. Nevertheless, had he been defeated, I could have got a nice chance, to carry along my dog meat all along, even in the office.

" *Pity*! " Ain't you able to think of the bunch of fried meat, hung over the fire for few munites, they came in a position to dropping aromatic fats and oils, where children and old women, place their hands and have it alright, even my father. I could remember when my father flogged my mother when they were eying for it, *Pity*!   Is it all?'

Ike must go into the matter and have a full first hand information, about what lost their rat meat. Though it was of delusory omen, but economists still state it as assumptions that aren't valid!

It was loafing of them, and could stir them into scoffing, if they had continued drap roaming, people pocked fun at *Gentle Elizah*, when a haze of sleeping, was enforcing her become frantic.

Soon they martified the rusal and started off, paying little or no heed, in grabbing the preliminary conception of the din mello-wing. The next place to go, couldn't be any place than as it usually be; unfortunate, too rigid and invevitable to crucial.

" What are all the lot following us for?"
" They might have deposited some amount with me!"

" What a commercial business is that? Any bank with you?

" Well if there is, there is Ike nodded and became very intoxicated about the matter. He hadn't been offended all the time, but that is no criterion.

" **Do! Gentle Elizah**, I am serious to know of the tragic reply you have registered.

If you'd be in the course to pursue it, so distorted as it is, you would also delve into the fathomless pove, of detecting the loss of our rat meat. **Terrible**!

"Well Ike, you must not go too wrong to pursue queries mostly, of this type. I'm surely aware that at the long run, it must end into a fix and immodest unchastity.

" If even I'd be in a position to fell this house, I must surely let the mouse run out. While making two ends to meet, I musn't create obstacles savouring barbarism!

" That's nothing. It is indeed nothing! "
" As the old English proverb has it, Nothing
comes from nothing. So you'd come down to
me, making beaufiful of yourself and welcoming
my lovely personality when ever you are called
for. "

" The lattest applies, in the form of a fatigue.
If it comes crisp clear, It must knock before
It reaches the goal."

" You all are born to talk in abstract So I
musn't. I'm much owed to this dubious argument running fast and free"

ADVENTURES
OF
THE FOUR STARS
✷ ✷ ✷ ✷

**The Life of An Adventurer Seems
Tough and Funny**

ADVENTURES OF

THE FOUR STARS *

———————◆———————

By

J. A. OKEKE ANYICHIE

══════════════════════

Published by

HIGHBRED MAXWELL

STUDENTS OWN BOOKSHOP,

17 Bright Street Onltsha—Nigeria.

Net Price 3/6d

*excerpt

Contents

D—For Deal

Dope of a Sure Horse

The Dame has it

Deal for Three

No Body's Business

The Dame is Though

Deal for Two

Deal in the Island

The Adventures of The Four Stars
dedicated to Samuel A. Okponku
And International guy whom I
chance to meet during the brief
writing. He says:-
"A quittes never wins, a winner
never quiter". That is to say,
"Once a Radical Star, always
A Star."

Author

The characters, places and names mentioned in this book are the author's creative imagination. If by chance they concide with a place, direct resemblance or allusion with any group of persons individual or Society dead or alive; in no was must it be taken as a material reality.

Author.

BOOKS BY SAME AUTHOR

The Magic of Success	—	In writing
The Radicals	—	In writing.

INTRODUCTION

It is with profound practical experience of what happened in the Old Western Countries, the era of Texas gunslinger, the Cow Boys and the Red Indians; the idea with which I set to write this Adventures of the Four Stars depeicting African guys in a set of Old Lagos Surburb.

In the Western Countries of America they call it Wild Old West, but here in Africa, it is the era of the dope addicts and peddlers; the Bad Boys of of Tinubu Square, the Wild Takwa Bar-Beach Boys and the jayi-jayi addicts of Idi-Oro surburb. Read of them in a thrilling and fascinating adventures packed in one.

Being a guy of repute, I am inclined to believe that once a guy, always a guy. As you read this book, you will find out that the only trouble with African guys is money. With a handful of money in pocket to reckon with, these stars are equally tough wracking brains and reducing the don'ts into the doings of some kind.

This Adventures in Ignorance portrays a class of Radical Stars whose love for adventure landed them into many troubles.

Their utter disrespect for the law is toughest. They started first as a group of three Boys and a girl whose Secondary Education was known as "The Four St r.", who rocked and crooked the surburbs of old Lagos; all the time dodging the law and the blue guys and the deals.

The saying that a Star is born and not made leaves the reader to prove if he is a Star or a mug. But remember a mug could be fearfully tough, sleck-headed and hard as a nut.

It is a shattering story for those guys who love to handle quids and adventure. This is an age of radical stars.

"Am I a Star?" "Am I ?"
Then read on and enjoy the fun. Once a Star, always a Star.

D-FOR DEAL

Kid Akabueze walked straight to the bar tender. He ordered a shot of Spanish Whisky. Light a cigarette and drew in a long bale right to the lungs. He sent out a chain of smoke and watched it circle the atmosphere. The bar was empty. He glanced at his wrist-watch and said:

"What in the hell? Is nobody coming around here?" I wonder what is happening in this awful town with the people talking politics. A game that is nobody's business."

He made a slight motion, searched his pocket trousers for an handkerchief. The bar-man was busy cleaning the counter. But his attention was not concentrated on his job. He has always admired the company of Kid Akabueze, because the latter has been his good customer when the going was good.

Kayode, the bar-man said: "Hope there is nothing wrong with the affairs of the State? I wonder why every mug in town is interested in Local and Semi national politics. These election days never bring us good tidings. To hell with these campaigns and damn everything."

"You know, Kayode", said Akabueze, "that things get muddled up and awful with the people making a lip service of political campaigns. A thing that is nobody's business. "A double shot of brandy. Remember my account and try to bring it up to date." "Got a packet of lucky strike cigarette?

Eh! Senior Akabueze! I bet your account now is four quids four bob. The Chief popped in and said no more deals as he is running shot of a coconut.

I wonder if you can square your account these days? Maybe I personally love to serve you on my account Believe it or not, you are a terrible guy whom I like to go for, even to hell. Shall we have a shot then in my account?

"Well Kayode, you have always been a nice feller. But I sometimes wonder if that Chief of yours is not an awful mug. "Meci mon Amigo."

"It is just one of those things", said Kayode, as he served Akabueze the drink. "My old mun has been architect of my good moral. One of those things she thought me was to avoid heavy drinking and cards. Today, they are good pre-positions that has helped to mould me. May she rest in peace." He made the sign of the cross,

The telephone by the side of the counter began to ring. Kayode made a fast move for the receiver, and said through the mouth piece.

"The Gay Palace Hotel, Broadway"

"Is Kid Akabueze around there?" said a faint voice from the other end.

"That", was the reply and hold on. When Kid Akabueze came to the receiver, he said rather demurly, Kid here, and who is speaking?" "Oh! Johnny just hold on. I shall be around in ten minutes".

He dropped the receiver and bade Kayode good bye.

Outside, he took a taxi and made straight for Hotel de Metrople opposite the Q-side Marina.

"Life is like that", he said. He thought of Johnny and decided that the letter is fearfully tough and level headed.

Johnny Ezekegbu has been a long boyhood friend of Kid Akabueze. They both left the Elementary School and also attended the same Secondary School together. At 24, Johnny is the most explosive thing. A four and half foot of a lad, in a tin and half feet of talent. The most explosive thing since the stom bomb. Kid was dressed on a Navy blue suit on top of an Italian bally shoe.

At Hotel de Metropole, Johnny is wearing a Navy blue trousers and a dark grey sports Jacket with a white bally shoe to match. He drained his last shot of Spanish Whisky and glanced at his wrist watch. He was thinking sort of mechanically. His conceived ideal, D., for a deal. The waitress was watching and eyeing him with interest. But he seemed to pay no attention. The thought of meeting Kid was uppermost in his mind. He is a guy who knows business from material pleasure.

Kid Akabueze paid off the taxi driver in front of the Hotel. Walked straight without turning. Inside the hotel, at the far remote corner was Johnny. He was searching his pocket for a cigarettee when Kid walked in. He lit the cigarette and sent out a circle smoke which he watched sailing the Air. "Life could be sometimes funny" he muttered.

Akabueze first made for the counter and ordered a bottle o Spanish Whisky and Soda. As he waited for the change, with the tip of the eye, he saw three individuals entering the hotel. The new entrants made straight to the table occupied by Johnny.

Salami Idowu is a crank from Idi-Oro. The notorious leader of a band of Back-Room guys and dope peddlers. A thug of the worst type. When he got to the table occupied by Johnny, he excused to share the same table. Johnny made no motion and pretended as if he was not aware of Idowu's presence.

"I say, excuse moi dedon", shouted Idowu.

"I hope that is not a decent order", retorted Johnny.

"Maybe you got to learn manners one of these days?", he added.

"Maybe you wana have some trouble, guy?', said Idowu.

"To hell with your trouble," was the reply.

At this moment, the other two fellers were on the standby.

They are aware that trouble is coming. And they were makers and they live by trouble and trouble is their second name. They were prepared for a show down.

All of a sudden, Idowu's face reddened. There was untimely and not very surprising. Idowu smacked Johnny on the face with a terrific force of his back hand. Johnny staggered. Idowu followed with another blow to the neck. He raised his hand for the final blow, a cool low voice from behind said:-

"I'll rather desist if I were you, mister."
As Idowu whirled around, Akabueze sent him a terrific hook to the jaw successfully followed by a short left jab to the ribs. Idowu lost balance and fell flat on canvas

His two friends were too cowardly to move. After ten seconds, Idowu tried and got up. He rubbed his face in search of blood. "But what was the raw deal with this ruffians?" What sparked the trouble inquired Akabueze, rubbing his wrist.

"Maybe the same old story. I definitely cannot say for granted what these thugs were after," said, Johnny. "Take it easy Kid," said Johnny. Before Kid could dodge, Idowu splashed a bottle of soda on the floor which he intentionally aimed at Johnny The bottle of soda water splashed on the floor. Kid was about to hook Idowu again, but Johnny refrained him.

At the counter a stout black fellow with terrible mark on the face mixed a double whisky and soda. The waitress who brought the whisky was so charmed at the display of fits from Kid that she stood staring at the Idi-Oro back room thugs who were ashamed of the show-down.

Idowu and his team were so ashamed that they left the hotel without a word.

The waitress was so charmed at the display of fits from Akabueze, that she stood staring and smiling at the two guys with deep admiration and want of company.

She said, "what an agile of a boxer you could be if taken to the stage."

"Has anyone ever made love to you?" he said.

"No, and maybe I shall expect you one of these days." The way and manner she talks goes to show she was well bred. Her brests were pointed over the white frock she is wearing.

This girl is superb' She has the good looks of an Arabian Princess. "One of these days, may be, he said, when the weather gets fine, I shall make love to you and may be carry you to the Barbeach and the Takwa Bay Beach. She smiled and mubbed her cheeks and said.

"You are sometimes funny Kid " I have always admired your company. But one thing is that you sometimes drink too much. And I have often wondered how a girl of my type could manage you. "Sorry as a nut," Baby. "My old mum has said these your exact words some couple of years ago when I was a higher school student." "You do not mean to say. You have been drinking right frcm childhood," says she.

"Wine is my second name in school. I have always thought of giving up drinking. But the moment I decided; "I'll get the attack of an acute illness that would develop into hysteria." "That is to say, that your nerves have been deadly and internally poisioned with wine.

"That's to say." So that is that. But you must in no doubt have appreciated the way, I worked on that thug of a mug. "That is where I got surprised at your heavy drinking that never wears you down." She whispered.

"But," I sometime forget that lovely name of your?" he said.

If you don't forget next time, we met you can call me 'Iyabo Martins.' "That I can't forget. I have always liked that name Iyabo. And maybe seeing you one of these days.

That is to say, summer day or night, said Iyabo. Whichever you choose, baby Iyabo.

But I never meant you should call me baby Iyabo. Was that the name I gave you?

No! But that name sort of reminds me of a cranky dame I met at Pitakwa. She says her name is Baby Iyabo, and Mama Iyabo all at a time.

"Was she drinking too much?"

Oh! hell Johnny here quite remembered our rough encounter with that dame. Believe it or not she was a real nut and a crank. At 19, she speak French and Arabic well. "She must be all nuts!" said Iyabo.

"Precisely what I mean." She is a real hand nut. The conversation was suddenly interupted by a young couple who entered and ordered four big bottles of Top Beer, Miss Iyabo Martins excused to attend to these couple. At this juncture, Kid and Johnny decide to make it at Gay Palace Hotel. The taxi stopped in the front of Gay Palace Hotel. Johnny paid off the driver. Inside the hotel, dance was going on. The thought of going into the dance floor without a partner was permicious to the guys.

Johnny searched his pocket for a cigarette. He brought out an empty packet of Lucky Strike. He inquired of Kid for a jot. Eventually they were both out of packet with a jot. Johnny decided to walk over the street adjourning the hotel for a packet of Lucky Strike cigarette. Just at this time, the guard by the gate walked straight to Kid and said that a Miss Shola Thomas left a message that Kid Akabueze should ring her at the Ambassador Hotel. The guard searched his pocket for the telephone number. She left behind. Akabueze thanked him and turned back to meet Johnny at the other side of the street.

The latter held a double packet of Lucky Strike cigarette which he handed one to Kid.

The idea of going back to Gay Palace Hotel was abandoned. Johnny decided to make straight for the Q-side Marina in case anything should chance. He promised giving a ring should anything unusual occur. So that is that, Billy.

In a matter of when you see me going too fast? You don't forget to halt me. Kid boarded a taxi cab and pulled in front of Ambassador Hotel, Suru-City. Paid off the driver and walked into the hotel. I was beginning to get worried as I lit a jot of cigarette in the hotel frontage. I reckon I should be worried because I have been dodging trouble for so many years that a little bit more is not likely to do me any good.

I have had every sort of trouble happened to me, and when things get a bit tough, I always remember the French guy who said that most of the things he had spent his life worrying about had not happened that guy I bet, definitely knew his stuff.

I got to tell you, fellers, about this French guy and my appreciation for him. Foli is a guy most of you would like to know, because he has spent most of his life wrecking his brains and reducing the don'ts into doings, of some sayings, to some other things. One of the things he said was, "A quitter never wins, a winner never quites." And that two-third of the world's trouble comes from "dames." When I say dames, most of you guys will understand mov. n'est pal?

Because a guy who has got a dame's trouble has got others anyway, I never met a mug, who has been worrying about a dame that has not got a pile of trouble to reckon with.

"Well life is just one of those things."

Right now, somethings goes into my brains as I watch the smoke from the cigarette thub in my hand circle the air. I thought for a second about Shola-that dame is tough and level headed. She is got a keen intuition. A dame that knows every bit of stuff about business and raw deals. I thought of the password, D—for a deal: That sounds like a hell of a jingo.

I give myself a little grin as I walked into the hotel floor. At the counter, I decided to go a beer and ordered a bottle of Top Beer to start with.

There, at the far remote, corner of the hotel is Miss Shola in the Company of two elderly gentlemen in grey fruits. I could register one of the guys to be Senior Okereke. The other's face, is not quite familiar I may, perchance have come across him once or twice. But could not for granted say, who is who?

This Senior Okereke is known to be a tough guy and handy with dollars. He is more or less a thick crook of the under world businessmen, who smuggled imported goods without the knowledge of the security Officials. That is to say, they are the fellers who invade import duty. He is the Director of African Pools as Alakon Marina.

His sayings, that the only thing a guy could do to a guy is to buy him off with dollars. It has been investigated that he often carries with him open cheques and some handful of cash. He is a guy that takes no chances.

With a bottle of Becks Beer in hand, I walked straight to vacant seat opposite Shola and her company. When she saw me coming, she dropped her eye lids in a rather attractive and inviting manner. I suited at her. And said, "Hello gentlemen' and sat directly opposite.

255

I was at alert for any eventuality.

Shola stood up and excused to introduce Senior
Okereke and his friend whom she call Amadu to
Kid Akabueze. The former expressed his delight in
meeting a member of the Four Stars, that International Organisation for the liquidation of Insurance
claims.

I was invited to join her company. Senior
Okereke ordered for a fresh bottle of whisky I fum-
bled into the pocket of my Jacket for a packet of
Lucky Star cigarette I served one to Shola and Amuda.
Senior Okereke made a deprecating gesture to not
being at smoking.

After two rounds of whisky shot, I excused to go
to the toilet room. Eventually, I made direct to the
telephone boot, dialled and waited.After some seconds, I heard a faint voice.

"Is that you Johnny?"
"Yeah! Kid and where are you calling from?"
"Right from the Ambassador Hotel.
"I can understand say, what"

"Senior Okereke and Amuda, his pall are right
out here with Shola. I was given this company but
you remember "things just sometimes rattle to make
a whole."

Say, "I am pulsating it appears the same old
business." "Yeah! And can you contact Thomson?
Tell him to hang around this pop and trial this
guy I shall beckon on Shola to play it the same way.

"That will be a hell of an idea, man!"
"When you see me going too fast."
"Don't forget to balt me."
"How does it sound?"

You 'll be surprised or what will happen. So long pal - And remember to give me a ring.

"Can get you if I want you. And now I got to scarm - And maybe seeing you."
"Like hell, you will" I say and hurry up.

I lit myself a cigarette and stood starring into the stilness. I reckon things are beginning to move a bit. Right from any moment now. Thomson will be hanging around this Ambassador Hotel, a deal that nobody's business, because what the other guy is doing arn't anyones business.

I made back to my seat and excused my friends for the night It was 11.45 p.m. when I got outside the stillness of the night. The night was chilly and cool sea breeze was blowing from the Beach. I looked round for a taxi cab. Eventually, I decided to walk the eight hundred yards on foot. At the Tinubu Square, I had to cut short the journey by going through Alakoro Lane.

Kid Akabueze awakened just after six O'clock. He lay on his back, his hands clasps in mediatation. He was looking towards the Marina and the calm sea. He felt placeful and rather amused.

Eventually, Akabueze got out of bed walked across to the window. It was a beautiful morning. The rays of the rising sun reflected to the waters below. A cool sea breeze whistled across the window shutters. A blue ribbon bird was heard singing on top of a palm tree opposite the window.
Akabueze turned from the window and began whistling to himself. After a moment he searched his pockets for a cigarette, got one and lit it, went into the bathroom and turned on the bath.

He lay in the bath for a long time wrestling decisions in the mind.

When he had finished dressing, he watched his time piece and noticed it was already 7.30 a.m.

What could be the next after thought?

He lit another cigarette and drew in a long bale right to the lungs and exchaled a circle of smoke which he watched circle the atmosphere. Momentrily, the telephone range. He passed for a moment and picked up the receiver.

The voice says "Hello Kid, how goes life?"

I nearly pulled a laugh because this is Thomson

I say, "Look! what goes around there and was the deal?"

"He says the deal was nice and fair."
"Any showdown?"

"The showdown was a hell, he bellowed into the mouth piece of the instrument.

I trailed of our good friend and his pal right to the Ebute-Metta round about. They must have been fearfully drunk. As they were about to cross the level railway crossing, something terrible happened. Senior Okereke, who was in the wheel ran straight into a moving goods-train probably the train was from Kano City. The car and the gentlemen inside were badly hit. I was the first man out. The rest of the story is nobody's business I can understand a raw deal, no doubt. It is an absolute and practical raw deal to reckon with. "But what happened to the guys inside the car?"

Oh! gosh! When I brought Senior Okereke out from the ruin, he gave up after three minutes. His pal Amuda was rushed unconscious to the hospital and he stands a little chance of making it.

"You are telling me."
"As if I don't know."

I say, can you put a call through to Shola. That girl will be shocked to hear this sad news. But to the stars, it is just one of those things

"Maybe the Stars will have something to reckon with in connection with their friend's death. And you can't beat if a Star was not the first person alive to get to the spot." Just tell that girl to meet me at the Q-side Marina in about two minutes, and I hung up.

At the Q-side Marina, opposite the Kingsway, Shola was paying off a taxi driver. I stopped out of a cab and whistled to her. She turned around and looked at me as if she had been axed.

"You out to be singing the signature tune. My dear honey. She says, "how goes life, Kid?"

I say, you'll be surprised. We walked straight to the Mogambo Hotel opposite the Street. The waitress brought us a bottle of Spanish brandy.

I looked Shola up and down and concluded this girl is a real nut. A real first class International dame whose flexible appearance merits being an Ambassador's foreign Secretary typist. She did a three years secretarial practice from the International Correspondence School, Paris. The only daughter of late Mr. Thomas, a wealthy Lagos merchant who left a quarter of a million pounds will, when he died. Miss Shola Thomas has been a childhood-found friend of Kid Akabueze. They met seven years ago when the former was a high School Student at Girl's

Grammar School, Lagos. She is the only female brain in the Four Stars. After the first shot of whisky, I said to her.

"Look Shola, I've got a surprise packet in stock for you, Maybe you do not love him really, my love. You were doing the next best thing. You were thinking you loved him. You fell all the quicker because you are much too nice a girl to go around the pops rubbing shoulders with rif-raffs that hang these bars and so called Club - cabins; setting them easy targets for "a raw deal."

Maybe when Senior Okereke came along with that damnable crook business of his, you were just ripe for falling. You fell all the quicker because you wanted a show-down. Maybe life is like that." Maybe you are right, Kid, she confessed. "We do periodically things happen or not as the case may be. We play red and black comes up. Well the black is up for you. Senior Okereke is dead."

There was a wild torrent of madness written across her face as she let out a wild cry. Tears were dropping her face, and she was sobbing. After some minutes, she asked how it happened.

"Oh! life is what we make it." She said.

I took out my handkerchief and wipped her face, and kissed her cheeks to ease her sobbing.

"Oh! Kid, sometimes you are awfully nice. You are comforting strongly enough. I always forget myself for you."

I do a little thinking. Suddenly I realise that this is the first of April. Over here, they call it, "All Fools Day." Maybe somebody was thinking of me when they call it that because I reckon you guys will have concluded by now that I am a bit of a mug, and maybe you are right.

At the same time, you will allow that it is a wise man who knows when to be a mug, if you get me. I am getting worried with this dame by my side.

My mind ran to all sorts of imagination. I lit a cigarette and served one to Shola. I sort of realise something funny is gonna happen, because I am sort of philosophical. I give myself another shot of brandy for a clear thinking and planning.

I told Shola to go home and relax to wait for a call.

After seeing Shola off, I asked the receptionist if any telephone call has been through from Johnny or Thomson. He tells me that he has not received any telephone call since the last forty five minutes. Me, I got to thinking fast about Senior Okereke. When a guy is at the point of death, little does he know of it nor where he is going.

I start pacing up and down the hotel room after another shot of brandy. Eventually, I give up thinking and go over the telephone both by the side of the counter. A magazine lay besides the boot and I picked up the first two pages, the cover of the magazine contained the portrait of Johnny Holiday, that half French and half American pop Star. I was about going over this magazine when the telephone jingles. I go over it and yank the instrument and say into the piece "hello."

"Hello! old horse, was the reply.

"Johnny! what is the game?"

Just the same old story. I have just come across Thomson, He said that the deal was a nice one. How was that dame?

You mean Shola? Well she was able to come over her shock. You could imagine that dame weeping in the hotel.

"You are telling me. Is she aware of the deal encountered?" Not yet. To tell of the ten thousand quids is to blow off her head. She will know when she might have come through her state of malancholy.

But how do we play this?

That will be as simple as A.B.C. and hung up the instrument.

The time was 4.30 p.m. when I entered the Gay Palace Hotel. I mixed myself a mixture of whisky. Lit a cigarette and puffed out a smoke of thick black smoke and watched it circle the ceiling. I am thinking about Okereke. Maybe I'm thinking it was very nice of Thomson to have pulled it clean and good with that cheque from Senior Okereke. I reckon this guy Thomson got a fast brain, because directly I told him of what I thought of Okereke then he decided to trial him. At the time of the accident, there were no cops, around and Thomson must have made a fast move to search the pockets. This fast deal of his has eventually yielded the sum of ten thousand pounds. The money is intended for a client of the African Pools to which the deceased was the director.

It happened that until the time of his death, this cheque for the ten thousand pounds was signed three days ago, but it was still stuck in the deceased other cheque book. Probably, the late Okereke, being a crook himself, had wanted to crook his client and was only waiting for the opportunity of a showdown before this fatal accident that has ended his life. This cheque is in no doubt, now a property of the Four Stars Insurance Bureau. And what happens to it is nobody's business.

THE DOPE OF A SURE HORSE

The time was 6.30 a.m. Akabueze poured himself a stiff mixture of whisky and brandy. A mixture that was not very good. He was thinking over what has chanced. He gave out a sigh of relief. He thought life is like that and that a lot of damageable things have been happening.

A taxi cab, pulled into a kerb with a jerk in front of Hotel de Metropole. Kid paid off the driver and headed for the call box by the side opposite the entrance to the hotel. He lit a cigarette as he picked up the instrument and dialled a number.

"I have got some pretty awful news for you Shola, I want to see you." Can you be at the West end in a quarter of an hour? It is urgent I should see you. Understand and do not ask why? She said thank you 'Kid', for she loves calling him 'Kid', and what about the deal you said?

"That will be fine." Things will have to work out by itself right. He hung up and walked into the hotel. The stiff mixture he had was not doing him very good So he ordered for only a shot of brandy.

Standing by the side of the counter was a dectative Inspector Olisa of the Iwaya Police Force, He was starring at Akabueze with interest.

"Can I do anything for you, Mister

The stranger took his right hand out of his pocket and handed Akabueze a small leather case with a transport celluliod front. Akabueze looked at it and saw it was a Police Officer's warrant card. It bore the name, Inspector Olisa of the Iwaya Police Force. The Inspector Olisa said, I'll like to have a word with you Sir. Am I mistaken, if I am not addressing Senior Akabueze of the Four Stars?

Akabueze made no motion and said what was the deal, as they moved away from the counter. He felt for his cigarette case, and led the way to a corner of the hotel room.

"What about a drink." said Akabueze. "No thank you, Sir, I never drink when I am on a job." said the Inspector.

Akabueze mixed whisky and Soda for himself pulled another armchair and beckoned the Officer to sit down, while peering the latter straight into the eyes. He knew the game was up.

He proceeded to drink his whisky and soda His guse that this was not a very solid and not a fearfully intelligent person. He concluded he would play the old game of the horse for a sure win.

Akabueze put his glads on a mantle piece. Lit a cigarette. He offered his packet of lucky strike to Olisa who nodded his head in a deprecating manner with a thank you.

Akabueze said quietly over the stick of jot in his lip. "This is pretty awful, can I guse your mission here is in connection with senior Okereke's death? I mean his fatal car accident 24 hours ago? The Officer nodded his head and said, "yes and that it was reported that he was last seen in your company before his death.

"Precisely," said Kid. Can you give any clue as to your last encounter? You see I just want to make report for the corner. Maybe you can tell us something? he concluded

At this remark, Kid Akabueze's face whitened and showed more of business preposition. He knew that in a coroners inquest, the Police report is always fine. He took a long sneering look at the Officer and said.

"By jove!" How can I help. But it was a car accident, you know? And it probably looked like the deceased was high and drove fast without seeing the goods train crossing the rail.

Well, we are definitely aware it was an accident. But I also understand your organisation has something to do with insurance claims? Oh! yeah! And have you seen that girl?"

I have not seen her yet. A comrade of mine tipped me to get you here.

Look Inspector, let us not waste time any more. But suppose Okereke got drunk and maybe moved too fast, as a result, he could not adjust his brake the moment he saw the moving train.

"That depends upon how we make it."

Kid Akabueze handed a four five pound notes to the Inspector who accepted with a jerk of the head. "I shall make a report of dangerous driving, as a result of alcohol." said the Officer.

Maybe got to be seeing you summer day or night. This time, he was satisfied with his game of doping the horse for a sure and easy win.

No sooner the Inspector left than Shola entered the Hotel. At the sight of Shola, Kid Akabueze whistled the signature tune of the Four Stars.

Oh! somebody stole my horse and gone away. Oh! somebody stole my horse and wagon. Left my heart in an empty cabin, now I'm going to the trial I used to ride. Some go younder the jungle way. Some volgars in Salamander-nothing younder because of my sorrows and my lose. And now I am going down to the canan. With no companion, by myself, and now I'm going down to the Oak tree, without morning food and everything. Oh! somebody stole my horse and wagon, left my heart in an empty cabin now am going the trial I used to ride. Stole my horse stole my wagon and my pride. And now am going to the trial I used to ride.

Shola walked straight and remorsely when Kid had finished singing.

He looked at her. "Look Shola, I know there is time for being fabious - and this isn't it."

"Yes, she retorted, and what about it."

He sat down and Shola took his hat and started cleaning it.

I've got some news for you, Shola, such that will shake the mallows of your bone. Our man Thomson came through with a cheque for ten thousand quids. And a Police Officer was just around her and his business was in connection with the coroners inquest.

Shola was stunned and she gave out an air of relief. "But you do not mean." "That is part of our business, baby." The game of doping the horse you mean. "It sounds strange and mystifying."

"Post! whoever that collected you three together is a real dangerous man." said Shola. "Not if you are a member, Four Stars.

"But of course there is nothing sort of definite about us Once a member, always a member.

Johnny has put a call through the international Bank, Broad Street, Marina. The Manager of the Bank has given us absolute support in confidence. The cheque will be honoured by the morrow.

THE DAME HAS IT

Kid Akabueze woke up to the glorious rays of a bright sun light morning. The invigoration air from the Barbeach was blowing merrily and gay. It was a beautiful morning; a morning that was full of vigour and the sweet of life. There was something potentous, something sister about the very feel of the air, the laughing brightness of the early sun dawn

Akabueze went over the window and looked far into the sea. The ships were happily anchored and few canoe paddlers were rollicking the calm bosom of the Lagos Lagoon. He went behind and began to dress. The page boy whom he sent to Q-side came back to announce of the strange car just pulled outside the frontage of 1179 Broad Street.

Most of you guys are aware of the fact that the English language consists of so many proverbs, and what have you got generally. Anytime a mug finds that he has lost some words to a dame and cannot explain something, he probably has to suck his lips and pretend to stammer. That is, supposing you are confronted as to what to say to a baby, you would like to read a book on human psychology.

That is why they say in Nigeria, a lot more is needed because a guy who is not handy with 'change' is a mug. And that is the better reason why many Nigerian teenagers seek their way to America or England for a surprise packet show. And when they come back after a period ranging from three - seven years they buy car and carry their girl friends to the Takwa Bay and the Barbeach. That is a real jingo, because the time was 8.30 a.m. and I am standing by my window still looking far into the sea.

With a bottle of star beer on the table. I got dressing up in case there should be any show down, all which goes to show you fellers that life can be sometimes funny and dull.

The guy who says this morning is cool for lovers, knows the language of his stuff.

Just at this moment I take a cool look towards the hall way; and believe it or not, I could not express my utter prof dity, for walking directly towards me is Alice Okafor I give a little grin to myself because Alice Okafor is the dame I least expected seeing.

Miss Alice Okafor is a dame every guy will go for. She is very attractive, charming, fastinating and has that alluring appearance that could make King Soloman shiver. I say this dame has it.

She steps some couple of paces and gives me one of those long looks. She smiled gayly. Her beautiful set of white teeth were glittering as a snow.

I say, Alice you are the craziest dame I least expected seeing, how goes life and that town of yours baby? She comes nearer and gives me a kiss, and say, "The same old Kid Akabueze." I held her for second kiss. She gave me a cool gentle smack on the face. I say, by jove, Alice, I can always forget myself for you But tell me how goes life in that crook republic of Ghana.

She says "thank you Kid" as I gently led her towards my apartment.

This marvelous. I am never happy as when I remain to think of you, baby."

She smiles and the more I like her for what she is. Believe it or not this Alice has all the natural attributes of a beautiful lady.

She takes a long knowing look at me as if to remember the glories of the past days we spent together and she said in a rather low whispering voice. "The same old Kid Akabueze". If I don't like you and your stuff, I'll call you the Prince of the wild old west. She smiles as she says this:

The fact I could not resist the charming personality of this young dame. She is wearing a light-grey frock with a tough green jacket and a white barely shoe. At 19, she finished in the second division at Mount Camilus Girls School, Lagos, before she took up an appointment at the Niger Embassey, Ghana. At this occasion, she is on a special Mission to Lagos.

"What of driving to the West end for a luncheon." "She says that will be fine!"

At the hotel, I ordered for a bottle of Spanish brandy and cocktail of chips and fried eggs with some pork pie.

After a bit, she takes a ship at the cocktail and runs her little finger over her lip and said, it tastes. "One funny thing, Kid, is that you have never even cared to visit me at Ghana Republic.

Never mind Alice, while there is life, there is double hope. One of these days when the weather gets fine, I shall make a trip to Ghana. But only I loot the malific influence of communism that is now the now the brainwashing adopted by Nkrumaists.

She smiles and says Kid you are very funny. And how goes life with Shola and the rest of the Four Stars, Johnny and Thomson?

They are fine, and are growing old every day. If you get me.

She says, Oh! Kid you mortify me.

I say, like hell.

I lit myself a cigarette and passed one between her lips.

"They sent a bounce of mugs; I mean the blue guys to trail our activities a couple of days ago. Besides which I have been making a mental calculation of what a swell mugs I made myself. I have been a top grade mug."

She flashed her eye lids and say, "You don't mean that Kid". Not you being a mug. But you don't tell me the blue guys had a fast one on you. I know your stuff. I'll rather dine with Cassanova than to think of you going wrong." "I know how it can be sometimes."

"Well I wish you were right Alice." But the activities of the Four Stars, hasn't broadened a bit these days. It looks we have been on the defence. There has not been much of a deal hanging on."

"That is bad.' She says. There is something like tears in her eyes 'If there is any guy who is permanently gonna keep his nose clean, that, guy is you. But I will try my hooks for the Stars.'

'The fact any deal with the Stars is fifty-fifty, Does that suit you? You Princess of the Niger,' 'Yeah! that's fine, When I got back to Ghana, maybe I shall cable you for a raw deal with the Danfosa gold and diamond mine, I use to know a lot of Africans who work there,'

'Okay Princess, the game is yours, I shall always look it an eventful show-down piece. But when do you go back to Ghana?' 'Maybe 11.30 tomorrow morning,' She said, I gave Alice a ten five pounds note, as we drive along back to my apartment.

At the Q-side Marina, Alice paid off the taxi driver. We were already waiting for her at the Quay, The thought of her missing Shola was not to her liking, because Shola was away from the Colony on a short business trip to Ibadan and would probably be back towards the evening.

Johnny handed a first class ticket he bought her. And Thomson gave a gold wrist watch he bought her from the Kingsway Stores. I stood smiling, and watching the show with keen interest and admiration. She could not conceal her bewildment over the surprise packets presented her. She accepted these gifts in a splendid condour.

The time was only ten minutes to go. The captian of the S.S. Black Star Line of Ghana, gave warning that all passengers should get into the boat.

Alice could not express her appreciation of the Four Stars generousity. She kissed Johnny and Thomson on the cheeks and promised to write them of the proposed gold and diamond deal. After looking me for ten seconds she said, "Oh! Kid, I can forget myself for you. I shall reserve your kiss when next I visit Lagos. May love and compliments to Shola.

I say, all for good sweet love, and remember to start your name always with a capital letter.

She says, "tough as a nut," I shall invite the Stars one of these days to Ghana."

"Aurevoir mon cheer amigo."

She borded the ship and in less than five minutes, the S.S. Black Star af Ghana, took off achore and in a gentle retimic procession of wave upon wave, the ship steamed out of Lagos on her maidian voyage to the Atlantic Ocean amist waving of hands and handkerchiefs. Far below the horizen is still the faint visible appearance of a green scarf with four black Stars boldly written, the Black Stars of Ghana.

Johnny, Thomas and myself walked across the
street to the Magambo Hotel. Johnny ordered a bottle of wisky and a soda. We toasted the health
and bonvoyage of Alice, back to the Republic.

After the first two shots of whisky, Thomas
produced a sheet of paper from his wallets. This he
sliped to Johnny who smiled after reading through.

I have told you fellers that this lad Thomas is a
tough guy with brains. The slip he showed us was a
written statement from the Manager of International
Bank, Broad Street Marina, giving honour to the ten
thousand quids cheque. There is another five thousand for late Okereke's life insurance and two
thousand for accident insurance.

Maybe that is hell of a deal to reckon with.

DEAL FOR THREE

"Am I a Star?"

"Am I?"

Most of you guys thought that whatever the other
guy is doing at the other corner of the street, is nobody's business. To hell with that cranky hell of a
jingo slang But as the red sun down was setting, there
was something sorta reminiscent about the general
feel of the atmosphere. The cool sea breeze from the
the Lagoon whistled through the atmosphere. Along
the parks adjoining the quay and the Lagoon, were
packed different types of cases with various plate
numbers.

This evening as I drive along the Marina, I was
thinking of Bob Osita and Samca Pius. I was not
too sure as to the particular environment that will
ease the tension trying to mount my feelings.

I gave out a sign of relief and decided to park in front of Hotel Bolingo. But just as I cleared to park directly in front of me stood a dusty car with a French plate number. Some tourists must be in town. I thought for a moment or while and had a second look at this dusty French four seater sports car. I decided something like a deal is trying to manifest.

Inside the hotel, I ordered for a bottle of cool ginger ale to case my biased feelings. I have no particular choice for any alcohol this evening except something chances that will warrant high tension.

The waitress mixed a strong mixture of brandy and whisky with soda in a three quarter bottle. I decided whosoever is going to drink that strong mixture has a problem to solve. I watched her add another shot of mun into the mixture.

"I hope that is not a very good mixture."

She looked at me and smiled "some guys whom I suppose to be International tourists just ordered it.' she said.

But I wonder what type of problem the guys got in mind. You know that mixture there is sufficient to send any mug real crazy. She laughs.

"This is the strongest mixture we have had this season. And I bet whichever guy that drinks this is all nuts. Believe it or not, I was scared when told to mix this "Man are some times out of mind to drink too much.'

The flavour of this strong mixture has entered and cleared my stomach appetite to drink. I order a double shot of Spanish whisky.

A guy comes behind me and says, 'Hello Kid' I turned back face to face with Samco Pius.

What in the name of the Saints?, This Samco Pius? 'What!'

"Qui la Bob Osita?'
"Je arriva avec Bob Osita"
"Ou la Bob Osita?"
"Il la la."
"Oh! Samco Pius! You must have been the last guy I least expected seeing?"

"Just one of those things' he said.

'How goes life mon ami'

'Same old story' Bob Osita is just around too'

You are telling me.

"Maybe as if I don't know the same Old Kid.'

We marched hand in hand with waitress utterly stupified at what has chanced. She was speechless and was only coming after us with a double admiration for my comrades.

'Hello Bob'

"To hail of that is not the Kid.' He stood up and gasped my hand. We nearly fell over when embrassing ourselves. Samco Pius has just told me you both alighted the town some minutes ago. What a happy jolly occasion.

"It was a hell of a deal to have driven all the way from Dahomey. The coming was tough because of the dry weather and the untarred road.

My jore! Two of you look like men just out from a gold pit. Why not go first to the bath and ease yourselves of the dust.

Our throat must have been dry and soar. The first deal in town is strong sink to shake off the warmth of the distance journey.

This Bob Osita and Samco Pius had been old class mates and boyhood friend of Kid Akabueze down the Kano City of the early fourties and middle fifties.

The going then was tough because they were then the mig leaders of the old Kano City, "African Cunning Boys." They were then styled rough, rascal, level headed teddy boys of Kano City and surbub. It was recorded in the police file, that they were the originators and the brains behind the Sabon Gari uprising in 1952. But for the arm forces, it could have been a civil tumult.

You must all remember the Kano City, Eldumia Cinema tragedy of 1951, these three guys and some handful of their teddy gangsters, were the only survivours.

At a latter age, they departed company to attend various institutions of higher learning in the country. Their first public appearance together was five years ago when both guys were involved in a thirty minutes gun duel with the Custom guards at the Idi-Oroko, Nigeria-Ghana relations when the latter accused the former of breding recalutrants and International bandits. That I am sure is now, no body's business. And that goes to account for what fellers these three guys are.

This Bob Osita, is a guy most of you know. He is tall heastone, sleek and level headed. He likes the company of beautiful dames.

"Samco Pius is a cool, thick, middle height ex-boxer. He is not very good in company of dames. His old saying that anything can happen to a tough guy, all because of a woman. This Samco Pius is a real International guy and a mystic. He is also a linguist, and can speak French, Arabic, Spanish and Samco added to the three main languages of Nigeria, very fluently. He is also very cool when talking but sometimes level headed and cunning.

Both guys have driven all the way from Dahomey to keep up a date with our Custom Officer. A
deal that is nobody's business.

I ordered for a bottle of brandy. This is an
occasion to remember in the annals of the African
radicals.

The waitress who brought the wine stood in admiration of a clear cut guy and two other dusty guys.
She walked straight to Bob Osita and smiled at him.
Bob who is a good company of dames concluded
that the waitress was charming and beckoned her
to sit down. He offered her a shot of wine from his
tumbler. He said·

"Has any one ever told you something, baby?"

"Such as"

"That you have something very alluring. I can
ever go for you in anyway." 'You do not really mean.'
She smiled, showing a set of her superbly white teeth.

One of these days I shall call for you and carry
you off to Dahomey. How would you like it? "That
will be fine." She kissed him and excused to go and
attend for a couple just entered. She promised dass-
ing the night with him, Samco Pius said, because of
a woman.

The time was 12.45 nite, Kid glanced at the wall
clock in the room and decided that the day is well
spent. His two comrades were already dozing from the
effect of the wine and the long after journey, Kid
excused to call in by the morrow. His two friends
have an appartment in the top floor.

Akabueze woke up to the glorious rays a bright
sunlight morning. The calm atmosphere, the Whistling
palm-trees, and the songs of birds on top of the
coconut trees along the quays were all that broke
silence.

276

He lay down on his bed wrestling decisions in his mind. He got up and went to the window and peered far into the sea. The rays of the rising sun reflected to the waters far below the horizon. The thought of Bob Osita and Samco Pius in town gave hime food for the thought. Went into the bath, the water was cool and soothing. After brushing his teeth, Kid began to dress. He selected American green sports shirt and a nevy blue trousers, a grey Jacket with a black Italian shoe, all to the match. Hurridly, he dressed, bit a stick of cigarette and hurried down the stairs.

"Lucky in deals, unlucky in love. Life is what we make it." Outside, Kid beckoned on a taxi driver. First of all, he decided to go for the call box opposite the Post Office. Took up the telephone instrument and dialled. After ten seconds, he dialled again and waited. There was no reply. He cursed and went back into the taxi cab and the driver headed straight for Hotel De Bolingo.

The car pulled to a jerk in front of Hotel De Bolingo and he paid the driver. Inside the hotel, the waitress was waiting for him. She ushered him into a special private room for V.I.P's. Seated doping Mariguana or concain was Bob Osita and Samco Pius. They smiled a happy good-morming and a pleasant day to remain together. Samco passed one wrap of stuff to Kid Akabueze. The latter after observing the dope concluded this to be a Lobito stuff of a very high grade.

His moulding of the stuff was superb Kid ordered for a packet of Indian Inscence to help abate the odour of the dope. His mould was conjectured to be a family mould. A bottle of Spanish wisky was on the table.

"Life is like that, men, when you play red, black come up'. And that accounts for your trump card. When Kid took the first bale of the stuff, he sent out a thick black smoke. "It is hell! this is a real Lobito Stuff. How did you come by it men!" he said

"We are at Las-Pamas three weeks ago" he said

"A Spanish dame we met in one of the International Hotels gave us about twenty tins of this special blend of dope. She said the dope was smuggled in from Beruit by a sailor she used to entertain. And I gave her only five dollars for the whole deal.

"That dame knows he stuff. Believe it or not, she must be a killer type of the dames we met sometimes.

Well, a good lot of things happen in international ports that is nobody's business. But here in Nigeria things are just the reverse.

I am sure Las-Pamas is another hell of a city with beautiful women and plenty of drinks. Take the city-on-the Niger for example, where every rich man is the thickest crook. In the day-time, they hang around with their long and luxirious cars. But at night, they become the masks men on the highway, all appearing like young elementary school boys in their school shorts.

These cabal of crook business men belong to a mean school of thought. None, but a coward will do what he is afraid to do in the broad day light, but choose the night as the target. It is hopelessly, hopeless.

The room was thick with black smoke encirculing the air. The fan was on and these three pals, as they sit in a semi-circle, were sparking ideas of what they thought of this country.

Eventually, the tone of the conversation took a different dramatic change.

Well, Kid, Bob said, we have always admired the activities of the Four Star. That is to say, we have always cherished the idea of having to work together for a show-down piece of a deal. The last time we met was five years ago in that Ghana-Nigeria boarder that sparked a hell of diplomatic course. After what looked like a tough gun duel with the armed guards, we all got escort free with no sly miscalculation", said Bob.

"I am pulsating with interest", said Kid.

"Bob, Mon Amigo".

"Vous aller pasque je suis cumpreine". Not to contradict the English word, we both made a fifteen thousand quids each out of that deal.

"And where do we go from here, Bob?", said .Kid
Well, today we are back to Nigeria for another thicker deal. This time, the deal will be with the "Customs Wharf".

"Oh! Jupitar, Oh! Zeus" postulated Kid. "How I love to be in one of the Streets of Paris".

During our last trip to Lass Pamas, a Pal, who works in the H.M. Port Novo, an Fgyptian Cargo liner, as Samco and I were making one of our daily routine of going to the Wharf in case anything should chance, we came across this old pal who tipped us of a supposed box of gas store for one Ahmed Trading Company, Onitsha. But the fact remains that this supposed box of gas stove contains nothing but a 35 lbs worth of gold, smuggled from Egypt. And that the supposed Ahmed Trading Company or Mister Ahmed, who ever he may be, is an international smuggler or International Crook.

What I did was to tip my informant, a sailor on board the Egyptian Cargo liner carrying this gold five hundred quids cash down, for a piece of his information.

In the night, while the sailors went out to the shore, my friend smuggled me in, and I saw what I knew to be a real deal. The motive of our journey right in town, now.

Kid Akabueze gave out a sigh of relief and said, "That got to be a real raw deal, pals.

This ship, I suppose, will anchor this evening at about 4.30. Our action is to hire out a boat and row out to the ship at night or do we propose to make it a clear deal with an Invoice? That is to pose as the director of Ahmed Trading Company.

"Personally, I prefer a clear genuine deal. The blue guys and the Officers in the Wharf are not fearfully tough."

It was concluded to play it in the cool way. Kid narrated of his old deal of doping the horse for a sure win, and all conclude it would work well.

"I shall probably make back to Las-Pamas for a short holiday after this deal", said Bod. This deal will be squared, fifty-fifty. We must play it fast and precisely." Samco brought out a packet of Pall Mall cigarette and handed one to Osita and Akabueze. After a moment while, the guns decided to embark upon the plans right out.

Inside the customs Wharf, was a Police sign board. "No Parking'. Kid cleard the car in the other side of the road. Eventually they decided to drive straight right into the Wharf. The two Officers on duty halted and asked to see their warrant for going into the Wharf. But at the sight of these guys well dressed, he decided they were decent citizens and opened the gate as Kid drove in and cleared at the left side of the ware house.

Kid Akabueze, Bob Osita and Samco Pius, the three guys superly dressed walked into the ware house office and demanded to see the boss. They were directed to a room. On the top of which is written, "Manager's Office."

Kid tapped at the door and a messenger opened the door.

"Good evening, gentlemen! Can I help you?"

The three guys responded the salutation. Samco presented an Invoice honoured in the name of Ahmed and Co. Onitsh for the claim of an electric gass stove shipped from Egypt.

The Officer after a close study of the Invoice, and the guys who presented it, authorised claim to the said box. The porter had no difficulty in sorting out the boxes weighing 80 lb weight of solid gold worth £35,000.

The labourer who helped to pack the boxes into the car was tipped ten bob. What becomes of the box and the gold inside, is no body's business. That must be, Deal For Three!

Kid and his comrades decided to call this a day to remember and after exposing of the box, drove straight to Gay Palace Hotel. They had dinner and a bottle of Martel Brandy.

The time was 9 30 Kid and his comrades left Gay Palace Hotel for Madam's cabin. The idea of having a second encounter with Idowu and his band of back room guys was not pleasing to Kid. But the fact, he must please his friends was another question. After a moment's thought, he made a final resolution to go to Madam's cabin and damn any consequence. But he knew Idowu and his thugs were there and that it would happen and soon.

Inside Madam's cabin, seated doping is Idowu His friends were around. He was bragging on what a swell guy he is. He was telling a story on how he encountered with two cops who threatened to arrest him for doping in the public place. All of a sudden, at sight of Kid Akabueze, he became cool and his appearance changed.

Kid Akabueze was watching him with the tip of the eye. A cushion chair was brought for his comrades to sit upon. Kid ordered for a bottle of cognac when Idowu started to grin his teeth. Madam was happy with Kid's news friends and was in deep conversation with Osita and Pius when Idowu maliciously wanted to push down the bottle of wine on the table under the pretence of being internally lit with wine.

Kid eyed him savagely. Idowu asked for a bottle of brandy from Osita. He was very rude in his request. The fact he wants to show off by trying to create a false atmostphere of being tough. At this, Kid asked him to learn to behave; And to have respect for strangers.

Idowu took it in the offensive and got up suddenly. Kid knew Idowu's evil intention and side stepped Bob Osita. Idowu grinned again, stood like one that has seen the trouble he long expected. He gave orders that he should be served with a double shot of wine. "I propose this is a mue's way of being tough and to hell with a double shot, said Kid.

Maybe your mum never thought you good manners. At such remark, Idowu burst out in a fit and took a sharp foot walk towards Kid with a well aimed blow. His eye blazing like fire.

Kid said, "Idowu, don't be a mug. This is not time for being tough. Madam will not like it, better stay put."

Idowu rushed on him. Kid over stepped and dodged the first blow, Idowu aimed at him. As Idowu lost balance, Kid suddenly exploded a double left and right hooks to the chin and the belly. Idowu fell flat on the canvas. Kid took him up by the collar and hit him so hard after pulling him up. He hit him again. Before Idowu could be up for the third time, Kid hit him by the jaw.

"Okay! Okay!" said madam, "take it easy Lid." You will do him more harm if you hit him again.

"Don't start anything else, Idowu," said Kid. I am sick of your reputation of being tough. Just take thing easy and stay put. If I hit you again, I'll hurt you.

NO BODY'S BUSINESS

Men, I am telling you what it means to be a guy Maybe a good lot of you appreciate what it means to be a real tough, cranky, swell, level head kind of guy! And what the other feller is doing at the other side of the Street, is no body's business. Maybe it sounds tough and cranky.

I have come across guys that are tough, sleek-headed and hard to penetrate. I mean those back room types and dope addicts and peddlers. Take a stroll right down the Idi-Oro bus stop. Directly opposite the station is a dilapidated 18th Century Story Building. Walk straight in and you will be confronted with what it means to be an addict or dope peddler. The eyes of those mush-room or back room type of guys is blazing like hell fire. "Yes Gehena?" The only supposed hell fire visible on earth and it is situated at the South-Eastern part of Jerusalem. What happens to these fellers in the den or jungle of oblivion where the black becomes white; the white becomes the red is no body's business.

Maybe let's take a cool walk in. I hope you will not betray the muggish aspect in you when it comes to being a paddy man down the deadly jungle. But not as a Palokas who feels he can be fearfully tough.

Are you bewild at those fellers you saw in round semi-circle, eyes blazing, countenance in a State of stupor, and the way they sit staring the stillness which tells you the men are half-dead and quite obivious of the menancing influence of drug they are subjected. Just say, "aellmen!" and they will all stir as if they have been waiting for the doom of this generation.

The first feller whom I call Axe-fear-no-wood makes a pass of something taller than the size of a pall mall cigarette to you, my comrade. Maybe you refuse to take. But the law stipulates that once a member, always a member. Or what have you come in to do? Maybe I excused you for being sick of Ako and maybe one of them palokas gets up to say "a blue guy is around." The others stir and on their faces is written with bold capital letters, "DEATH" And you wonder what all this meant. But rightly, I got to bail you out, And I say "Men! never you all mind any damn about this guy here. He is no blue guy! He was just discharged from the crink now. Maybe he felt it wise to take purge to wash out the deadly beans he has eaten these eighteen months behind the iron bars".

One of them gets up. He appears to be the leader. "Men! we believe this our guy friend. What he kinda say just now is true. That feller, he says (pointing to you my comrade); is really damn sick. But before he is allowed to go free, he must make us some show. They all say, "yeah! yeah!". Jack-fear-no-body, you are correct!

They shouted, "he must make some show".

I say, cool and take it easy men! Maybe you all never heard of Kid Akabueze. I have been a swell type of International guy this seven years. Pasque, je compra bonfrance!

I place a one quid red note on the table and say, "this for more stuff, jots and some bottles of beer. They all jump up as if to worship Nebuchadnezer the then King of Babylon. And I tapped my comrade on the shoulder, telling you that we must discharge. And don't ask me of what has happened to the quid.

i give myself a second thought. Life is just forging ahead like the carcas of a dead horse by the Niger Dam. I searched my pocket for a jot. I was lucky to run my fingers across one rumpled lucky strike cigarette. I lit and sent out a thick circle of smoke.

I let my mind draft to different types of false imaginations. I was just wondering what it means to be tough. The thought of some old celebrated Weststern Films I used to go began to dawn upon me. I thought of Four Guns to Mesa; Tony Curtis in adventures of Robin Hood; The Carribian Gold and all sort of Western Cow Boys of yester years.

But here is black Africa. Where the idea of old Wild West of America, the days of the gun slingers and hired gun men, was a mere dream. With these thought, I decided that it would take another decade to produce tough guns. I mean like Robert Wanger, Billy the Kid, Jessy James and Durango Kid.

At the Tinubu Square, I stopped to gaze at the fountain with its dizzling waters as bright and white as snow. Pigeons of different colours were busy taking bath in the fountain. The idea of these heavenly creatures filled me with warmth and admiration. I thought life could be very funny and sweet. Just then, a pair of white pigeons flew up some two feet from the ground. The one I gazed to be the male crooing, drew near and was pinching the female with its beak. The thought of these little creatures in their romantic embracement stirred a deep philosophical emotion in me.

I would not help thinking of Platos exact words in his book, the 1st Republic in which he stated that man is a political animal, born in association with other men, he cannot attend either virture or happiness as an isolated individual.

How I love to be an under-graduate in any leading World University. The idea of qualifying in an honours degree in Pychology was weighing my thought.

I began to whistle amicably as I strolled down the square to the park. I stopped and lit a cigarette. A car passed by. The memory reminded me of the past activities of the Stars Burean. "That is be or not to be." I thought of Shola and the idea of when you see me going too fast, you don't forget to halt me. The Slogan of the "African Cunning Boy" which every guy ought to know in case any eventuality or miscalculation subsides. A saying that is no body's business.

I hailed on a passing taxi and told the driver to drive straight to 1129 Broadway. I paid off the driver and fumbled for the key to my room in my pocket trousers.

When I got into the room, the bed room was rough and un-kept. After a two seconds self brain washing, I remembered that I had not slept on this bed for two nights. I must have been mentally un-balanced, I decided I should go and see a psycha-rtrist for a sort of brain anylisis. I lay down on the cushion chair and soon fell asleep.

The next morning, Kid was driving along Bright. Street. After driving for three hundred yards, he took a sharp bend to the one way street. His idea to dodge the slow traffic hold up was vague. Sudden-ly he accelerates and was driving at 60 m p h a speed that was not very good in so busy a thoroughfare. Pedestrains and cyclists were all jumping to one side of the road. Some passers-by were shouting, "one way"

Opposite Martins Street was a police control post. With the sign "No entry" Kid ignored it and drove through in time to avoid colliding with a Po-lice Van coming from the opposite direction Instan-tenously, Kid clutched and the Car took an atomatic stop that was as sudden as it was mysterious. The car was bumping when a Police Officer alightened from the Van. The passers-by were aghast at what nearly looked like a terrible accident.

The Police Officer with a pocket diary in hand approached Kid and demanded of explanations on three count charges of traffic offence.

First, he made Kid aware of having failed to halt at the major road, driving through a one way traffic and finally reckless and dangerous driving.

Kid who was dumb founded at his mysterious escape from death stood speechless, flying and twisting the cares key in his little finger, occasionally he glanced at the Officer.

" I say Mister", said the officer, "let me see your driving Licence."

Kid paid no heed. He was staring at the crowd thronging to watch the show.

The Officer demanded the second time to see Kid's driving licence. The latter replied that his licence has no material bearing whatsoever with what really happened.

"I don't know until we get there" was the reply. But I can guarantee you that your lieence will be impounded for the next twelf months:-

You are trying to kill two birds with one stone, Mister, I,ll rather drop that charge if I were you. But whats the idea standlng in the mist of these hungry crowds who cannot just get about their business!

But the idea of a civilian trying to be tough with a law officer was not new in this part. The officer was embarassed at the youngman's guts. He decided of the possibility of applying force to this young civilian under his arrest.

He later gave up the idea of using force. After a moment interval, the officer said, "by the by Mister, who are you and what is your business?"

Kid handed him his complimentary slip card and in a low cool voice, said, "Do we just take few steps away from this mob? It is better we talk real business and fast. I get sick with men who will not mind their own business."

For the first time, the high tention and the serious countenance of the officer began to ease down. Kid concluded, psychologically that the same old story when in doubt, wrack your brain for a deal. Maybe a way too.

The crowd of people assembled were beginning to disperse but some unly stood to see the end.

Kid produced a packet of envelope from his pocket and handed it over to the officer, saying, "My driving licence and particular are in that envelope, Mister. Can I be allowed to go. Maybe I shall see you again in about two hours at the Police Station"

The Officer who was experienced in his duty received the envelope of a suprise packet from Kid and allowed the latter to go, telling Kid to call at the Station to collect back his particulars.

"I am sure you want to teach me the law", said the Officer.

"Maybe we are not after the law yet."

"I suppose you will ask that at the station", but just let me see your driving Licence. I wonder why some fools, after drinking, cannot comfort themselves well, but would choose to be a menace to the traffic and thereby endangering the lives of other Innocent people. But I'll set an example of you to other young men."

Kid wished this Officer should avoid insulting remarks and talk business. But the Offier was on his demand for the Licence.

"By the way, where did you get that heavy drinking Minister" said the Officer.

"How I wish you forget all about drinking and lets talk business", added Kid. His face showing red.

"But you must go with me to the station", repeated the Officer.

"What the hell is in the station?" Said Kid.
He tipped the Officer a two quids note and that was all.

THE DAME IS TOUGH

Miss Shola Thomas woke up to the glorious ray of a fresh sunlight morning. She went over to her window Cabin and toofi a long look far into the sea. She thought for a moment or while. The idea of having spent the last thirty two hours in the sea was refreshing. She thought of meeting Kid and the rest members of the Four Stars. She went to the well furnished cupboard in her appartment and produced a bottle of Spanish brandy.

A cool sea breeze was blowing merrily and gay. The wishpering coconut grove and the endless palm trees far of the horizon presented endless view. A bird was heard singing at the conifer tree by hotel international. Nigerian flag was flying at the ten storey International hotel.

At the habour is a Nigerian passenger boat from Germany. Shola thought of her trip from Duala. There was a mild shout of sweet 'welcome home' some enthusiastic crowd gathered to welcome relatives from Over Sea.

Finally, the ship anchored. There was a long quean by passengers they line to hand their luggages for searching by the Custom-guards.

Miss Shola nearly overstepped a beared young man directly in front of her. She apologised and took her line. This guy in thick sun glasses looked her up and concluded this was a beauty.

Shola was only four yards to the nearest customs-guard when Kid whistled.

"Anything you can do I can do better" she flashed her eye lids and smiled.

When it was her turn to be searched, the Officer with a tribal mark on the face looked her up and down and decided he has never seen this beauty in all his life.

Instead of the routine of searching through the travelling bag in the Lady's hand, he beckoned her "How do you do, baby? Hope you had a nice trip?"

She said, "Oh very well thank you" He wished to know where she will put up in town. But the fact she told him she would be flying by the 11.30 Plane to Enugu and that he should not worry about her until she chanced to travel by sea again.

This Official in his bid to know where this dame leaves has utterly failed in his duty as he waved her Okay sign to pass. Thereby, he failed to notice £20,000 worth of diamond. Shola brought along with her on her trip from Duala Via Ghana, when she called and stayed with Miss Alice Okafor for the deal.

Outside the dock, Kid Akabueze and Thomson were waiting for her. At the sight of Kid, she whispered" I can do anything better than you."

She rushed and embraced Thomson, kissed Kid on the forehead and let out a sigh of a happy Bon Voyage.

"How are you, Shola?" said Thomson.

"Oh! very well Thomson and how goes life with you and this first son of an Arabian Knight," pointing to Kid.

Oh! that will be fine. Hope you had a nice trip?"

Sure men; It was a real experience she said, she tapped Kid by the jaw and said jokenly, "You son a pirate, what has made you so cool?"

"Oh! just one of those things, honey." He said, Lucky in deals, unlucky in love. But shall I call you the princes of the jungle? You have a tremendous charming personality. Your alluring looks can easily win you through any diplomatic secret service, he concluded laughing at her.

"Oh! Kid, what a lovely nasty and untamed lad you have grown to be?"

When I was on the high Sea, the more I enjoyed my trip, was the more I remembered those betwitching blue eyes of yours. As for my trip, you will be suprised, she said.

"How, is Alice, Shola" Said Thomson,

Oh! she sends her love to you all, She promised to visit Lagos some time next month. She has kind regards for you, Thomson

Oh! ha, ha, Boy, that is to quote you are in love with Alice, Say Boy"

"There is nothing secret about it, Kid, I shall engage Alice when the weather gets better. We shall make a trip to the States for our honey moon," Said Thomson.

"Alice even told me that she has placed orders for a wedding ring", said Shola.

THE STATEMENTS OF HITLER BEFORE THE WORLD WAR*

PREFACE

This very short but highly amusing drama called "The Statements Of Hitler Before The World War" is intended to entertain you much anywhere you may be: whether in office, or market, or workshop or house or in journey.

The statements and other characters in this very little booklet are purely fiction.

Interested Schools and other organizations are free to stage the play.

However, if you are chanced, you may notify me.

(Okenwa Olisah)
The Dramatist

*complete text

Characters of Play

1. German sons, daughters, Soldiers, Police Band, Hitler, crowd.

2, Joint British and French soldiers.

3. French Authority.

4. Japanese troops.

5. "Hindu" Indian fighters, their snakes and other charms.

6. American soldiers.

7. The enemies.

The dramatist will welcome constructive criticisms and suggestions aimed at improving my play writing.

—OKENWA OLISA

Scene 1

IN GERMAN GOVERNMENT FIELD

German sons and daughters sing war song, and after fifteen minutes later, Hitler in a terrible army uniform enters, (*amids cheers and clapping of hands*) followed by army soldiers and Police band.

Hitler: War song and police music all stop (they
stop) Say Germany the power!
Crowd: Germany the power!

Hitler: Please repeat it seven times with very audible voice so that your voices may travel five thousand miles down to England, our common antagonist

Crowd: Germany the power, Germany the power!
Germany the power, Germany the power   Germany the power. Germany the power Germany the power.
(applause)
Hitler: Yes, Britain has heard our voices. They are terrified. We must win the war at hand a n d declare England our colony, willy-nilly, inspite of her Independence, and we will torture the remaining citizens. England has no sufficient weapons for this war. She depends merely on tricks and diplomacy which are now so uncovered. British cunning ways will not help them in this world war. Only power and disastrious German weapons will triumph. Under top form secret, I now disclose to you that my private informant, a British traitor, has informed me that her country will seek the help of America wh :

when the war reaches a critical stage. France and other nations will also join forces with England and support her atom bombs. But no single German will die of such bombs. Germans bear in mind that we must do what?

Crowd: Win the war! Woe bettide the aggressors.

Hitler: It must interest you to hear that we have two wonderful military weapons specially manufactu-red for this live or die war, the first weapon is called AUTOMIC EXECUTOR (applause.) This travels ten thousand miles when fired and no human being, tree, animal, could be alive again where it passes (applause) As far as w a r is concerned, Germany commands the "technical know-how."

Crowd: Hit Hitler! Hit Hitler!
Fire Hitler! Fire Hitler. The strong man of Germany. Your name terrifies the Britishman as tiger terrifies an ordinary man.

Hitler: The second weapon is called WORLD DESTOYER (applause) This can finish the whole world within five minutes when fired. The t w o wonderful weapons are now lying with anxiety in the Army base. Germany is the most powerful country on earth. Joined other nations together, Germany could face and crush them in war

We will destroy many cities particularly the bea-utiful Paris. Our military aircraft are all ready. They will bomb even the youngest baby in any hostile nation. The ORDER,—"BOMB any breathing obje-ct" means that they will be killing both human beings, animals, and so on and so forth.

Absolutely cock-sure, most Germans have not rea-lised that their Hitler (he points to himself) is partly a HUMAN BEING and partly an ANIMAL. (Wonderful! Wonderful! Wonderful! shouts the crowd

My mother is a human being but my father is an animal. It was a very strong animal called—Gorrilla who conceived my mother.

(Wonderful, Wonderful, Wonderful! shouts the crowd again.)

So my blood is mixed up— human blood and animal blood and that is why I am very very strong and could kill an elephant with a single blow. (applause)

Crowd: No wonder, The mystery of your power is now over.

Hitler: If Germany wants to have more strong men and women, strong animals like gorrilla and lion must conceive some of our women. Those women who are willing to produce strong Germans for us through the communication of strong animals should now raise up their hands (many women put up their hands) (prolonged laughter)

I am very glad that Germany has many devoted sons and daughters.

Reference to the war again, all of you must fight to a finish, several countries will attack us but victory will be ours. Before saying further, the Police band should give us that music which puts power in a warrior and makes him to cheer up in the face of stern attacks.

(Now the Police band entertains every body and every one including Hitler dance.) Hitler sings as he dances about:

"Music is the power of a warrior.
"Music is the power of a warrior.
"All dead Germans should rise up that war day from graves and fight
"A—day-old baby must fight on that war time.
"A lame and blind man must fight.
"Failure of the Germany to win the war must make me to disappear forever. Many people will s a y that I am dead.'

"But God forbid. Germany must be victorious. Visions have revealed this to me. Prophets have seen it." *(repeated four times.)*

(Music wounds up.) All of us are happy. I am much annoyed with England. What most of the business houses there do is this: after manufacturing inferior things like matchet, they mark it— "Made in Germany" because they know that Germany is reputed with superior quality and that any article with German trade mark must sell quicker than "hot cake."

There is grave unemployment and hunger in England. She relies upon her colonial countries, and that is why she hesitates too much in granting independence to them.

England cannot do without her colonies, and she persecutes and jails freedom fighters in those her colonies. Britain indirectly practices racial discrimination. She calls Africans black monkeys. She regards blackman inferior.

You see England (an officer from the Ministry of Information comes in before Hitler could utter words further against Enlgand), What is wrong? asks Hlitter.

Officer: According to our usual reliable information source, there will be war at any moment from now at our frontier with the our neigbouring country. The information further says that joint British and French troops will take an offensive.

Crowd: Let's go t' fight. We want the war. Our AUTOMATIC EXECUTOR and WORLD DESTROYER must conquer the enemies with disgrace.
Hitler says with very loud voice:

"There must be billions of deaths, severe injuries, Sickness, agony, hunger, suffering, losses, and destruction o f state buildings and important cities including Paris, London and Washington. " I must fight like my father gorrilla.

I must fight with all t h e forces a t my disposal and command in order to fulfill my promise to the Germans—to win the war and retain the dignity of Germany. (appaulse)

" No matter how brave and precantions Churchill may be, my Army-dogs must capture him along with the King of England. Needless revealing how I would maltreat them until they enter into my harmful hands.

Everybody kneel down and let us pray about the war. (Everybody kneels down.)

Oh! God of Germany, God of Universe, Messiah, Jehova-a-Emmanuel, Alfa and Omega.

Crowd: Holy

"Hear our prayers. Your children in Germany are persecuted. Please protect us, save us from our enemies, witchcrafts, evil spirits and avert any obstacle which may cause us lose the inevitable war.
Send down your military angels including Angel Michael on those war days for them to help us win the war and I must as a promise sacrifice my most beloved son to you, if Germany wins the war, as a Thanksgiving to your Lord.

We earnestly beg that the angels may massacre our antagonists at every war scene with their swords. However, if our enemies repent as from now, God of mercy, forgive them, but if they don't repent, let the Angels use their swords against them, and your hot anger fall upon them.

Please bless us and whenever we pray o n c e, answer us seven times for the sake of our Lord Jesus."

Crowd: Amen, Amen, A-men.

CURTAIN FALLS

302

Scene Two

WAR BEGINS AT FRONTIER

German soldiers fire British-French armed forces and the enemies also fire in return. Hitler commands his troops while the Police band entertains German troops with music two miles away from the frontier.

Commands Hitler: Fire, fire, fire! Don't allow them cross the border. Kill the aggressors. Hitlerites, remember our promise to the nation. Leave no stone unturned. Fight with all t h e forces at your disposal. Don't let your country down. Take heart. Cheer up. Open continuous fire. The enemies seem tired. Oh, That's their commander — Churchill. Open fire on his side. He must not go alive.

(War becomes worse and spreads. German troops shoot to death many enemies. The frontier battle lasts for five critical days.) Casualties are carried away by ambulance. The Germans defeat the enemies at the frontier. The fight ends there with the "Surrender Flag' lifted by the other hostile party. CURTAIN FALLS.

IN JAPAN

German troops advance to Japan. However, they have it hot there. Japanese troops are underground fighters. They fire German troops through the holes in the ground. Germans begin to destroy important buildings. After 30 days war in Japan where a lot of German soldiers lose their l i v e s, war ends there.

(CURTAIN FALLS)

Scene Three--*In India*

In India, German troops have it hot also. The "Hindu" Indians fight with charms. Snakes chase German troops, and the "Hindu' Indians apply other medicines to fight German troops. Machine guns are used to kill the snakes by Germans but abortive. The German troops run away from India because of the activities of the poisonous snakes.

(CURTAIN FALLS.)

Scene Four--*In France*

German troops now advance to France in a bid to destroy the famous and beautiful Paris City. Hitler with a very audible voice from paratrooper orders: Destroy Paris, the Pride of France! But automatically the French Authority raises a 'Surrender flag' to German troops and they accordingly pass the Paris with a victory song

CURTAIN FALLS.

Scene Five-At Frontier Again

America joins the world war and gives German soldiers very tough time. Hitler cries out where he hides when American Army dogs overpower h i s soldiers at the frontier:

"Oh the world is against Germany, for what? Tiger is held by trap!   My hope is shattered My heart is broken. My life is now worse than useles; I am disappointed. Oh what a vanity in human life? I am in the worst lamentation

A common fly is better and stronger than me now. Oh I am very sorry for my fellow Germans alive who will be mocked as a result of this war.

May the souls of Germans who are dead in this war rest in perfect peace.

May the souls of our antagonists rest with t h e devil in hell!

304

"I will disappear before the war ends entirely. Many people will falsely say that Hitler is dead." After two hours Hitler said these above, his enemies capture him where he hides in lamentation. His hands tired behind his back, fired a shot, but Hitler disappears unhurt. Hitler's disappearance shock his enemies. They shout: Oh this risky man has disappeared! We would have offered the birds of the air his corpse to eat."

Immediately a Radio broadcast from London says: The war is over. Great Britain and allied forces are victorious. Hitler is dead and he is buried in a forest 500 miles from Germany. May God save the king.'

The British National Anthen is blown.

Everybody disperses

CURTAIN FALLS

THE END

AUTHOR'S WAR COMMENT:

Many people were enriched by the world war, because in some African countries, some people broke into the people's shops and packed goods openly. The breakers were not prosecuted because the situation was uncontro -lable by the police. By that time, during the war, some African soldiers were taking articles by force from the owners. They performed mess. They could see a woman in the street and carry her by force.

The Army were feared much by that time.

There is a strong allegation particularly in the Eastern Nigeria, that the soldiers were responsible for the high bride price.

The allegation went on to say that when the soldiers returned from war, they began to pay high bride price, thus set a very unfortunate example. However, I praise our youth who joined the army during the war, because Army work is very risky, and our Government should do some good to our Ex-servicemen. It is not yet late.

THE LIFE STORY & DEATH
OF
JOHN KENNEDY

The Late President John Kennedy who was Assassinated on November 22nd 1963.

NET PRICE 5/-

THE LIFE STORY AND DEATH OF JOHN KENNEDY*

The Death of John Kennedy.

The 45 year old late John Kennedy was assassinated on Friday November 22nd, 1963. As President Kennedy was going in his car, he was in the middle while the American Army and the Security men were at the back as well as at the front. Unfortunately Lee Harvey Oswald was standing and measuring them with a rifle at the two storeyed building in Dallas City Texas. Immediately President Kennedy's car came, Kennedy was shot by Oswald and the dangerous bullet affected him at the head and gave him severe injury.

Taken to Hospital.

Kennedy was at once rushed to the Parkland Hospital Dallas, Texas in the United States where he died shortly after his admission.

But before the death of President Kennedy, he opened his mouth and spoke the following words:

What President Kennedy said before his Soul left the world.

"A Country must protect her vital interest. The weapon with which she endeavours to do so are diplomacy, economic influence in the form of financial and c o m m e r c i a l restriction, Propanganda and armed forces on land, at sea

*excerpt

and in the air. These are weapons of attack and defence alike. A peaceful country to protect her vital interest, must have all these weapons, but never uses her armed forces except in defending herself against an attack by the armed forces of another country or in a civil war.

The highest form of Strategy 'grant strategy' as it is called with which a peaceful country should endeavour to protect her vital interests should so intergrate her diplomacy, economic influence, propaganda and armed forces, that her resort to war is to render these unnecessary, except when she is attacked with armed forces, in which event she goes to war with the maximum change to victory. Diplomacy which embodies foreign policy is thus a major weapon of any peaceful country and also fact of an independent America. For America should remain a peaceful country never to become an aggressive country.

Foreign policy therefore (For a peaceful country) is a defence weapon and it should aim at reducing the number of the country's enemies (that is those who oppose the total interest of the country). The enemies may be actual or Potential.

The best strategy for any country for reducing the number of her enemies, actual and potential, to a minimum is for her to organise as many countries around her as possible, into a closely knit political union of which she must be a member or, if such a union is already in existence, to join it. From the defence point of view, the union aforesaid is real: its size, people and natural resources when even only partially developed will render any armed attack aginst her costly and ineffective. Since this union cannot be realised immediately, the countries involved in the project being many and varied, other association convinced solely as defence measure should be aimed at. Nevertheless, the policy and plans for achieving the creation of the ideal Union of World Nations, can be put into operation even if I happen to die.

As a matter of fact, I am extremely sorry for the person who shot me because of what might follow my assassination and his actions. I have done everything to establish peace and law in the world and make all the people equal to law, hence God created us equal with exemption of colour. Obviously, I am quite aware that I will die, from this pain.

(1) What evil have I done to wicked men who planned against my life? I think I have been fair if not good. I have tried my best and even missed my bread to save the world from danger. I have worked hard to see that peace with happiness is everywhere in the world.

O! devil why are thou so wicked, why people plan against the innocent. O, the land of America, the negroes and people all over the world may lose a friend. I am really very sorry for the young people who will mourn my death. If I happen to die, my spirit will live with you. The creator and Father of the world will send another person to rule with peace.

I never knew my life will end like this. Whatever may be the result, whether life or death, I still maintain that without peace, respect, justice, and love to all human, there must never be happiness.

O! I am sorry for the people who will be much worried over my death. Some people will be struck with horror when the news will be broadcasted over the radio. Some may not even believe it in time and some will ask within themselves, why is it that he was unable to save his life from the enemies. And the answer to this question is, I did not know that they have planned to kill me. However, I am very happy for the historic role I have played. My name will still remain on the lips of people after my death.

It is good to live and die for righteousness, I can still remember the brave men who were killed for righteousness, the missionaries and other countless friends. They were killed by wicked men because they were doing their best to establish peace and make everyone equal to the law.

God have mercy on my soul and that of my killer, because he knows not what he did. "Blessed be the land of America" "Blessed be the people and rulers of the world" "Blessed be the soul of Abraham Lincoln who died because of slavery and slave trade abolition in 1864."

"Blessed be my dear father and mother"

"Blessed be my brothers and sisters"

"Blessed be my wife and children"

"Blessed be the American Negroes whom I am sacrificing my blood for their own safety"

"Blessed be my soul and good bye to my friends".

After these historic words, and sorrowful events, President Kennedy slept for ever.

Kennedy's Assassination: Azikiwe Speaks and

Warns African States.

President Azikiwe of Nigeria on Saturday being 23/12/63 warned African States to ponder seriously before deciding to trust in a Government elected by American electorate.

This he said, has become necessary because, "It is now crystal clear that certain influential sections of American public neither respect human dignity nor regard the black race as human beings who deserve to be treated with respect, decency, and equality".

WHAT IS LIFE?*

(A book of outstanding precaution,
with genuine facts intended for
the course of true living,
moral activity, and for
self utility Love).

~~~~~~~~~~~~

*And lovely read, in
the advance of the book,
the story of once Rapacious
Rufus who wanted whole of himself,
and was later perished on the track.*

BY

FRANK E. ODILI

*excerpt

Revised edition for your more complaisant
and easier readings

———

First Published January 1960

This Edition . . . . July 1961

Printed in Nigeria by
THE STAR PRINTERS
NW6/1 Onireke Road,
Ekotedo, Ibadan.

FOREWORD

It has been my candid believe that authors are born and not made. The case of young Frank E. Odili affords a living example.

In his fascinating book—"What is Life", he has been able to sportlight the activities of a boy, rapacious as he puts it, and by name Rufus. The trend of this interesting book shows that upbringing paves the ways of life. Thus poor start entells a poor end. What a shameful end was it for poor Rufus in his attempt to own the whole world?

Rufus is not alone in this race of selfishness and foolish endeavour. So many are like him and their ends are equally the same. Mr. Odili has the both foresight and ability to write. He prepares the reader first and allows him to go on with interest and zeal to what he has for him. Thus the book starts with a general comment on all aspects of life, and the main story—an interesting and captivating piece follows.

The part of Rufus' wife is a good lesson to all women and that of Rufus himself an unforgetable sermon to all men. Thus the story is meant for all—both boys and girls, teachers and students, traders and buyers, and men and women.

All good citizens should endeavour to read this book and find out what the young author has in stock for them. The book is interesting and affords a good reading.

I esteem it an honour and a rare opportunity to be asked to write a foreword to this book. Should I fail in my attempt to give the best I have, I should be judged by my experience rather than by my age.

JOE. N. C. EGEMONYE
AUTHOR OF BROKEN ENGAGEMENT
AND
DISASTER IN THE REALMS OF LOVE, ETC.
P. O. Box 18,
Nnewi, Eastern Nigeria.

PREFACE

"WHAT IS LIFE?" has been my first attempt as just any in any field of authorship; and more reverentially as this. I would not have risen perhaps to handle a pen, or find myself a writer of and for the mass if not the intense disagreement of conduct I gasped over the life and its recipients. This gasp is not for the highly pleasant acts I witness my men do that introduces me this stir, but more for the wrong folds to which their motives are born. And that is the sure aim of this work.

Because men have mistaken the sense of this our life, and therefore turned to the vainglorious, painful and penal acts of it, such as: has through the love of enthusiastic monuments extended the contemptuous and retributive actions of this our age; has for the whole love of contending and tasting easy and quick riches endangered their times of joyful prospects; has through fondness of the more senseless women we are left with, winged off their portion or share of achievements; has through beershop attendances and other profitless and useless undertakings fallen to baneful consumption of their possessive incomes; has conjectured the dear love of man and God a true backwardness in them; accepted deceit, fraud and stealing as a means of winning over success; the world/life therefore has been a total fruitlessness, hunger and bitterness. It is this, my friends, that I have taken myself (mindless to the many difficulties it encounters to explain at better understandings), to allay them to you if for best you can hear me or do to that errand to which the life and purpose stimulates for you.

This work then can (if read with good care, and with an enthusiasm of consent), inspire you the spirit of love, wisdom and concern. This is not even all I have for you for a partner of this work—entitled "ACTS TO GOOD CITIZEN" is there being endeavouring for you same. That, when it is come, (perhaps now), will supplement to total, the great accounts/bindings you are got of this life. That is all for you, and read on.

Before participating in adjournment to this Preface, let me humbly owe my deepest regard to Mr. Joe N. C. Egemonye of the Iheme Memorial Grammar School for kindly writing the Foreword. Same I owe to Mr. Mich. A. C. Nwosu of Saint Teresa's Nsukka for kindly too writing the Acknowledgement.

And finally, I limn my congratulations to the undermentioned eminent personalities who through their aids and love, have encouraged authorship to a destination success: first is my headmaster, Mr. L. N. Anwunah of Saint Patrick's School Awka; Mr. Okenwa Olisah, an author of well supervised quality, Onitsha; and Councilor S. U. Okwumuo, Central Press Manager Onitsha. And congrats are due to many other friends whose cheers, wishes and emboldenments are exclusive the list.

—FRANK.

ACKNOWLEDGEMENT

Frank, a growing writer of good intellect, has presented this work in the eager sense to unfurnish that main diseases of our life—ignorance, (but which he based mainly to that of the lifely knowledge and its propulsion than more you could think of it), hate, greediness, and sin. In his durable capability to this as one who has posed himself deeper speculation over the life, and more of humanity, I can without any hesitation maintain that he has given an excellent view points which should be a practical lessons to all.

His work, aim, and mannerly presentation are thoroughly creditable. And although he bore the thought of the talents before maintaining this writing, yet, the average he never forgot at all. I therefore maintain that the precinct of this whole work is flavourly good, and agitative to taste for the confiscate reading. I have read it through; and although works without critics are barely counted few, yet, in this one of Frank, boastful I am to recommend the greater restraint he manifested never to keep you totally bestirring to this char.

You should therefore read to the curiousity of benefitting to your contribution rather than contriving to minor, useless, and profitless criticisms which has nothing really or solutional unto you. It is complaisantly an investment of pride to any of you who has a copy of this pamphlet, and advise you (after reading) to pass it on to your friends or recommend it to them. Do you hide what is pleasurable and good?

I am then thankful and grateful to the right of honour I possess in acknowledging this book.

Yours Faithfully,

MICH. A. C. NWOSU,
Saint Teresa's College,
Nsukka, Nigeria.

319

Contents

i   The Foreword

ii   The Preface

iii   The Acknowledgement

iv   Hint Over The Life

v   Section (A). Thinking To The Life

vi   ,,   (B). True Life And Goodness

vii   ,,   (C). Match Keeping and Early Choice

vii   ,,   (D). Thinking To Purpose

ix   ,,   (E). The Purpose Enhancement

x   ,,   (F). Friendship Among All

xi   ,,   (G). Personal Emolument

xii   ,,   (H). Man's Last Problems

THE RAPACIOUS RUFUS' STORY

xiii   The Loving Hours of a Boyhood Start

xiv   The Change of Expectation

xv   True Friend Advises

xvi   The Preparation For Life

xvii   The Trade Business Affairs

xviii   Winding Off Occassion

xix   A Wife For Rufus

xx   The Marriage Joys

xxi   The Strip of Relaxation

xxii   The Complete Fall

xxiii   The Step of Replacement

xxiv   The Division For Shares

xxv   The Split of Greedy Rufus

xxvi   Remarks

xxvii   A Wise Note For The Propellers

xxviii   Note For You

HINT OVER THE LIFE

IT IS IN FACT a point of matter that if life is to be endured perfectly, and in a more enlightening way than burden-like occupancy, it is a rule of general importance that we should apply a solutional thought into it. It is a doubtless fact that our life has been an endurance of unpleasant one, yet, if dear and appropriate thoughts are to be forwarded into its fare, we must at least find it not all too bitter too. If I were to define the life to you (though which I am not concerned to do of entitling it thus rather than to point out those obligations your concerns and meditations are due) I would indeed tell you that the life is no little a mystic enthralment to man; not mystic by the way it comes to exist when we think of God same, but by the way it functions unto its resumers. Sensing likewise into this, we wouldn't be less instructed on that same point that our life is just a platform of acts. You may not know this until you have been to a cinema theatre, and what do you witness there? Any different sight of your daily lifely scenes? Not at all for those are the scenes of this life, and each fellow is an actor. The question then is: do you act better in the way your scene will be pleasurable? All actors have their good instructions before they act, have you then received yours and act accordingly? Let all Dick and Jack bear this question upon themselves and know how they play their parts.

Have you ever had a dream? Then don't think more of what your life is. As a dream is a total nothingness—nonentity, so is just the life we live in but more nonplus to us. Because the life is nothing to us rather than Him that owns it, each one is subject to an end; why then are my men not catchy upon this? Actually they are not, hence my pen is busy, otherwise, what is the sense/solution telling a fellow what he knows and actuates it? Because our life itself is deceptive, fruitless, unveracious and anomalous, the inhabitants living has mistaken it, therefore practised all unhumanitarian ways (evils) as a means of solving it;

but does it actually solve through that consistency or participation? Not at all my fellow mates, and hence this writing has been specially dedicated for you— chiefly to mark up your corrections and know better to those heads where your ignorance chokes.

I therefore accelerate to this expostulation by introducing these masterly questions which will enable you think better of yourself and the life in achieving its thorough end. Here we go, but....don't flag.

Section (A). Thinking To The Life

Are you good in life; known the purpose of your being so, or being brought up the life at all? Do you then maintain to the ability of its sensational goodness? Or are you yet straining to wild hopes, therefore living to depression of perfect activities? Are your doings of fair worthy praise or merely surviving to the mournful portion of your characters? Which of these doings are you duly happy; an acquaintance of true living or the snobbish concurrence of tending the rightfulness? Which really if not the self-true-motive or goodness to which your whole binding is due? Are you with the mind of griping the worldly abundance, thereby contravening a humanitarian loss unto yourself? But why think much on the world and its containings than the good concerns you are bound over to it? Does all that whole make the end of human desires? Then, why bother so highly upon them and just to that, intercede curses upon your periods of contriving happiness? Do you hate being happy in the life you have come? If not, why not abide in a legitimate serenity wherein you will be all confined to this? Aren't you striving to the summit your strength could mount of this life? Why not it keep you happy and genuine before yourself and the Creator? Are you really achieving nothing out of this life? Shall I believe you so? Who is then achieving? Does any agree upon this? To truth you might have circled here but are you begging your diet? No, and what more achievement expects you in order to be happy and good of your life?

Well readers, in the above, think/act better, plan

fairly, recounting your fears of life, remain unbewildered and firmly in all the courage of your life. Reasoning and fear is your true forepass of life, contention and justice—your virtual recount, while wisdom and consideration brings you asssuage and your ways adornment. And to all basic of reasonings, think deep and strike fair always.

Section (C). True Life and Goodness

Are you not sincere and just in life? Are you envious and wicked; why? Do you yearn very eagerly and so, think the world alone for you? Are you bearing the thought of becoming rich a day? Have you reasoned before this desire? Do you forsake money to live a hateful and dishonest life? Are you annoyed when you are poor? Why not you the money in order to be all satisfied? Why not your state find you the most pleasurable one of mankind since you are not the worst of that proportion (whatever your circle is)? Why even despair and look on others as if better life they have come more than you? Please, never you deceive yourself for each fellow is there with the trouble or tormentation that guards him. The only difference is this: some are burdened with lighter loads, and others heavily—each of these loads are mighty to the shoulderers.

The fact is there that our life is indispensable of consideration hope, love and charity. Should we reason rightly in the sense of this life, and more to those put to you above, the life is no much better to any than the way he accepts and lives it. See to this: by the good thought and courage we have on the journeys of this life; by the candid love we have on our fellow mates; by the fair considerations we render to things to make it suit tolerably; by the full contentions we have over our possessions to avoid greediness and stealing; lies our true happiness of this life, and more the forfeiting of those great burdens/hardships to disturb our footstep of progress.

Considering far and wide to this extent of our thought, we could ask: what is that great need of man in this disastrous life of ours that make us plunge with every bitterness, eagerness, disunity, greediness, hatredness, and many other regardless attainments of us to battle unto the things of this life? Frankly speaking, it is my strong conviction that men hardly reason at times when they emulate on pursuing blindly into the exposures of this life. Why aren't we partaking to reason susceptibly unto ourself and the life before we take to gathering its fruits? Since the life itself is not for any but are all mere speculators to it, why not with patience, love, and others to cope it than remaining complete thorns and menaces to our fellow mates? Why do we constantly joy upon evils when even the creation has no solution to us by that? It seems to wonder me great that very many people are little like me, and in thought, reason much the opposite way as I do it; otherwise, why is it that we cannot just live a very peaceful and thorough-minded life to ourself and depart whenever it is time due of us? But what keeps my certain men very low in right thinkings? I wonder!

Since men (no matter what rank) are equal of creation, and the last enemy of man (death) awaits both the good and bad, and the poor and rich; since the life is nothing of men's possession, and the riches and pleasures in it all for the moment we sigh or even get them; since our desires are fast greater upon the exposures of that life than the main concerns we are scheduled of it; since man has never the contention upon whatever ranks his state; since the world itself is mainly composed of trials to all its dwellers, and at a point to bring high the low and the high backward; since the much nonsenses we do are not of God's own likeness and kindness to us; what then a sensitive life do we claim ourself? Let us mindly think my friends, and act practicably unto this I tell you below.

Think deep and extend far your changes towards the ability of faithfulness, love and passionate attainment to others. Our life is short and yours may soon exist no more. Would you be pleased to die an evil death before our Creator's own hate for projecting bad His wills? To this think I not—engraving ourself into

324

the unknown perishment of evil habitation but for owing to the rigorous extent of men's dishonesty sake, we build on that track. The acceptance of man in forwarding no contempt survival is as well striving to God's placidity.

And for the true sense of this, survive a virtuous, lovely, passionate, generous, and peaceful life in order to please the Creator since that in collocation cries the need of our purposeful existencé. Life is of full joy when the fear of God is tended first in heart. And these being done, the sense of creation is partly tended to.

Section (C). Match Keeping and Early Choice

What type of company do you dearly keep? The company of lazy or the hard-working match? What is this company looking upon you to others? Is that the precept of your being loved, or just a burden-shape with your tending acquaintances? Do you tend to something doing or just perishing to bad companies? Are you without the knowledge that lazy and idle companies make you think of nothing profitable/good of this life? Or are you the one practising it to others? If so, then why; or does the good of life not taste you? Even though it doesn't, who is to labour for you when nothing you know of the labour? Or don't you take to eating? Have you chosen the accursed way of living— stealing for want of stamina to produce up needs? Perhaps, you havn't, and what step have you taken therefore to supplement or act rousingly into this desire? Are you planning now it is right of you, or until it is too late to find your step? Why look time perishing upon you than you could ascert earnest use to it? Do you think a time gone is back coming; or that an opportunity foolishly wasted is worth regaining back? Too senseless you are whoever cracks jokes with his time, and leaves depression to all his lines of prospect!

This whole of "C" is among the rigorous facts that substantiate in the true and encourageous forepass of life. The first of its contents lies the very step by which we probe ourselves to the real gesture in which the life will find us its dwellers. In that way ofcourse, we could know by what order of good or bad the life would find us pannelling to it since the question of the company we keep has much which it plays in that affairs. Then comes the plans we undertake to build up the life itself.

Sensing more or better into this last point, let us fully convert ourself that we to the life are totally meaningless and more of bitter herbs if we don't confine earnest plans to ourselves on how to cope the life we are all. This is sure an important affair to anyone who finds himself a sharer of the life, and to elaborate into it, he has got to think to himself to know what circle he is to couple himself. Infact, without reasoning there should be no betterment in this, and to reason, one must have known better the circumstances that bind him of this life. Through this commendation can any success or the lifely merit be conducive, otherwise, what need or sense is there fooling when great things lay ahead for ones care? I am saying this not for the elaborating ones who catch the meaning of the life and attempt their abilities into it, but for the more idle, dwindling and flinching others who look on to the life as if it has more parcels of good to bestow upon them rather than the breath it has left unto them and others too. And through this busiless gazing and self tantalizations, have much of the spoils they conspire over themselves.

But I say to you my friends: beware and free yourself from idleness and laziness. If I am to inform you correct into this chronicle which I weigh as one (if not the greatest) of the demolishing and demoralising practices in some of our burden-like men, I can tell you that this is the root of all evil conceptions of this life; (but is not, for so many are on the labouring and getting state, yet, are the more counted in this do, but on the move that they want to capture whole, and in a day's time too!) I am sorry I can't continue you far in this until just that next work I promise you; though I am lacking space of furthering you, yet, these are sufficient for the wise to know and be concentrative!

Section (D). Thinking To Purpose

Have you reasoned deep of yourself, others, and main stand of creation? On what aim are your main existence binding? Do you ever know and think of it? Havn't you got duties to perform of this life? How far have you elaborated yourself doing them? What are the alikes of these duties? (I leave this to your imaginations till you read that book I promise you—"Acts To Good Citizen" and you will know better of them; price 5/6d, and may have been published in your reading this). Coming back in our question again if you now sense of the duties, do you ascertain the correct shows of it or merely wingling yourself on a deceitful pertinence? Do you then convert the ignorant, sighing others into the practicable good of your kind whereby your life is solely materialistic? This you must do if the love of God and His wills are really burning in you.

Section (E). The Purpose Enhancement

To enable you project better these wills/duties, the question however is: how much great have you thought upon your Creator and the aims totalling your existence? Have you then kept pious and eleborated to this aim? Or have just the unsatisfying—evil characters of others kept you counted to their numbers of oneless concerns? Should you imitate the reckless and the fools, would you like bearing the same records with them? Or are you just ignorant to the fact that all person's agitations or contributions to this life are equally put to records? Why then ignore this fact as to permeate little zeal in featuring all that durability and worthiness are necessitating from you? The fact is only there that you must reason deeply before your standing lots as to actuate the orders and likenesses of our Creator.

Section (F). Friendship Among All.

How far have you shown appreciations in others and wish same from them? Do you claim much superiority over yourself, and then act stupendously in the ways needed for your care? What is that possession or gift you have that thrusts you very rude before the eyes of men? Is there anything so new in this stretch of our living? Why mad then with just the very little you can boast of? I am sorry to mention: it is not riches that captivates you nor is it your unapproachable graduation: nonsense. It is but mere stupidity, senselessness, and pomposity that engraves you to the sorrowful and angry looks of men! Are you away the sensation that a haughty and impudent somebody is easily alighted to dislikeness and hate? Are you ignorant or forgetful to that word of our Redeemer that whoever takes himself high must be brought low, and the meek (though to whatever poverty or greatness) must be cherished? Doesn't this happen all occassions in this our living, and have you not often been witnessing it to your own sight and realizations? Why then practise it, and at very miserable points to note? Let me tell you plainly before I wind up this point: I am the one writing to you who hates personally to see any proud fellow along my side: all because I don't practise it; I yield to anybody according to his very due; though my appearance or seeming may deceive sighers to classify me to what I am not, yet, in my self and spirit, I know who I am.

So, my good friends, these are my advises to you: Do all you may but try to free yourself from pride and rudeness in whatever measures you can. Remember that this if attained to, has not only the dislikeness of God upon you (as He hates it even more) but the hatredness of mankind too. Everybody hates pride itself for you could even imagine the proud too who hates to be prided to; who would therefore accept his when he doesn't tolerate that of others? This will consequently show you that that pride itself is a word of total hate than practise. You may ask from where this pride takes your name, but I tell you: take low yourself as if nothing you are but yet something; greet every heights you see, and pay homage to every rats and donkeys of your ways; it will cheer you till end beyond your expectations. Less of these biddings, be you the earth, and not nation controller, you are alrightly looked the meanest of all. And here readers, I wind-up.

It quite substantiates a burning fact that many survivors today has very little to reason to the sphere or subjection by which our life is a magnificient sanctity—that is, that ways by which our life is said to be pleasurable, either to the top one or low, and yet, is not pessimistic at all. This is consequently from the strain in which we lack the understanding or step of a perfect, gradual progress in pursuit. This is so because, we seem to know little that by hurriness and greediness towards wealth, we very little catch it too (if at all we could), and by precautionable and modest stir—without any malice/contempt towards our neighbours, we surely assume the decree of it. It is just because, our present life is full of whims and enthusiasms, hence our creation or manifesto into the very noted uncontention, evil deeds, and hatredness all over. Should all these not have dwelt to our rapacious and gluttonous tastes, who would not have sensed to wise for good? But too ignominous and childish a thought we confine ourselves if that be the regulative ideas since the life itself cannot remain erect or much meaningful without all these monuments for its temptable sentiments too.

After all, weren't we all told that this present stretch of living is made for our temptations? Who finds himself ignorant to this, and why do we fall constantly to it? Not only that we fall to it (which punishment lies better for us) but are being tortured momently by it too. By the way, why don't we reason accurately to ourselves to know that this world is a total blight if not nonemtity, and is yet something of importance? Peeping into the world today, I can very much understand that not even the so called propellers are at a satisfied groom to his portional dividends/shares. But what all these cause, since the women too (though not of them presently or at all) are at their worsts; the men both high and low, small and big, much alighted to this concern? The fact is there; we all yearn too greedily.

Sure, these are certain points by which we keep ourselves desperate on the move:— (1) We assume no thought on how to battle good of the life and win it. (2) Our honours and concerns we lack; loom in what is unexpected of us. (3) We hate ourselves and love money above all counts. (4) We think less of the Highest or Creator and loom very much in our life gifts, forgetting that all these are basically towards His wish and powers. And these few points of ingenerous acts and thoughts being born and panelled by us, we must therefore understand (through the miserable esteem) the much lost of God's acceptance which we accounted ourselves by a tensive, odd illumination.

In this sense then, when we have got to assume a hearty reasoning to all the events of this life, peaceful and amicably, we could understand that the step in which most pertain as their true way and conquer of life, is totally away of the reality to a perfect sane of creation. In steering on with this too, when we most think of the things of this life—beauty and attractions that come out of it; when we even think much of the main purpose and likeness of man which is money, and the speedy pursuit men assume to have it full; when we ahead ungenuinely without a guiding thought to check us true in all we could desire benefittably; when we do not even reason of the main purpose of life we reside and the knowledge it has meant for us; why can't we then by a sight of the poorer classes have our ways genuinely straightened in the aheading of betterly pace? Why can't we think little of this worldly possessions if we could rather smell of achievement in the rightful go of God's own appreciation?

How do we at all expect benefits and prosperities without the good works of us and God's best assignment of pleasure in it? Have we got any share in this peculiar display of worldliness? Can't we therefore reason deeply when we concern ourself to rushing it over? Who brought or owns it then when we could only sigh the existence and leave it same as we have seen it? Is your much greed to grasp it wholly and selfly the wish of the Possessor before introducing you to it? Why dwell senselessly greedy then? Isn't this the cause of our many failures? Are we all thoughtless in the full concern we are meant of this life, added to the acceptable routine for merit? Let us just think if we can.

In this true joy of life, possess the reasoning thought to guide you true in all the matters of it. Reason better, the existence of God and all His mercies, wills, and the perseverance He maintains towards us and our hearty ones, pray to Him for more assistance while you keep on with the orders of this life being needed from us. He is there for you as you are for him, and for this, become of the best personage. Think little on all lifely things for mere spectator you are, and have very narrow chance to them. Plan better and have all your hopes upon the Father; the thought for anything is all of His powers and gifts, and through this, force betterly and less when He's not yet of you. Bother less to your stand in any state it might be found for such He lets to you than you for yourself. Remember Him always to your prospective doings for a virtuous step in life receives (among other things), peace and happiness to its return. Being you are too much unaware to when your longings and all will cease of this life, it is therefore necessary for you to keep the best routines of it.

Reasoning deep to the creditable reach of this life—contents and states, then think yours very forward and pleasant; all because, you are not the worstly founded to note. If this be the case, look at the other, poorer, ranks of you, and perhaps being hated by the earthly goods to have remained in an untranquilling quest; what of them; are they not surviving alike? So, in this life consideration, forsake not the evil of men, or the state of life to turn you bad in doings; keep you hate to others; make you forget your creator; make you injure; make you grow unsane; make you senseless or regardless in out/inward looks; and make you lose the placidity of life. Let all become your joy and lead you to straight forwardness. All is your creator's gift and so, accept it likewise while you struggle to the best you, can to the tale of your life conquer. Your state cannot remain for all eternity to the gravity it may participate but could be changed the morrow; all is perceptive because, no state in life is ever solid, but loose. In tendering less to these delusive aspirations in us, survives then our upright go in a respective endly record.

Section (G). Personal Emolument

Have you reasoned considerably, of yourself, life, position and death? What remarkables have you then made to long your life, yet dead? Have you planned extremely better for the true judge of you? Have you made better the needings of you in life or yet hoping unto hopes? Have you reasoned to merit those expectations? What are these that you have got to merit? Have you not been a descendant and then making sure of yours? Have you then made good and happy preparations for the coming of them? What is that expectation on you in the making of these preparations which reads headly the completeness of your survivor? Do you know of this and aim at it? What is it then the expectation? Are you not yet on the verge or rankling state of parenthood? Are you remaining happy to that state or did you plan unpleasantly before taking yourself to it? Are your descendants then entirely happy, or have you brought them through to rub the agony state of this life? Is that your project/schedule? If so, are you looked right before the sight of man and God? Did you restrainably think to this before your effection into the marriage? Doesn't it look such a curse to you for seeing those your descendants in too much a state of grievance or without any better schedules? Having learnt this, do you then stir reasonably to do something to it—their trainings and up-keeps? Aren't you withingly proud as a father to see these your children hoist in a very prospective mood in the future? But, can they easily remain as the said without your much ado upon them? What if they remain pleasurable, can't you be exaggerated, though of cheers and respects from your side, looking individuals? Who speaks rash or evil upon good? Then, such a miniature is no less an evil to himself, nor has done anything profitable to count of him. This will show you that good deeds to this are always praised worthy. And that through this will peacefulness and love shine your very step of this life. You cannot aim or leave to others what binds you personally to do. Now, think yourself to others, gratifying the likeness they owe towards you and your deservable doings, and ask yourself this: what is life, my bindings or what creation stands for me?

These thinkings being so practically in tune of our realities, what is it then our gravity in becoming home masters? What disasters in the manner could keep up uncertain and peaceless homes if we could be self cautious to endow the pride of a virtuous home maintenance? Are these not the home bindings which mainly entells the variety, completeness and worthy reach of a man's honour in this scene of living? Aren't our desires so unshyly born in this sense of becoming home masters and is it not the less collocative reside of these manly routine that keep most of the unprepared men in a shrink of outstanding look while in pretence of seeming less interested at its joys? The stretch of wilful obtuse to go in marriage leads a guiding knowledge of man in achieving an endly reach of it while hurrily and ignorant record to secure, leaves a detest to him.

Tending the full point of consideration to this high repose of definition, your adornment and respect effect the honour from the very root of your home which shines outwardly for the spectators notification. In this sense, your rank of honour or no honour takes effect through this demand on you. Aren't you mindlessly put to boo when the sight of your home is a complete ignomity to what spectators will look forward to grant? Surely so for while few will be rebelled to troubled looks upon you, others are solely attached to mocks and hurtful blabs to paint you up! That is why it is necessary for you to be cautious whenever you manage a home for not only will you remain unpleasant for lacking this, but will receive the much gossiping and meanly looks of men. Unto these I have said to you, take the best care over your homely managments by using the natural sense you are given; accept peace too as your motto to all the undertakings, for wherever a peace is found in a home, it is just happiness and love which rules the dwellers, while prosperity at the same time knocks at their doors. It is only by this and other undertakings will we so conquer those our great lively bounds.

Section (H). Man's Last Problems.

Are you now at the reasoning hours? Do you question deep to your life characters? Are you fully cleared in thought and deem too good of yourself? Do you heartily reason of your last breath on earth? Do you feel it sharp and deep when you sense of it? Are you ever perturbed when such thought of death flashes to your imaginations? What's your very concern in death affairs? If you think of this, then, isn't it the very necessity binding me, you and others? But what do you sense for your fears or bound when to that very remembrance of death if really you can reason? Aren't that fear the very clamour of all your life concernments? And which are those concernments? Now, have you concentrated or assumed whole all your lifely purposes? Should you think of, or to this, isn't it the full meditation you ought in all your worldly cotemplations? Do all men bear this thought beside them when they emerge effectively to their doings? What is that need of man in this sided dwelling; and which same are those needs of many others: do you know? What are the true wisdom and ignorance of this life battles? Do you know? And all these to your fullest imaginations. Why are your bindings so wilfully important to be fulfilled, especially in the thorough wish of our Creator? Do you at all reason intensively and externally to all the rightful and firmly search of this life? Are you of the better or worthy count when you are found not completing these needs of your purposeful existence? Do you try then in this aspect to execute or actuate all these expectations? If you try, then aren't you happy before yourself, doings and your Lord? Have you not been to a purpose or ado before coming or been brought into the widely being? Have you therefore, started dexteriously in a graceful manner of strivation and living whereby you are founded?

In the full considerations to the above, our life is completely less of a home to the rating prospect of any as thinkings and seemings are due to concern. We think too much of earthly bargains in the sense of losing our true manners which deem full and expectedly from us and allow the worst to survive unabolishable. This to check in our humanitarian circlement, is a mark too mistaken and unbecoming of us.

Whenever life is to be thought over, when you shall remain in want of all worldly possessions, when pleasure will all overcome your grief, whenever the sweetness and love of things may endure much more of your standing life, when the love of God would be kept behind and that of money put too forward, what are you then; and where is your stand? Are you ever to depart with all these earthly ownings if the Lord wants you surrender up? Are these not for the earthly ownership as empty you have come? Whom are you struggling for after all: are those not for your descendants? If they are, why not please do that in the most delightful manners as to retain that good blessing of God to them? Reason you shall, otherwise, debauch.

Are you expecting to grasp all the gifts of this life, and therefore embarrassing yourself in the queerish way of activities? When the thought of departure as a human being comes across you, why not devote gratefully and mannerly in all your manly steps of life? Do you think a non-satisfying step of countless possessions to world things would ever restore you a security or rest, inspite of many of us today who labour a complete amiss? Why not to your spiritual interest in God keep the good rule of your main created life? Are you actually redundant in fetching up your needs when you are physically looking fit to that? If you are not, then, what is your more greatest need of the life? Do you want to gather more than your strength's production? Then don't be greedy. After all, are you a beggar who only depends on charity? If you are not, then why not contemplate with satisfaction to that little or much you can find yourself? The greedies are always tortured while the satisfied are countlessly peaceful.

Do you on earth's living pray to gather more of others' self productions? Meaning just a curse to yourself? Do you not beg for more strength and to live by your productions? Is that not the best demand of a sensible fellow wishing for prosperity? If you are uncontented to yourself, do you think your imagined person of fulness quite satisfied to himself? Do you not reason most on this worldly affairs and what it plays to the passing times of men? Do you not know that things in this life are quite samely to the other? Do you think that there is a best place for happiness or the best of riches in this present life we are? Who do you think on earth or could guess by self-thought that in riches, has the full percentage need that he bothers for no more, or in happiness claims himself alone to that mood while others are not? It is accidental if seen.

This would enough encourage us through if we could by our senses consider most of these helpless claims on the part of our struggles which never give us an end. Some in the position so uncontented think the world a possession of some, but it is absolutely a big mistake on the estimating point of such reasoners. Life is not for any at any reason and men not for themselves. We are all at many shakes alarmed of beseiged suspicions, with sentiments to our stimulating anxieties. This is all we should know of life: we have nothing in the world; the world is dead open and the people living are pitapats. We have no hope of piquant stand, and expect nothing out of hope, and are flutters of trials and deeds.

Why do men feel always too uncontented to themselves and yearn very greedily? Are they always away to the sensational doings that life is nothing to man than a passing time of counts? Could they not at sense stay joyful to all the imaginations of their life by the little or more they may possess while they man their ways in the fullest modesty needed by all in the life? Why do men not reason when antipathy is the true horror of men nowadays? If we blame ourselves for being poor and then to do unwise, what is life then more of us if we decide inconsiderate to our doings? Do we think riches the high pride of man in this hopeless survival we are? What is riches to our capital desire of life when we attain to the best doing of our creation? Which is the most proudest and rejoiceful state of this life: evil possession of riches or the true steps to the wish of the highly Observer?

It is a great shock of horror to the poor-states-men when they reside to cry on riches which give them out of no possession to last badly ends when they greedily loom in the tastes of hurrilly possessed ones. Poor ranks to do on every creep of riches, with the sense of unexpected manners to the possessing pursuance, is a great displeasure to them! Just imagine a queer minded folk, at the verge of evil riches, how do you expect him happiness? An evil man is never hapyy; not only for himself, but his opulence too. Considering this I tell you, you could so same imagine that of the poor but good minded fellow at the best of strivation to this riches, how do you watch the steps rise? All are not forcible at all; they are slowly and steadily coming as in godly needed one. After all, is it not little drops of water which make a mighty ocean? These facts are sure and situated for us, yet, little thought we share to them. We supplement our desires of a day's rich, and yet, penalised by it, why can't we presently find our lessons?

It is for the objectivity and confirmation of this truth I tell you that I have indulged in putting forward this fiction to you. It was not my good aim to include or introduce this when I am only faced with the desire of advising to put you into the thorough match or way, but circumstance of good reason has manipulated me this better sense: the story is not at all for interest alone; it is more for the conveying of lessons which I so meant. It may not meet your full demand, nor of what I consolidated or meant before letting it, yet, I certify it is all for your greater advantage. So, while you read through it, kindly do that for lesson sake which the tale really aims at. It is interesting as well and so get it:—

AFTERWORD

"My body may be here
but my mind's long gone with the Ibo."
—Paule Marshall, *Praisesong for the Widow.*

This collection partially owes its existence to my friend and colleague, the late William French of the University Place Bookshop in New York's Greenwich Village. For nearly fifty years the shop specialized in, as their Yellow Pages advertisement read, "*Everything to do with the Negro.*" It sounded antiquated then and it was, as was a significant portion of the significant stock.

More souk than shop, nine floors above Broadway the vocationally marginalized bookseller/scholar curated an imaginary Africa representative of the real Africa. Here I encountered the bibliographical construct of a world deconstructing itself faster than my own: the file cabinet archives of a downed Black Panther, drawers of bus station paperback blacksploitation, the now fly-speckled negritude of Léopold Senghor and Aimé Cesaire, Brooklyn's quasiscientific self-published Afrocentric Egyptology, deep, florescent-lit stacks of university press evidence of the lost civilizations of the Sub-Sahara, chronicles of the Black Atlantic diaspora, nineteenth-century minstrelsies' imprints in dialect, the belles lettres of Civil Rights, the bullet lettres of Chester Himes, a photo of Idi Amin Dada nude—all rescued from the oblivion of neglect by Mr. French. Rather than travel in pursuit of Africa, he chose instead to Africanize the familiar, to invert the near shores to their other side, to the "Africa within." Which is where we met.

Among Mr. French's treasures were the anthropologic poetics of Onitsha's market literature. His was one of a few collections to survive Nigeria's destruction of things Igbo, all of which are presently outside their country of origin. Their collecting he considered paramount in his professional and personal accomplishments. The authors were his contemporaries. He was able to procure 220 pieces dating from before the civil war. I have his catalogues and invoices from Messrs. A. Onwudiwe, Highbred Maxwell, and Njoku & Sons, "*Books Sellers*," *Importers & Publishers,* Main Market, Onitsha. His last order was mailed to Biafra, August 9, 1966. Nine months later the books would arrive but his check was never cashed. There was no response to further inquiries until I made mine a decade later.

Rare, in the book business, is a vague term used to mean there are few copies recorded and thus very few on the market. It might mean scarce and it might mean precious. Too often it means neither. In the case of the pamphletry it meant both. The five and seven dollars apiece Bill French asked me for his duplicates I knew to be wildly disproportionate to the pamphletry's value but appropriate to the demand, as our shared interest knew no other market.

During the late 1970s and through the '80s, I scavenged University Place Bookshop as I scavenged all of New York's Book Row, Greenwich Village's Fourth Avenue from Ninth to Fourteenth Streets. The five blocks of mostly grimy secondhand bookstores presided over by grim often-grimy elderly bibliophiles was a wonderful place for anyone entertaining my literary pretensions. And they were entertaining. Through an association with a bookshop on the Upper East Side, I found myself mau-mauing the literary interests of an educated, affluent, and acquisitive clientele, gifting the erudite mistresses of, appraising, configuring, and cataloging the libraries of, and curating the collections of the Upper East Side Medici.

As their private librarian I learned to appreciate the book as a thing as well as the narcotic state of mind I sought between so many covers. Catering to uptown's connoisseurship, I acquired an understanding of motives and criteria that, frankly, had never interested me before as I was far too busy reading. It didn't occur to me that the book as an object was of enormous interest until it was brought it to my attention by financial incentive. While some of my clientele were shallow, seemingly in direct proportion to their vanity, the majority of this effete elite were serious bibliophiles to whom I offered the curatorial and bibliographical services they hadn't time to perform: appraising, arranging, augmenting, cataloging, collating, inventorying, and restoring their carefully cultivated interests.

The mechanisms of collecting support the quest not just for the best but for knowledge. At the heart of these interests I recognized a discernible need for truth, a wanting to know the origin of the thing in order to understand the nature of its message, that I responded to with sympathy if not sentiment—which is where the dealer goes wrong. For collectors, first editions possess an elemental signature, a proximity to the author, that qualifies a symbolic validity later editions don't possess. In collecting incunabula, for instance, the content of the book is often dwarfed by its stature as a relic, a milestone in the history of literacy.

People who find book collecting a vain pursuit are always goading me to confess to having clients who are trying to buy class by buying fancy books. These people, who claim to be bibliophiles, generally quite sensible people, differentiate themselves from such frivolity by imposing puritanical and proletarian constraints on book buying they would never consider when choosing anything else. They say it isn't necessarily because they're cheap. They'll insist they don't care about the edition they read or its condition and like to infer that to consider the book as a thing of interest in itself is crass materialism. They insist their interests are strictly academic and their reading has never been touched by sentiment. As book lovers they're as impotent as the most dilettante fashionable readers.

I admit to being a rather dilettante "hip/phony" myself at times. Uptown's effete elite contributed to my education as an antiquarian and this collection owes a small but significant debt to the clientele that brought the pamphlets within my ken. Likewise, the milieu in which my appreciation of the pamphletry lived, south of Fourteenth Street deserves its honorable mention. By downtown standards they functioned within the tenor of the time. Downtown, my social circling beyond the pulp mines mamboed about the incipient graffiti/neo-expressionist art scenes and beyond to the wild style third-whirl electric boogie all New York City borough highlife scenes of the times.

In the seventies and eighties, each of those scenes assimilated Africas like the one I have always known. These Africas were neither a place, a philosophy, nor so much a style but a dialectical touchstone, one that implied more than it ever explained. The aesthetic said it. Its destruction-ist mentality is similarly about breaking down existing forms and putting them back together. The paradoxical nature of the pamphletry, its promise and demise, its invincible ignorance, its pop splendor, and its outsider status all appealed to my black heart and the black hearts of my artist contemporaries and their models, who were entertained.

As the pamphletry intended. Unlike, say, the signed first editions I'd accumulated, the Onitsha books interested people who cared nothing for dicty books or Africa. They spoke directly and simply to a sensibility that felt confined by the literary. The Igbo authors' enthusiasm for their new media captures the spirit of experimentation drained from our contemporaries' prose. Once the first flush of fab curiosity wore off, the little books retained their grip. Once accustomed to reading the unhomogenized prose that's sometimes called Young, Mad, or Uncooked English, the polished prose of my time's publishing wore comparatively tight in the crotch.

❋ ❋ ❋

In the winter of 1993 Bill asked if I was interested in buying his pamphlets. While he was desperate for money he gave them to me at cost. We shared the troubles of the times. In the early nineties, other affinities New York City shared with Africa were the AIDS epidemic and economic blight. I'd lost a family member/best friend, five close friends, and one hundred and fifteen acquaintances. Bill was losing his wife and his livelihood. The recession and technological changes took a great toll on independent booksellers at the time and we knew several bankrupts and suicides.

That spring I was afraid I was losing my young son to an

autistic state of mind I couldn't conceive. That my son's involvement with the spectrum threatened to preclude his using language gave me nightmares. He didn't speak and only a small sparkle in his eye indicated comprehension. In oral and written cultures, these people of the fourth dimension are sometimes outcasts and sometimes seen as holy madmen, emissaries of a world primary to the illusionary realm we inhabit. If it is difficult for the literate to conceive the unwritten world, it has been near impossible for either to grasp autistic consciousness.

I became highly aware of the literary constructs I couldn't take for granted if I wanted to save my son. Words meant as little to him as they meant in the oral world from which the writers of the pamphlets emerged. They, however, provided me the key. *Find the key and it leads to the Word.* Literacy employs mnemonic devices I intuited within his capacities. To understand my son, it seemed to me, as to understand the pamphletry, was not so much a romance (a literary construct) as a love affair.

The pamphleteers warn us not to misconscrew the two up and never to mix them up with money. The complete title of Sunday Okenwa (*The Strong Man of the Pen, The Master of Life*) Olisah's pamphlet of useful advice this book takes its name from is *Life Turns Man Up and Down, Money and Girls Turn Man Up and Down.* Olisah, one of Onitsha's greatest existentialists, cautions us to the perils of romantic notions confusing practical solutions. For all the doggerel of his evangelical didacticism, his forewarnings argue against the presumptions imposed by the world without.

As does the great Igbo author Chinua Achebe, in *Things Fall Apart.* Literacy as much as colonialism is the catalyst for change in Nigeria. Literacy, similarly, was the tool I used to effect change for my son. Incomprehensible and apparently uncomprehending, he was read to, year in and year out, all the books I never read when I was a kid. Books written, like Onitsha's street literature, to an audience with the equivalent of a third-grade education. And it worked. I'd been reading to him for two speechless, ritualistic, mystical and mystifying years when, on my skimming over a word, he supplied the word, his first. It was as if he couldn't speak until he could read.

Until the Word heard became concrete, alphabetized and grammatically ordered, cause and effect seemingly eluded him. With the Word he could reason. With it we could talk. The market writers' perceptual differences oftentimes mimed the kid's, bringing me the same answers by different questions. I do not equate oral and autistic consciousness, save to relate their differences with the literate state of mind. Neither can withstand it. Both fight it. Autism, I hypothesized, is to illiteracy as illiteracy is to literacy but in the other direction: equal but separate.

Neither illiteracy nor autism are synonymous with stupidity. They are states of mind. To understand either is to grasp a consciousness no more illusory than our own. Igbo consciousness underwent no less radical effect when it grasped literacy than my son did, and it happened in much the same manner. Literacy has always been a means of coming to terms with a technologized environment that never comes naturally. It is a sanctuary in a life that turns man up and down. It is full of hard lessons and good laughs. It is full of friends and family, imaginary and real. I want to thank my son for impressing me it doesn't much matter which. I want to thank him from the bottom of my heart for emerging.

Bill did not emerge. New York University absorbed the shop's stock, paying his debts, just saving him from bankruptcy. *The New York Times* and *The Village Voice* covered the shop's demise in much the same manner they'd cover Sotheby's sale of the city's last Checker cab. He wasn't the last of Book Row, but he was the last of its great authorities. And now he's ceased to be, on purpose.

❋ ❋ ❋

This selection of pamphlets owes a great debt to Dr. Emmanuel Obiechina, whose works on the Market Literature are indispensable to its appreciation. Mr. William French accompanied my introduction to the pamphletry with Obiechina's anthology from the African Writers Series, *Onitsha Market Literature,* and his unsurpassable critical study, *An African Popular Literature.* I can make no greater recommendation to the interested reader than these books. Read him and reap.

I have Arthur Nwankwo of the Fourth Dimension Press, Enugu, to thank, as we all do, for sustaining an independent literary voice in Eastern Nigeria during the dark ages following the Biafra War, as well as facilitating my search for copyright holders during the as-dark ages of Sani Abacha's thoroughly corrupt regime. Communications with Nigeria came to an impasse when I needed them most. Neither postal nor telephone connections functioned sufficiently. Arthur and his associate, my friend Udenta O. Udenta, worked with me to find anyone who might hold copyright to any of the market's publications. Without their instruction and friendship my study could never have come so to life for me. *Justice, Peace & Progress.*

Bernth Lindfors, Peter Hogg and Ilse Sternberg have been very helpful to me in my studies and have my gratitude. As do the librarians of the Schomburg Center for Black Culture and the New York and Brooklyn Public Libraries.

For a variety of good reasons I would like to thank my

family, Fran Lebowitz, Peter Heaney, Julian Asion, Edwin and Barbara Weisl, Courtney Ross Holst, and Erroll McDonald.

And for even better reasons, this book is dedicated to my son, Adam Adolfo Thometz, and the former Camilla Jackson Huey, who we just love.

A READER'S GUIDE

Coming to international attention as Igbo land became Biafra in 1966, the study of Onitsha Market Literature during the war better served the purpose of acquainting the world watching the slaughter with the Igbo than the television, but couldn't attract the audience. Peter Hogg and Ilse Sternberg's *Market Literature from Nigeria: A Checklist* (London: The British Library, 1990), remains the thorough bibliographic guide to the pamphletry. With the possible exception of the twenty-five items in my collection absent their cataloguing, there is nothing to add but there is a great deal to recommend.

Beyond the scope of that work are several books that enhance one's appreciation and entertain:

The Life of Olaudah Equiano, or Gustavus Vassa the African, Written by Himself is the first and, until Chinua Achebe's *Things Fall Apart,* best account of Igbo land by an Igbo. I like very much Paul Edwards' facsimile of the 1789 edition (London: Dawson, 1969) but prefer reading it in the more readily available paperback editions. *Efik Traders of Old Calabar,* containing *The Diary of Antera Duke,* was edited by Daryll Ford and first printed for the International African Institute in 1956 and reprinted by Dawsons in 1968.

While touched on in Sir Richard Burton's and Mary Kingsley's travel memoirs of West Africa, the writings of

Onitsha's adopted son, the "Ubiquitous Coaster" and palm-oil ruffian John Moray Stuart-Young, contain the most entertaining, enlightening, and certainly the most eccentric insights into Eastern Nigeria produced in colonial times.

British anthropological studies skirted the gutsy subject of the Igbo until the women's riots of the 1920s. The resultant spate of interest, coinciding as it did with anthropology's entry to the syllabus, produced the first objective studies. Very interesting are M. M. Green's *Igbo Village Affairs* (London: Frank Cass, 1964) and Sylvia Leith-Ross's *African Women* (London: Faber, 1939) on the domestic life of the time. There's much to recommend C. K. Meek's *Law and Authority in a Nigerian Tribe* (London: Oxford University Press, 1937), but K. Onwuka Dike's *Trade and Politics in the Niger Delta, 1830–1885* (London: Oxford University Press, 1956) is perhaps the most authoritative of the studies on the Igbo land of nineteenth century, benefiting as it does from the indigene's intimacy with his subject.

Victor C. Uchendu's ethnographic study, *The Igbo of Southwest Nigeria* (New York: Holt, Rinehart and Winston, 1965), enjoys that same advantage over Daryll Forde and G. I. Jones's groundbreaking survey, *The Ibo and Ibibio-Speaking Peoples of South-Eastern Nigeria* (London: International African Institute, 1950). Their supplementary bibliography, by Mark W. DeLandey (reprint 1963), shows just how small a literature existed on the subject before the Biafra War. Very lovely are Jones's photographs of his subjects, which can be seen on Indiana University's website, http://www.siu.edu/~anthro/mccall/jones/.

The Onitsha writers seem to precipitate a sudden interest in the field of letters and learning with the "Orality Problem." Interest in the differences between oral and chirographic cultures, between the written and the spoken word, coincide with the pamphletries discovery outside Nigeria in the early 1960s. Walter Ong's *Orality and Literacy* (London/New York: Methuen, 1982) crystallizes the concepts Marshall McLuhan's *Gutenberg Galaxy* (Toronto: University of Toronto Press, 1962) and Jack Goody and Ian Watt's essay "Consequences of Literacy" (1963, reprinted in Jack Goody, ed. *Literacy in Traditional Societies,* Cambridge: Cambridge University Press, 1968) address.

These seminal works found their pretexts in Igbo land's crosscultural collision. McLuhan refers repeatedly to West African literature exemplifying the premises of his *Gutenberg Galaxy.* Jack Goody was acquainted with the pamphletry from his fieldwork in Ghana. Both were in touch with the scholars from the University of Michigan doing fieldwork in Onitsha, who are thought to be among the book's first collectors. With *'Public Opinion on Lovers': Popular Literature Sold in Onitsha Market'* (Ibadan: Black Orpheus, Feb. 1964, 4–16), Ulli Beier describes the literature McLuhan inadequately identifies.

The start of the Nigerian Civil War in 1966 ended the pamphletry but created new interest in the Igbo that their study did something to satisfy. As with the Women's War of 1924, Biafra provoked a new round of scholarship, most of which came to press just as the fighting stopped. Some of the best found substance in the pamphletry. Harold Reeves Collins's wonderful work, *The New English of the Onitsha Chapbooks* (Athens: Ohio University, 1968) and the obscure Kraus reprint facsimiles of twelve Onitsha pamphlets, *B. Chinaka, Thomas Orlando Iguh.* . . . (Nendeln: 1970) speak eloquently of who the Igbo are. S. Okechukwu Mezu's very scarce five volumes of *Igbo Market Literature* (Buffalo, N.Y.: Black Academy Press, 1972) in reproduction is the same but so much more so.

The Igbo literary scholar Dr. Emmanuel Obiechina, Jack Goody's student at Cambridge, published his analytical study of the pamphleteering as *Literature for the Masses* with Arthur Nwankwo's Nwamife Books concurrent with the armistice in 1971. His anthology and invaluable introduction, *Onitsha Market Literature,* appeared in Heinemann's African Writers Series in 1972, and in 1973 Cambridge University Press packaged the critical study revamped with three facsimile pamphlets as *An African Popular Literature. Language and Theme: Essays in African Literature* (Washington, D.C.: Howard University Press, 1990) collects much of his best work. I cannot too highly recommend these books to anyone interested in this topic.

Igbo Traditional Life, Culture and Literature (Austin: The Conch, 1971), which Obiechina edited with M.J.C Echeruo, is invaluable. It includes A. E. Afigbo's comic masterpiece, *The Igbo Under British Rule: Aspects of the Human Dimension.* Afigbo's difficult-to-find *Ropes of Sand: Studies in Igbo History and Culture* (Nsukka, Nigeria: University Press Ltd. with Oxford University Press, 1981) should be read by anyone with a serious interest in Igbo history.

Wole Soyinka's *Art, Dialogue and Outrage: Essays on Literature and Culture* (New York: Pantheon Books, 1994) was crucial to understandings that made a serious difference in my life, though I'm not sure I interpreted his essay *The Autistic Hunt* as he meant it, as well as my appreciation of matters Nigerian. In Oliver Sacks' *Anthropologist on Mars,* the autist Temple Grandin influenced the same thoughts I was having with her *Thinking in Pictures* (New York: Doubleday, 1995), an extraordinary entry to another way.

Without Robert Farris Thompson's *Flash of the Spirit* (New York: Pantheon Books, 1983), without Robert Farris

Thompson himself, I wouldn't have enjoyed those matters half as much as I have.

Bernth Lindfors's *Critical Perspectives on Nigerian Literatures* (Washington, D.C.: Three Continents Press, 1976) is extremely helpful to putting the subject in context. It includes a piece from Don Dodson's thesis, *Onitsha Pamphlets: Culture in the Marketplace* (Madison: University of Wisconsin, 1974), that deserves publication. Peter Hogg and Ilse Sternberg's aforementioned *Market Literature from Nigeria: A Checklist* (London: The British Library, 1990) entertains as few bibliographies do. It is the only significant work on the subject after 1975.

Cyprian Ekwensi was the only writer to graduate from the Market to international publishing. Heinemann's African Writers Series keeps several of his titles in print. *The People of the City,* the first fiction by an African to be published internationally (London: Andrew Dakers, 1954), and *Jagua Nana* (London: Hutchinson & Co. Ltd., 1961) are highlife chronicles without peer.

Among those conspicuously missing from this selection are works by the great Ogali Ogali. Reinhard W. Sander and Peter K. Ayers have collected his extraordinary contribution to the literature in *Veronica My Daughter and Other Onitsha Market Plays and Stories* (Washington, D.C.: Three Continents Press, 1980). This fact underlines the limitations of my unrepresentative selection from the Market. Only very small segments of this collection have seen reprint. My criteria was to make available pieces from my collection that haven't been previously made available to the common reader.

While Amos Tutuola was never published in pamphlet, his works are amongst the *Maddest* works I know in English. They served as my and many's introduction to the possibilities inherent in West African's contribution to literature. There are few works of literature as *outside* as *The Palm-Wine Drinkard and His Dead Palm-Wine Tapster in the Deads' Town* (London: Faber & Faber, 1952) and *My Life in the Bush of Ghosts* (London: Faber & Faber, 1954). Grove Press published them in the United States. As a young bookseller in Minnesota I read everything Faber & Faber published, no matter how dull. This was back when publishing imprints had characters; Tutuola epitomized their reputation as purveyors to the sexual and intellectual avant-garde. Tutuola was not dull. He made the exotic erotic without even mentioning sex.

Chinua Achebe's *Things Fall Apart* (London: William Heinemann, 1958) and *No Longer At Ease* (London: William Heinemann, 1958) appeared abroad before *The Sacrificial Egg and Other Short Stories* came out from Etudo Limited in Onitsha in April 1962. It is the most elegantly produced of all the pamphlets. Achebe is back in 1971, on the cease-fire, to rekindle Eastern Nigeria's presses with his *Beware Soul Brother and Other Poems* (Enugu: Nwankwo-Ifejika & Co. Ltd., 1971, a.k.a. *Christmas in Biafra.* Garden City, N.Y.: Anchor/Doubleday, 1973). His collected works cannot be too enthusiastically recommended. In *Morning Yet On Creation Day* (London: Heinemann, 1975), "Onitsha, gift of the Niger" is an expanded version of his preface to Obiechina, 1973. It is as beautiful as anything by this magnificent writer. His works are key to understanding all of the above and more. Word.

The material reprinted in this book originally appeared in the following publications. I have made every possible and several impossible efforts to locate the legitimate copyright holders of these pamphlets, without success. My debt to the writers of the Onitsha Market is immense. Should anyone know the whereabouts of any of these authors, please contact me in care of Pantheon Books.

K.W.T.

Rosemary and the Taxi Driver by Miller O. Albert. Onitsha: Chinyelu Printing Press, 1960.

Man Has No Rest in His Life (*Since the world has broken into pieces, truth is not said again*) by Your Popular Author, THE STRONG MAN OF THE PEN [Okenwa Olisah]. Onitsha: B. C. Okara & Sons, All Star Printers [no date].

Beware and Be Wise by Olusola. Ibandan: Adee Works, 1967(?).

No Condition Is Permanent by The Master of Life [pseudonym for Sunday Okenwa Olisah]. Fegge-Onitsha: Njoku & Sons, Umeh Brothers Press, 1964.

Money Hard To Get But Easy To Spend by Sunday Okenwa Olisah. Onitsha: J. O. Nnadozie, New Era Press, 1965.

Lack of Money Is Not Lack of Sense by Felix N. Stephen. Onitsha: Chinyelu Printing Press, 1962.

Miss Comfort's Heart Cries for Tonny's Love by Cyril Nwakuna Aririguzo. Onitsha: Chinyelu Printing Press, 1962.

Drunkards Believe Bar As Heaven by Sunday Okenwa Olisah. Onitsha: B. A. Ezuma, Chinyelu Printing Press, 1960.

Beware of Harlots and Many Friends by J. Nnadozie. Onitsha: J. C. Brothers Bookshop, revised edition, 1965.

How to Avoid Corner Corner Love and Win Good Love from Girls by Thomas O. Iguh. Onitsha: Gebo Brothers, Okwume Printing Press [no date].

Why Harlots Hate Married Men and Love Bachelors by C.N.O. Moneyhard [pseudonym]. Port Harcourt: C.N.O. Moneyhard, Fenu Press, 1960.

Mabel the Sweet Honey That Poured Away by Speedy Eric. Onitsha: A. Onwudiwe & Sons, 1960.

How to Write Famous Love Letters, Love Stories, and Make Friend with Girls by N. O. Njoku. Onitsha: Njoku & Sons Books Co., All Star Printers (Nnewi), 1972.

Saturday Night Disappointment by Miller O. Albert. Onitsha: Chinyelu Printing Press, 1960.

Adventures of the Four Stars by J. A. Okeke Anyichie. Onitsha: Highbred Maxwell, Mbewu & Sons Press, 1965.

The Statements of Hitler Before the World War by Sunday Okenwa Olisah. Fegge-Onitsha: Aloysius Umunnah, Atlantic Printers [no date].

The Life Story and Death of John Kennedy by Wilfred Onwuka. Onitsha: J. C. Brothers Bookshop, 1971.

What Is Life? by Frank E. Odili. Onitsha: N. Njoku & Sons, 1961.